W9-BNM-484

D1613435

HAIFA

HAIFA
City of Steps

Nili Scharf Gold

Brandeis University Press *Waltham, Massachusetts*

Brandeis University Press
An imprint of University Press of New England
www.upne.com
© 2018 Brandeis University
All rights reserved
Manufactured in the United States of America
Designed by Eric M. Brooks
Typeset in Arno Pro by Passumpsic Publishing

For permission to reproduce any of the material in this book,
contact Permissions, University Press of New England, One Court
Street, Suite 250, Lebanon NH 03766; or visit www.upne.com

Yehuda Amichai excerpt from *Great Tranquility* and
Dahlia Ravikovitch excerpts from *The Window* reprinted with
permission from Sheep Meadow Press.

Library of Congress Cataloging-in-Publication Data
NAMES: Gold, Nili Scharf, author.
TITLE: Haifa: city of steps / Nili Scharf Gold.
DESCRIPTION: Waltham, Massachusetts: Brandeis University
Press, 2017. | Includes bibliographical references and index.
IDENTIFIERS: LCCN 2017019025 (print) |
LCCN 2017029772 (ebook) | ISBN 9781512601190 (epub,
mobi, & pdf) | ISBN 9781512601183 (cloth: alk. paper)
SUBJECTS: LCSH: Architecture — Israel — Haifa. |
Haifa (Israel) — Buildings, structures, etc. | Haifa (Israel) —
History — 20th century. | Gold, Nili Scharf — Homes and
haunts — Israel — Haifa. | Gold, Nili Scharf — Family.
CLASSIFICATION: LCC NA1478.H35 (ebook) |
LCC NA1478.H35 G65 2017 (print) | DDC 720.95694/6 — dc23
LC record available at https://lccn.loc.gov/2017019025

5 4 3 2 1

To the Hadar HaCarmel that was,

to my teachers and principals at the Alliance School in Haifa,

to my beloved family,

and to the memory of Paula Hahn

CONTENTS

HAIFA

*

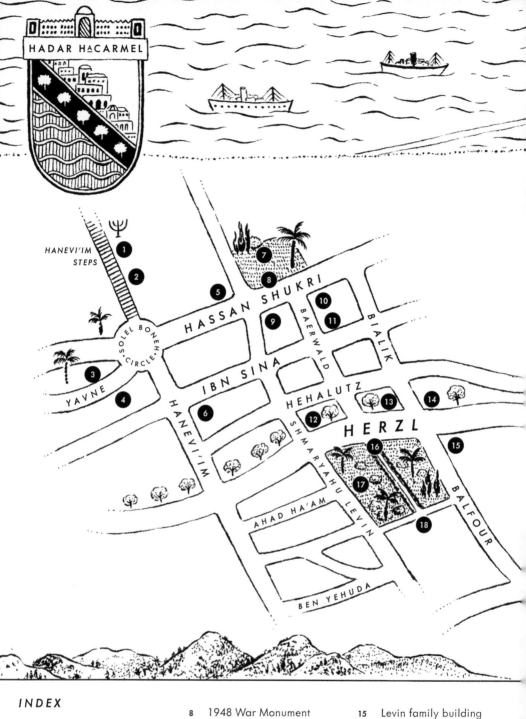

INDEX

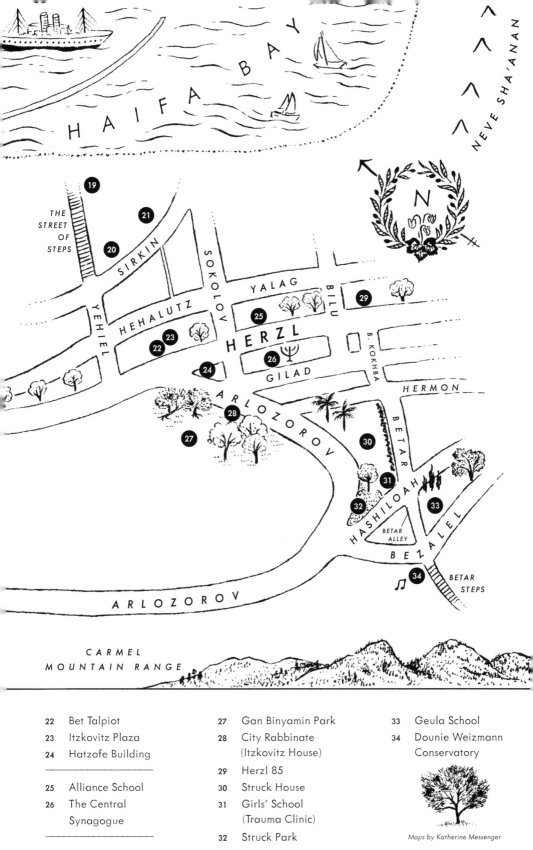

HAIFA BAY

NEVE SHA'ANAN

N

THE STREET OF STEPS

19

21

20

SIRKIN

SOKOLOV

YALAG

BILU

29

HEHALUTZ

25

HERZL

YEHIEL

23

22

24

26

GILAD

B. KOKHBA

HERMON

ARLOZOROV

28

27

BETAR

30

31

HASHILOAH

32

BETAR ALLEY

33

BEZALEL

34

BETAR STEPS

ARLOZOROV

CARMEL MOUNTAIN RANGE

22 Bet Talpiot
23 Itzkovitz Plaza
24 Hatzofe Building
_____

25 Alliance School
26 The Central Synagogue
_____

27 Gan Binyamin Park
28 City Rabbinate (Itzkovitz House)
29 Herzl 85
30 Struck House
31 Girls' School (Trauma Clinic)
32 Struck Park

33 Geula School
34 Dounie Weizmann Conservatory

Maps by Katherine Messenger

INTRODUCTION

*W*hen *I was seven or eight years old*, I thought that when you swam toward the shore from the sea, you would always encounter a forested mountain with a golden dome sparkling on its slope and white blocks of houses climbing upward. The caress of the warm seawater and the tree-strewn heights of the Carmel, like their blue and green hues, merged and became a part of my being. I took them for granted like the air I breathed.

When I would take the train back to Haifa from my studies at the Hebrew University in Jerusalem, it was not until the Carmel rose into view on my right, the sea neared the window on the left, and the palm trees appeared along the tracks that I felt at peace. When I traveled even farther afield, I would search for substitutes — a river, a lake, an ocean — but none could hold a candle to the beauty of that dramatic moment when "the looming mass of Mount Carmel comes down to meet the waters of Haifa Bay."[1]

The "Haifa" of this book is not the entire city. When I say "Haifa" here, I mean, first and foremost, Hadar HaCarmel—and not even that Jewish neighborhood in its entirety but a defined route, the route of the first eighteen years of my life, during which the city was my home and my entire world. My family lived in Hadar HaCarmel, midway up the northern slope of the mountain facing the bay.

In fact, my Haifa is an entity limited in both time and space: one slice of one neighborhood as it existed between 1948—the year of my birth —and 1966, when I last lived in the city. But just as people have parents and grandparents, children and grandchildren, so it is with buildings and cityscapes. Therefore, the period the book explores is not confined to the block of time between 1948 and 1966. Sometimes it looks forward to the ensuing decades, but mainly it stretches back to the beginning of the twentieth century. In those early years, when Hebrew Haifa was a mere glimmer, an idea, most of the city dwellers were Arab, and the minority was a colorful mixture of Jews, Turks, German Templars, and others. The name that Hebrew Haifa was eventually given is from Isaiah 35, which prophesized that when redemption came, the desert would burst into bloom: the lush "splendor of the Carmel"—*Hadar HaCarmel* in Hebrew—would be bestowed on it.[2]

This beautiful place where I grew up has a memory: the people who drew its blueprints, designed its houses, paved its streets, and planted its gardens. This place also preserves the story of the making of a community and the struggle for life against the backdrop of a unique landscape at a unique crossroads that was at once geographic, political, national, and historical.

I was born in the Bether Hospital on Pevzner Street, one of the tree-lined streets of Hadar HaCarmel. My father, Jakob Scharf, arrived in Haifa Bay in 1939 from Vienna, via Dachau, which he had barely escaped. When the rickety boat full of illegal immigrants approached the shore, the passengers, all refugees, were ordered to throw overboard every object or document

PREVIOUS PAGE The view of Haifa Bay from the Carmel
Courtesy of Dr. Dahlia Levi Eliyahu

that could reveal their country of origin, in case the British caught them and sent them back to a burning Europe. His boat successfully avoided the British coast guard, and he settled in Haifa, where he had relatives. In my father's stories, the capitol of His Highness Kaiser Franz Josef was a fairyland, but about his birthplace of Obertin in Galicia, he said nothing.

My mother, Dora née Preminger, recognized early on the imminent horror on the horizon, and in the spring of 1933 she left Europe, never to return. Chernovitz, the half-Jewish city where she was born, had been a part of the Austro-Hungarian Empire. Since 1918, however, it was Romanian and a favorite playground for the Kuzists, members of Romania's two antisemitic parties. My mother, then a young Zionist around twenty years old, saw a Kuzist yank out the beard of an Orthodox Jew. At that moment she decided to immigrate to Palestine. As she knew that her father, a strictly Orthodox disciple of the Sadigura Rebbe, would oppose her move, she did not tell him she was leaving. Her mother gave her a ruby ring, and her brothers, money for the journey. She settled in Hebrew Tel Aviv, which became increasingly crowded over the following years as the circumstances of European Jews worsened. In 1940 she moved to Haifa.

My mother and father met by chance a few years later in one of Haifa's European-style cafes. The German language, which my father brought with him from Vienna, and which was also still spoken by the Jews of Chernovitz, connected them, as it did many of their contemporaries in Hadar HaCarmel. It was the language of their love. They guarded in their hearts the remnants of the obsolete, enlightened Austro-Hungarian Empire, even while living under the dubious protection of the British Empire. In Haifa during the first half of the twentieth century, this was nothing exceptional: the city and its inhabitants, both old and new, were well versed in the frequent comings and goings of large empires.

In Haifa at the turn of the twentieth century, two empires met: one that had already begun to crumble and one that would fall a few decades later. The Ottoman past met the British future. And to this small but developing town at the end of the sultan's rule, a multitude of peoples began to flock. But within a short time World War I erupted, Haifa's infrastructure collapsed, and the city was abandoned by many of her inhabitants. During that same war the land of Palestine was wrested from the Turks, and the other major powers divided the spoils among themselves. The British had long coveted Haifa and, indeed, attained it after the war, along with all of Palestine, for a nearly thirty-year-long mandate of dizzying development. Meanwhile, a new empire, an evil one, was growing stronger. It never reached Palestine's borders, but its shock waves did. And inadvertently it contributed to the prosperity of the city. Haifa's burgeoning importance, however, began years earlier, at the end of the nineteenth century.

The city lies on the coastal strip on the southern part of Haifa Bay, the largest bay in Israel and the only one that sits at the foot of a mountain that grants it spectacular views and defends it.[3] It is a natural transportation hub, the only one of its kind in Israel and a rarity in the entire Middle East. Haifa has a harbor that is friendly to ships, free of nautical obstacles, and protected from winds by the mountain. The harbor is located on a major land intersection: to its east is the only easy passage toward Transjordan and Iraq; to the north the route along the coast conveniently leads to Lebanon, Damascus, and beyond; and the road south heads toward Egypt.[4]

Despite these advantages, during the first two thousand years of Haifa's existence, as mentioned in the Talmud and other ancient sources, it rarely surpassed the status of a fisherman's village or a little town.[5] Even during its short moments in the sun, Haifa ranked lower than its northern neighbor, Akko. It was not until late in the eighteenth century that Haifa became a major player, under the leadership of Bedouin chief Dahir al-Umar of the Zaydan clan, who conquered the Galilee and made his capital in Akko but ultimately annexed Haifa because of its port. He destroyed the ancient settlement and in 1762 built in its stead a fortified city on the southeastern point of the coastal strip, in a place that would assure the city's status as a key port in Palestine long after the end of his rule. The wall around New Haifa, or Haifa al-Jadida, was shaped like a symmetrical trapezoid and had two gates—eastern and western—through which the King's Highway passed on its way toward Akko and Jaffa. In his new city Dahir built a market and a mosque, and on the slope of the mountain he erected a tall, rectangular fortress equipped with cannons, called Burj al-Salam, that looked out over New Haifa and protected it.[6]

Haifa became an important commercial center with the conquest of Palestine in 1831 by Ibrahim Pasha, the son of the ruler of Egypt. When Akko's port was damaged by Ibrahim Pasha's attack and again when the Turks reconquered it in 1840, Haifa was the beneficiary. The reforms that

Ibrahim Pasha enforced during his nine-year rule, called the Tanzimat, granted more rights to non-Muslims and made Haifa more attractive. Following this tolerant policy, a massive immigration changed the city's demographics as it absorbed Christians from Lebanon; many merchants and craftsmen, including some Jews; and consuls representing various European countries, who brought business and economic improvement and protected their countrymen from discrimination.[7] The majority of the Jews who settled in Haifa during this period of relative security were from Morocco and Algiers and so were protected by the influential French government. When Lord Moses Montefiore came to Haifa in 1839, he visited their community.[8] Even after the Egyptian conquest ended, the Ottomans continued to grant foreigners and representatives of other countries an autonomous status, attracting investors and entrepreneurs from all over the Middle East as a result. Haifa's tolerant, cosmopolitan character was thus established between 1831 and 1840.[9] That period also saw the formation of neighborhood patterns that would continue into the beginning of the twentieth century: Muslims and Sephardic Jews settled in the east, while Arab Christians and, eventually, German Christians and some Ashkenazi Jews settled in the west.

Perhaps thanks to those reforms, about thirty years later, in 1868, location scouts for the German messianic sect, the Templars, decided that their community should settle in Haifa, "one of the few places in the land that could be considered a city in the eyes of a European observer." A flow of ships visited its enlarged port and new harbor. Haifa was then home to about twelve European consuls and enjoyed an international atmosphere — Greeks, Turks, Italians, and Armenians as well as various religious leaders all lived there. In 1867 the Hebrew newspaper *Hamagid* declared, "Haifa is a large city that trades with nations."[10]

As the century came to a close, Haifa's status was further strengthened by Sultan Abdul Hamid II's decision to connect the city and its now-expanded port to the Hejaz Railway. This ambitious project tied Haifa to Damascus in the north and the holy city of Medina in the south. It was completed in 1905 and motivated economic growth and a large immigration of not only Muslims and Christians but also European Jews — businessmen, clerks, and artisans.[11]

The modern Zionist movement also reached a peak around that time.

In 1897 Theodor Herzl convened the First Zionist Congress in Basel to
"lay the foundation" for a national home for the Jewish people. After he
visited Palestine in 1899, Herzl wrote his utopian novel *Altneuland* (Old
New Land). Published in 1902, it portrayed Haifa and the north of the
Land of Israel as he envisioned it would be in 1923. The descriptions of
the city and its port, written by the statesman with the soul of a poet, are
quoted to this day—with praise or scorn—in most of the books about
Haifa's history.[12] The beauty and passion of Herzl's language may explain
Altneuland's profound impact:

> Thousands of white villas gleamed out of luxurious green gardens. . . .
> The mountain itself was also crowned with beautiful structures. . . .
>   Now the city and harbor of Haifa lay before the entranced eyes
> of the travelers. On the near side, the broad bay with its zone of gar-
> dens . . . a magnificent expanse lay spread out before them. The sea
> glittered blue and gold into an infinite horizon. . . .
>   Below them lay Haifa like a sea of light. In the harbor and the
> roadstead as far as Akko the lights of the numerous ships were re-
> flected like stars in the mirroring waters.[13]

Herzl's utopian vision captured people's hearts, and, partially due to
his influence, Jewish organizations came to see Haifa as the Zionist center
of northern Palestine, the city of the future. But it was the non-Zionist
Ezra Association of German Jews and its forgotten leader, Paul Nathan,
who initiated the project that would impact the fate of Haifa for generations: an academic technological institution the likes of which did not
exist in all the expanses of the Ottoman Empire. They chose Haifa as the
home of the Technion because they saw it as a neutral space, not dominated by ethnic and religious tensions, like Jerusalem, or pioneering Zionist political ideologies, like Tel Aviv. The temple of science that was
ultimately erected with cooperation from the Zionists would become,
within a decade, the kernel of a city within a city—Hebrew Haifa, Hadar
HaCarmel.

In an effort to raise the money to acquire land around the Technion and
emphasize Haifa's importance, Arthur Ruppin, head of the Palestine office
of the Jewish National Fund in Cologne and the founder of the Palestine
Land Development Company, wrote to German donors in 1914, "Haifa is

the future port of the Land of Israel. It is already the center of Arab and Jewish intellectuals in all of northern Palestine. Our influence in northern Palestine depends on our prestige in Haifa." The purchase of large swaths of land was made possible in part because of the political insecurity that reigned on the eve of World War I. The German Templars worried about the value of their lands, as did the French-affiliated Carmelites, who were considered enemy agents by the Ottomans. Consequently, both groups sold large areas of land on the mountain and the slope to the Jews.[14] Despite warnings made by Arab intellectuals against the Zionist newcomers, some Arabs sold land to the Jews as well.[15]

By the end of Ottoman rule the entire area around the city was built up, stretching beyond the German colony in the west and the old fortified city of Dahir al-Umar in the east.[16] At that point, its population had reached twenty thousand inhabitants: 45 percent Christian and 40 percent Muslim. Jews made up 15 percent of Haifa's residents, but their portion of the population grew at the quickest pace. The roots of Jewish Haifa, then, preceded the British Mandate and even England's Balfour Declaration in 1917, which publicly supported Palestine as a "national home for the Jewish people."[17]

After World War I the British became the masters of Haifa. They imposed military rule until 1922, when the League of Nations granted them a mandate for Palestine, with the Balfour Declaration serving as part of its rationale. The British wanted the city to be a strategic imperial center, serving as a military base that would secure the northern hinterland of the Suez Canal as well as both a nautical access point to Iraq and a transit center through the Persian Gulf all the way to India. The city was also the hub of the Mediterranean railroad system. The British turned Haifa into an imperial, Westernized city and transferred the supreme military command of the region there. It is worth noting that the expansion of the port, the draining of the surrounding area, and the development of petrochemical industry, which included the construction of oil refineries, stemmed from imperial calculations, not local ones.[18] Nevertheless, at first glance it seemed that Herzl's dream of "the city of the future" was being fulfilled.

The Mandatory government brought in city planners and architects who were clerks of the empire and who had worked in all its colonies. In 1919, on his way to Bombay, Sir Patrick Geddes, perhaps the most eminent British urban planner, arrived in Palestine at the invitation of the British governor as well as the Zionist leader, Chaim Weizmann. Together with the city engineer, Assaf Ciffrin, he suggested an overall plan for Haifa. At Ruppin's request, Geddes's particular focus was on the area east of the Technion, where Hadar HaCarmel would eventually reside and where an unpaved grid of roads had already begun to form. He praised the location of the planned residential neighborhood because it was close enough to the commercial center of the lower city for convenience, but distant enough to foster healthy, quiet living in a green area with spectacular views of the bay. Geddes "was enamored of the Carmel ridges, with their fabulous view . . . to the sea," just like Ruppin, who named his daughter Carmela.[19] He envisioned Hadar HaCarmel as a "garden city" in accordance with the progressive urban design ideas of the period, fostering a connection between man and nature—low houses with narrow lots and façades, and gardens on each side. He suggested creating wide, parallel streets along the contour lines of the mountain, with steep, narrow streets, step paths, and alleys connecting them while looking down on the bay. In 1921 the Palestine Land Development Company wanted to translate Geddes's principles into an architectural blueprint and invited the young Jewish architect Richard Kauffmann to do so. He designed the Jewish neighborhoods of Haifa. Kauffmann's plan for Hadar was a flexible and adjustable system that served the city for sixty years. Like Geddes, he too worked with great respect for the city's natural vistas.

The first houses in Hadar HaCarmel in the 1920s stood like "palaces in the wilderness." In 1921, when there were a mere two hundred residents in the neighborhood, the Committee for Hadar HaCarmel (Va'ad) was formed, which functioned as an almost autonomous municipality until the establishment of the State of Israel. That year, 1921, was marked by violence against Jewish settlement in Palestine, and the head of the Va'ad emphasized the need for a central Hebrew neighborhood to act as a fortress "that will ensure our existence in the city of the future, in Haifa."[20] The committee wished to build a model neighborhood, a green, manicured garden city with trees adorning its streets. Here was the first modern sewer system and the first public park in the land. As early as 1925 the streets were lit with electricity. Around that time Jewish laborers who had completed British-initiated public works in the Galilee began to flow into

the city, forming what would later be known as "Red Haifa," a city dominated by leftist workers' political parties. In the late 1920s Jewish Haifa also
began the search for a modern local architectural style that would unify
European forms with eastern motifs, even as the Mandatory regime was
trying to preserve the existing style through laws that required cladding
houses in stone. Indeed, in 1926, the architect Yohanan Ratner designed
the pioneering Labor Council's central building, one of the first modernist structures in Haifa and perhaps in the entire land.[21]

Yet, the revolution in the development of Hadar, from both political
and architectural points of view, happened later and was connected to the
bloody events of 1929. Due to a second wave of violence against Jews, the
Hebrew garden city, which was supposed to rely on the commercial infrastructure of the mostly Arab lower city, was disconnected from its supply
sources. Additionally, Jews who had lived in Arab neighborhoods fled to
Hebrew Hadar, creating a dire housing situation. The public buildings that
were then constructed in Hadar HaCarmel — first and foremost, the Business Center on Herzl Street — are a testimony to the abandonment of the
residential, suburban nature of the neighborhood and to the fact that the
architectural pendulum had moved from conservatism to modernism.[22]

In Mandatory Haifa, British architectural conservatism merged with
Middle Eastern forms and German Jewish avant gardism. A new Hebrew
city was created independently of the ancient Arab one, by architects who
came from distant places and brought new and modern ideas from Europe.
Most of them arrived in Palestine between 1933 and 1939, graduates of the
German-speaking technical institutes at the forefront of architectural education of the time. These young architects in their twenties and thirties
had innovative ways of looking at the world; they were rooted in their new
land but still connected to their cultural past. The architectural style that
they developed in Haifa was marked mostly by a German imprint from
the period of the pioneers of modern architecture, the Bauhaus and International Styles. In particular, the influence of Erich Mendelsohn's work
from Berlin in the 1920s is recognizable.[23] Together with Kauffmann, he
translated the Bauhaus and International movements into the idiom of the
local climate and culture.[24]

By the end of 1939 modern architecture dominated Hadar. A movement
that had been considered a passing fad became an accepted language that

spread to every domain: residential housing, schools, public structures. A consistent environment was created in Hadar — a totality of modern urban fabric. Haifa, therefore, earned universal significance in the history of architecture and planning for its concentration of modern architecture, unparalleled outside the centers of the movement at the heart of Europe. As noted by the authors of *Bauhaus on the Carmel*, what elevates the architectural story of Haifa beyond the local to one of great international importance is the phenomenon of taking the British avant garde in city planning and the central European avant garde in architecture, then rooting them on the ancient shore of the eastern Mediterranean.[25]

In the early 1930s fascism in Europe spurred a large wave of Jewish immigration. The British tried to stop the accelerated growth of Hadar, the Hebrew "garden city," which was now absorbing the immigrants, but they finally surrendered and granted permits for three-story houses. The British even located their colonial government buildings — the courthouse and city hall — at the edge of that neighborhood. Jewish Hadar spread southward, up the mountain. By 1935 it numbered twenty-three thousand. In 1936 a third wave of violence broke out, known as the "Arab Revolt." Continuing until 1939, it was the longest and the harshest wave, including a general strike, protests, and violence against both the Jews and the British. Again, refugees moved to Hadar, Jewish residents fleeing the Arab lower city, and, again, construction began on a mercantile center that would secure the independence of its food supply — this time it was an ambitious initiative for a modern, Jewish market. The Arab Revolt was socioeconomic as much as it was nationalist.[26] The rioters were poor Arab workers protesting against Jewish and Arab elites alike and against the British, whom they saw as supporters of Zionism. The fear of and opposition to Zionists that had budded during the Ottoman period grew into an integral part of Arab nationalism, one that increased along with Jewish immigration. To appease the Arabs, the British issued the third White Paper in 1939, a policy that marked the British retreat from their earlier support of Zionism. It harshly curtailed Jewish immigration at the very moment when the fate of European Jewry was decreed. This restriction was felt acutely, especially in Haifa: because of the topography, people could see from their terraces and roofs the drama of the coast guard expelling and sending back shiploads of illegal immigrants who had fled Europe.[27] On

May 18, 1939, tens of thousands in Haifa demonstrated against the White Paper. In 1940 Italy entered the war and started bombing the city on and off until 1943. British Mandatory Haifa's intersection of roads, its industry, and its port served the war effort throughout the Middle East. While the war raged, the Arab Revolt was suppressed, but tensions still simmered beneath the surface. Once the war ended, however, they erupted, and the struggle within Palestine intensified.

On November 29, 1947, the United Nations voted for the partition of Palestine and designated May 15, 1948, as the end of the British Mandate. The Arabs rejected the plan. With the declaration of independence of the State of Israel on that date, Arab countries boycotted Israel, isolating it from its natural Middle Eastern hinterland. Haifa's life as a mixed city in which Arabs and Jews lived side by side reached a sudden end. Walid Khalidi, the eminent Palestinian scholar who established the Palestinian narrative of the events, argued as early as 1959 that the Jewish takeover of Haifa in 1948 was an outcome of a British-Zionist conspiracy.[28] Jewish historians contend that the British were neutral if not hostile to the Jewish cause.[29] Regardless, in April 1948, when the British soldiers abandoned their posts on the borders between the ethnic neighborhoods, hostilities between Arabs and Jews became full-fledged battles.

The organizational and topographic superiority of the Jewish forces brought them victory on April 22, 1948. Thus, Haifa was the first large city in which Hebrew rule was founded. Within a short time after the Jewish victory, nearly fifty thousand Arabs left Haifa, joining those who had left in the months following the United Nations vote in November 1947. Ultimately, out of the seventy thousand or so Arab residents before the war, only three thousand remained. Haifa was now an independent Hebrew city, but it was completely disconnected from any land access to its neighbors. Looking back on the closed borders to the north, east, and south, the head of the board of Israel's commercial fleet noted, "Israel is like an island whose inhabitants must use sea and air routes."[30] Sadly, the trading city now had no neighbors to trade with. Haifa lost its geopolitical status as the gateway to the Middle East and became an unimportant, midsize, regional city.

And so what was a great victory for many in 1948 marked the beginning of Haifa's decline. With all the land borders closed, the train lines no longer led anywhere; no oil flowed from Iraq to the refineries near the bay;

and the oil containers left Haifa Bay, never to return. The port served the country for two more decades, until the Ashdod port surpassed it. Haifa ceased to be the city of the future.

In the 1950s and 1960s, however, the city was not ready to admit that it had forever lost the dominant status it held during the British Mandate. A million immigrants, many of whom were Holocaust survivors, arrived in Israel through the port of Haifa during the first years of the state's existence. They masked, to a certain extent, the emptiness left by the absent Arabs.[31] Some of those newcomers were housed in the homes the Arabs had left behind. In 1950 Abba Hushi, the head of the Histadrut, the city's powerful labor union, was elected mayor. He implicitly assigned Hebrew Haifa a new national mission: to act as the flag-bearer of the working class. It was surely no coincidence that Labor's construction company, Solel Boneh, built its headquarters not in Tel Aviv but in Haifa. That building was the first quasi skyscraper in the city.[32]

Haifa faced great challenges, from unemployment to a shortage of appropriate housing.[33] But those problems were aggressively and energetically heeded in the first decade of Israeli Haifa's existence. Additionally, a large effort was made to ensure Haifa had the institutions due to a large city. Plans for a full-fledged university began early in 1953, and a theater was built — the only one constructed, funded, and staffed by a city anywhere in Israel.[34] Hushi also promoted the building of community centers, including the first Jewish-Arab cultural center in the country, on HaGefen Street in a mixed neighborhood.[35] The only underground train line in Israel, the Carmelit, was dug during that period, connecting Haifa's three centers: wholesale commerce near the port, retail and entertainment in Hadar HaCarmel, and luxury housing at the top of the mountain.[36] With all this ambition for growth, the municipality decided to gradually move the Technion campus out of Hadar HaCarmel, starting in the early 1950s.[37] While the institution did require additional space, the fact that it was extracted from Hadar in its entirety contributed to this historic neighborhood's eventual decline. Hushi tried to preserve the "greatness" of the city, but Haifa was already doomed to slowly fade into the periphery.

— ✳ —

This book stems from my life in the city. Its course follows my own personal map and preserves the corners and intersections, the houses and staircases, the stores and parks that shaped me as a person, as they did for many of my contemporaries and compatriots. Without being aware of it, we were the first Israeli Haifaians who lived in Hadar HaCarmel — little children who grew up inside the independent State of Israel. Throughout the following pages the district reveals itself in clusters, each with its particular character, each representing for us a piece of our existence: the seat of power in the northwest plain, overlooking the port; the institute of higher learning on the hill; the center of food shopping at the indoor Talpiot Market; our schools and houses of worship; and the playing fields of our youth movements. Many of the buildings that surrounded us and which are featured in the book were built in the fourth decade of the twentieth century, but each chapter focuses on a different aspect of the city's life and that of its young inhabitants.

The terrain of the book, for most of its five chapters, follows the main thoroughfare of Hadar HaCarmel, Herzl Street, as it goes from west to east. From that central axis of Herzl, tendrils stretch to the north and south or, in Haifa-speak, down toward the bay and up toward the mountaintop.

At the western end of the district is my first home, where I lived near old Arab houses and not far from the government buildings that had been built during the British Mandate. These structures, their stories, and their status in the history of the city occupy the first chapter, together with literary works that reflect the particular nature of that area. This chapter is where the memory of the city is stored: the Ottoman remnants, the British colonial imprint, and the indelible Arab presence.

From there, we travel southeast in the second chapter, to the buildings that create the busy crossroads of Herzl and Balfour. This is the intersection that stretches its steep arm upward all the way to the monumental Technion building, the genesis of the Hadar HaCarmel neighborhood and its heart for decades. This is also the locus of Haifa's architectural turning point and a favorite site of Haifa authors.

The third chapter takes us farther east, where Herzl Street meets the only diagonal street in Hadar HaCarmel, Arlozorov Street. There, the book's route digresses downward toward the sea and passes the modern architectural masterpiece, the Talpiot Market, along its way. This is where

Hadar touches the former Arab neighborhood of Wadi Salib, Haifa's politically and socially charged area, which was also reflected in the earliest
Israeli novel written about a city.

The fourth chapter covers the smallest amount of ground — it is composed of a mere two buildings, although its size belies its great significance.
The two face each other across Herzl Street — the school that I attended
beginning in third grade and the central synagogue of Hadar HaCarmel.
Each represents a different architectural and philosophical sensibility: the
insistence on the pursuit of comprehensive education opposite the bastion of conservatism and religious dominance.

The fifth and last chapter features my last home in Haifa — the house
where I lived since the time I was six, the house where my father died
and where I stayed until I left the city at the age of eighteen. From that
house near the eastern end of Herzl Street, the route climbs up through
small streets and banks of steps until it almost reaches the ridge of Mount
Carmel. Ultimately swallowed by Hadar HaCarmel, this area, previously
called Ge'ula, bordered the original parameters of the district in the east.
As it climbed up the slope of the mostly uninhabited mountain, it became
a prime adventure park for a generation that came of age in Haifa.

The total area I have described here is very small. The footsteps of a
child can cover most of it within a few hours. But owing to Hadar HaCarmel's topography, its geographic location, and the fact that it is laid out as
a grid, the greater vista is always present, even in confined areas. At every
intersection, one needs only to turn left or right to see the mountain or
the sea. This is how we learned that the place has no limits and the heights
and expanses beyond await us. Hadar HaCarmel, then, and even the short
route of this book, is not small at all. It has no borders, its horizons are
wide, and it stretches to infinity.

The time frame of the book loosely overlaps the years that I spent in the
city from the day I was born until I left to study in Jerusalem. Although the
discussion often goes beyond the bounds of those eighteen years, everything relates to them. If a structure was built in 1913, for example, but was
still standing in 1948, it enters the book. If a literary work was written after
1966 or its plot takes place after that year but encompasses the streets and
houses of the Haifa that I knew, I include it. It seems that 1963 is the invisible line that divides those who know my Haifa and those who do not.

Authors born before that year still share the image of the city or, rather, the image of Hadar that I remember. The book focuses on the period before the 1967 war, which turned everything upside down and changed the country beyond recognition.

In Haifa the 1950s and 1960s were the years of Mayor Abba Hushi, who was elected in 1950 and served until his death in 1969. Even though he was motivated by political ambitions, he cared about the city more than any who came after him. He lived on the elegant Yerushalayim Street in Hadar HaCarmel and pampered his neighborhood as he did the entire city. The story goes that Abba Hushi walked the streets at the crack of dawn every morning to make sure the sanitation workers had done their jobs faithfully and that the streets had been swept.

Almost a lifetime has passed between the time I lived in Haifa and the time I sat down to write about it. With the help of poems, stories, and novels; with architectural textbooks, tour guides and history books; with blueprints and documents from city and state archives; with endless walks and conversations with good, knowledgeable people, I began to decipher the spell that the city casts over those who know it well. First were the literary works, and sometimes their authors as well, who taught me to produce the right sound and tone. The writers who helped me tell the story of Haifa are all Hebrew writers who lived in the city for a significant period of time: some were born in Haifa, some grew up there, some arrived as young adults. The portrait of the city is not necessarily the focus of their poetry and fiction, but its true face hides between their lines. They guided me around my city and showed me how to see it anew through adult eyes. Some of the authors generously told me in interviews about the various ways in which the city is woven into their texts. Their words — both written and oral — play a vital part in forging the various stations of my book.

Haifa's authors use the city, its streets and landmarks, intersections and steps, as a language, words and sentences through which they reveal their inner worlds. I am trained in reading texts, but I discovered that buildings too may be read as texts that speak in a language with their own cadences, rhythms, and idioms. I learned that each building tells a story in the way it is constructed, that a building can serenade its environs. This book is a meeting point of different art forms and space, memory enshrined in literature and landscape.

1

THE SEAMLINE

Where Memory Is Stored

"*Ibn Sina 4, Ibn Sina 4. Don't forget.* Ibn Sina 4. If you get lost, find a policeman and say, 'Ibn Sina 4. I live at number 4, Ibn Sina Street.'" This was the mantra my mother drilled into me. And one day I did, indeed, get lost. I was four years old. My mother; my baby brother, Gadi; and I were strolling through Memorial Park (Gan HaZikaron, literally, "The Garden of Memory") on Hassan Shukri Street, near our house, when suddenly my mother and the baby carriage disappeared, as if swallowed up by the earth. I was standing there all alone. But I didn't panic. I remembered, "Ibn Sina 4. Find a policeman and say, 'Ibn Sina 4.'" I looked around and there, at the entrance to the park, was a policeman. I walked over to him and, without shedding a tear, asked him to take me home. When he knocked, my mother opened the door. Afterward, she would proudly recount how

Memorial Park fountain *Photograph by Aviv Itzhaki*

impressed the police officer had been by my maturity and the fact that I knew the address.

Like Memorial Park, the other landmarks inlaid along Hassan Shukri Street — as well as the side street, Ibn Sina, where I lived until age six — enshrine both Haifa's past and my early childhood. Together they create a treasure trove that is municipal, architectural, and personal.[1] Memorial Park, which we frequented throughout my early childhood, had wide, paved paths surrounded by grass fields and flowerbeds. The waters of the tall fountain at its center leaped up and hit the pool beneath them time and again, their sound blending with the voices of mothers and children that burst forth from the nearby playground. From the colonnade at its northern tip, one could gaze out onto the port and the ships and even the Lebanon Mountains on the other side of the blue bay.

Opposite the park, on the southern side of Hassan Shukri, rose Haifa's glorious city hall, the pride of the city and, even now, the street's most distinguished tenant. Its soaring entrance-archway; the green, manicured plaza that distanced it from the sidewalk; and Memorial Park, which extended as a continuation of that plaza — all announced the building's authority. West of the park, across a narrow alley, sat the police station; it was an old, heavy, stone building with a decorative wrought-iron gate. Across from it, city hall's older, more modest neighbor, the courthouse — or "Law Courts" in British parlance — stood like a dignified aristocrat.

Side by side these two stately buildings—city hall and the courthouse—bestowed confidence and trust on all who visited the street. These buildings and even the name of the street on which they stand are echoes of the Arab-Jewish coexistence that was forged in the city before 1948. The strict symmetry of their design gave each building the appearance of a scale with two balanced arms, a visual expression of equality as if to proclaim, "In Haifa, each side used to be given the same weight; Jews and Arabs were treated equally." Indeed, this was the attempt before the war of 1948, after which most of the Arab population departed the city.

While Hassan Shukri Street, along with Memorial Park and the British colonial buildings, were the northernmost border of my early childhood map, Ibn Sina Street felt like a friendly extension of our home. I was only faintly conscious of the bustling HaNeviim Street, which touched the western tip of both my Ibn Sina Street and Hassan Shukri at the Solel Boneh Circle, yet two of its smaller branches had a great significance to me in those early days: HaNeviim Steps Street and Yavne Street. The former dropped north, down toward the sea, a steeper continuation of the flat HaNeviim Street. I used to skip down those steps with my father on Saturdays on the way to the Hadrat Kodesh synagogue. Yavne Street turned westward and descended gently toward Wadi Nisnas. My mother used to take us to Yavne when we were sick, for one of its secret-shrouded buildings housed our health clinic.

This area west of city hall, which was eventually swallowed by the Hadar HaCarmel neighborhood, used to be known as Al Burj, named for the Arab stronghold Burj al-Salam (Fortress of Peace). The fortress, erected in 1762 by Dahir al-Umar al-Zaydani, the Bedouin ruler and founder of new Haifa, stood where Memorial Park now sprawls. Its last remnants were gone by the middle of the British Mandate period. The cornerstone of the prestigious residential Arab neighborhood of Al Burj was laid in 1908, when a rich Lebanese Maronite, Salim al-Khouri, built his "palace" there and enclosed it with an expansive garden. Later Al Burj developed into a "kind of a winding *seamline* of Arab and Jewish houses that were interlaced, one with the other." This seamline, *kav tefer* in Hebrew, was not a border but rather a line that both separated and connected, like the seam of a garment. It was populated with ornate buildings in varied styles, some built through Arab-Jewish real estate partnerships.[2]

The seamline and its landmarks are etched into the memory of the city's inhabitants and its authors—the ethnically ambiguous characters in the novels of the Haifa author Sami Michael cross through it, as does a conflicted protagonist of the postmodernist author Yoel Hoffmann. The footprints of this area are also scattered throughout the letters and poems of Yehuda Amichai, who lived in Haifa before making his name as one of Israel's greatest poets. When the seamline's landmarks surface in literary works, they are akin to spatial Freudian slips, as partial, involuntary revelations of the urban subconscious, where the collective past of Haifa is stored. These are nonverbal slips—street corners and structures, not words, that hide history's secrets.

During the British Mandate the main street of this neighborhood, Burj Street, was an extraterritorial plane of sorts, and the British authorities selected it as the ideal location for government buildings—most significantly, the district courthouse and city hall. At the time it was convenient and accessible to all the city's residents, and it connected the ethnically mixed Al Burj with the rapidly developing Jewish Hadar HaCarmel. It passed high above the lower city on the mountain ledge, near the two Arab neighborhoods of Wadi Salib and Wadi Nisnas. After the courthouse was finished in 1932, Burj Street was renamed Courthouse Road, but ever since 1940 it has been called Hassan Shukri Street.

A Mayor for All

Hassan Bey Shukri served as Haifa's mayor from 1914 until his death in 1940, albeit not continuously.[3] He was a kind of enlightened revolutionary, a man with an antiwar vision who consistently and publicly promoted interethnic collaboration.[4] The attitude that he conferred on the municipal government contrasted with the policies of his Arab counterparts in other mixed cities.[5] He demanded that Jewish rights be upheld, even though he was an Arab leader in a city that was, at the beginning of his tenure, predominantly Arab. All told, he was a kindhearted, incorruptible man who supported equal representation for Arabs and Jews in municipal committees and posts and had the minutes of city meetings recorded in Hebrew in addition to Arabic.[6] He adhered to this policy during the Arab revolt in 1936–39, despite betrayals by his friends, and even after vilifica-

Portrait of Mayor
Hassan Bey Shukri
*Courtesy of Haifa City
Archives*

tion, threats, and assassination attempts by Arab extremists that ultimately
forced him to temporarily leave the city.[7] For Shukri, the good of Haifa as
a whole was always the priority, and he bestowed this ethos on the conduct and values of the municipality of Haifa for years to come.[8]

In the very first council meeting after Shukri's death in 1940, his heir,
Shabtai Levi, proposed renaming the street on which city hall would be
built to Hassan Shukri Street. This way, Levi said, "the name of the deceased will have an enduring connection with the [city hall] building."
And so, before the first stone was laid—even before the design was final-
ized—the link was cemented between city hall and the legendary mayor
who had "invested enormous efforts" into the construction of Haifa's most
illustrious building but who did not live to serve in it.[9]

In fact, the Jewish Shabtai Levi was Hassan Shukri's closest friend. Levi
had been a Haifa citizen since 1905, city council member since 1918, and
the deputy mayor starting in 1934. Like Shukri, he was of Turkish origin.
Throughout all their years together and the changing times, Turkish remained the two friends' intimate language. Zechariah Froehlich, the
last living witness to their unique bond, divulged this detail to the city's

unofficial historian, Eli Roman, some seventy years afterward. Froehlich had begun his career in city hall as a delivery boy in Shukri's office in the 1930s and could still effortlessly recall that period.[10] It turns out that both Shukri and Levi were graduates of the Imperial School of Civil Administration in Istanbul, established in 1859, which trained the Ottoman Empire's administrators and instilled in them its tolerant culture. It was said that the graduates of that school placed public service first and Turkey second, as expressed in the Turkish rhyme, "Önce Mülkiye, Sonra Türkiye."[11] In Haifa, Shukri and his deputy-turned-successor applied a similar guiding principle of "Haifa first, ethnicity second." Their courageous partners — the Arab and Jewish city council members — behaved in a similar fashion, acting "for the entire population" in a "city that belongs to each one of us."[12] The Jewish council members supported improving the quality of life in Arab neighborhoods, even when the expenses exceeded the budget for Jewish ones, while the Arab council members cooperated with their Jewish peers despite outside threats and intimidation.[13] Together, they steered Haifa's ship through the stormy waters of the British Mandate and national conflict with mutual respect, tolerance, and friendship.

Early in the twentieth century, before the rise in immigration from Europe, the municipal representatives of the Jewish population — Shabtai Levi, among them — were mostly members of the Sephardic community who came from North Africa and the Levant.[14] The roots of this community were planted in the nineteenth century and earlier.[15] Their homes and synagogues sat side by side with Arab homes and places of worship in the eastern part of the city — in the Jewish Alliance School, for example, Arab Muslims and Christians studied alongside Jews.[16] In those neighborhoods the relationship between Arabs and Jews mostly fluctuated between friendship and neighborly decency, even during times of tension.[17] Haifa's Sephardic Jews were fluent in Arabic and were intimately familiar with Arab customs.[18] This contributed to the mutual trust and ability to cooperate on municipal matters when obstacles arose.[19] When European Jews joined the municipality, they continued the policy of separating civil administration from the outside political conflict. Indeed, Haifa was the only ethnically mixed city that continued to function even when violence erupted.

Turning Points in the Life of City Hall

The eighteen years (1924–42) that passed from the first initiative to construct a headquarters for all the municipality's departments until the fulfillment of that dream overlapped with one of the most crucial periods in the history of the country and, perhaps, of the Middle East. The piece of land allotted for city hall was located on the seamline between the "lower city" and other Arab neighborhoods and Hadar HaCarmel, the Jewish neighborhood sprouting up around the Technikum (ultimately, the Technion).[20] This lot blended strategic advantages: geographically, it was on the northern border of Hadar, at the cusp of a mountain ledge from which one could observe the Haifa bay; demographically and politically, it served as an intermediary between the two populations.[21] The Mandate authorities decided to build the courthouse there in 1928.[22] The municipality of Haifa understood the area's importance and joined the effort to centralize administrative buildings along the seamline. Shabtai Levi, then a city council member, assisted the British in acquiring more land for the courthouse, and in 1932 the impressive building was inaugurated. At the same time, with the support of the city council, Mayor Hassan Shukri embarked on extensive negotiations with the British to buy a lot for a new city hall.[23] After years of lobbying, the British high commissioner finally approved an exceptionally large loan for the project on the cusp of 1940, despite the tension that dominated that period.[24]

The minutes from the meetings surrounding the land acquisition and erection of Haifa's city hall are a spellbinding historical record of Arab-Jewish cooperation in Haifa in the 1930s and 1940s. At the beginning of 1940 while World War II was raging, the city council adopted the equitable principles that would guide the construction. A building committee of two Jews and two Arabs composed a detailed work contract that serves as testimony to the integrity of its authors and their desire to right previous wrongs.[25] A Haifa resident, according to this contract, was anyone who lived in Haifa, regardless of ethnicity: "all the workers . . . will be Haifa residents . . . the term 'Haifa resident' means a person who, according to the opinion of the employer, is a true resident (with a pure heart) of Haifa." Furthermore, they agreed "that the sums that would be paid to Jewish and Arab workers would be equal."[26] One may, then, interpret the structure

Front view of city hall *Courtesy of photographer Adi Silberstein*

of city hall itself—its stones and doors, floors, stair railings, and meeting halls—as a monument to the unique web of relationships forged between the Arabs and Jews of Haifa before 1948.[27]

The posting that advertised the search for a contractor and related positions was published in the three official languages—English, Arabic, and Hebrew—and the project was expedited because the municipality's previous office building in the lower city had been bombed in 1940 by Italian airplanes. The economical proposal submitted by Solel Boneh, the Jewish cooperative construction company, was selected, and in 1941 the foundations were laid.[28] The war caused some cuts to the original plan, but the building was completed within sixteen months.[29]

The invitations to the inauguration of Haifa's city hall flaunted a drawing of the new building and indicated that "his highness, the high commissioner would be present." Arab and Jewish leaders from all over the country attended the ceremony on Monday, June 29, 1942. During his speech Shabtai Levi thanked all the laborers, artists, and craftsmen, both Arabs and Jews. He ended with an expression of hope that Haifa "will be able to fulfill its mission of peace as a connecting link between east and west, north and south, not only for the benefits of its inhabitants, but also for the entire Near East and Middle East."[30] Sadly, Shabtai Levi's words were scattered to the winds before even six years had passed. The period during World War II was not marked by overt tensions between Arabs and Jews, but soon after the war ended the tensions erupted again due to the disputes regarding how to handle the masses of Jewish refugees and the persistent suggestion of Jewish statehood as a possible solution. During the early months of the 1948 war, most of Haifa's Arab inhabitants left, the city remained empty of half its population, and Haifa was no longer able to fulfill its "mission of peace."

After November 29, 1947, when the United Nations voted to terminate the British Mandate and partition Palestine, hostilities between Jewish and Arab paramilitaries erupted, and Haifa too entered the cycle of violence. Firefights, snipers, explosions, and car bombs dominated the city and its vicinity, and many of the Arabs — especially the wealthy and prominent — left. The fierce, bitter battles climaxed on April 21, 1948, the eve of Passover of the Hebrew year *tav shin het*, after the British announced that their military guards would leave their posts between the Arab and Jewish neighborhoods. On the morning of April 22, the Jewish Hagana declared victory.

In British armored cars the Arab leaders — both Muslim and Christian — were driven to a side entrance of city hall to sign a ceasefire agreement.[31] The wood-clad conference room in city hall became the stage for the wretched penultimate scene of the drama. This was part of a seemingly fated chain of events whose actors recognized its horror but, as in a tragic play, were unable to stop it. The fact that some of the members of the "cast" were friends, who had successfully overcome their differences in the past, made this break even crueler. In the same conference room where they used to discuss the fate of the city, in the presence of the Jewish mayor Shabtai Levi and the Jewish city council members, as well as officials from the Hagana and the British Mandate, the Arab deputy mayors and the leaders of the Arab community examined the details of the ceasefire agreement. When it seemed that the document was ready to be signed, the Arab participants suddenly asked for a twenty-four-hour extension so they could receive approval from the military command in Damascus. Despite the objections of the British and Jewish participants, the British pledge to protect the city's Arabs, and the mayor's promise to personally guarantee their safety, the Arab representatives insisted on the extension.

Finally, all agreed to meet again in city hall in a few hours. When the time came, however, only the Christian leaders returned — but not to sign the agreement. Instead, they announced that they and the other Arab representatives were going to instruct Haifa's Arabs to leave the city. This is how the fate of the Arabs of Haifa was determined. Shabtai Levi even ordered cars equipped with loudspeakers to circle the city streets, announcing to the Arab residents that they would not be harmed and urging them to stay, but there were other forces at work, which drove the Arabs to leave.[32]

Scholars from the various sides of the conflict do not agree as to the content of the orders that the Arab representatives of Haifa did or did not receive from their commanders abroad.[33] The mere definition of the Arabs' departure is suffused with pain and discord: Was it flight? Abandonment? Expulsion? Was there a sincere attempt to convince them to stay? Were they exiled? Were they victims of a scare campaign accompanied by shelling? Was it a departure that stemmed from a flawed assumption that soon the Jews would be defeated and Arabs would return, as victors, to their homes? Or perhaps it was a combination of these possibilities and interpretations. The answer is beyond the scope of this book. In any event, the immediate result of the Arab leaders' refusal to sign the ceasefire agreement was the mass flight of tens of thousands of Haifa's remaining Arabs to the British-held port. Despite differences regarding the preceding details, according to all accounts, within a few weeks the city lost about 95 percent of its Arab population, and within a few months those who had left were barred from returning.[34]

Snipers on 4 Ibn Sina

When I was little, my mother told me that after the Hagana won, cars drove through the streets of Haifa with loudspeakers, entreating the Arabs in Arabic and Hebrew to remain. At the time my parents lived in a ground-floor apartment on 4 Ibn Sina Street, which they rented from the house's Arab owner, and its story reflects that of many others like it. In the Haifa City Archives I found the blueprints of the building, one of the many stone houses constructed in the area in the 1930s by wealthy Haifa Arabs to rent out to Jews.[35] Built in 1936, 4 Ibn Sina was the property of Mr. Salim Azam. After the establishment of the State of Israel, however, my parents no longer paid him rent — the house was transferred into the hands of the government. The mysterious, incomprehensible word *Harekhushanatush*, which was repeated in the adults' conversations about the apartment, was the name of the secret entity to which my parents paid rent every month. Years later I learned that *Harekhushanatush* was actually two words, *rekhush* and *natush* (*ha* means "the"), that meant "abandoned property." According to Israeli law, this was the legal status of real estate that belonged to Arabs who had left.

I never met my parents' Arab landlord, and until my visit to the City Archives I didn't even know his name, but I heard the story of his departure from my mother: during the battles in the city, she said, the *effendi* (lord or master — what my mother called the rich Arab landlord), who used to live on the top floor, left the house at 4 Ibn Sina, together with his family. Near the opening in the stone fence that surrounded the building, his sixteen-year-old son turned around and addressed my mother, who had accompanied them with her gaze: "We will return," he said, "and then . . ." And he completed the sentence with a sign everybody understands — he slowly sliced his finger across his throat, meaning, "we will slaughter you all." During the weeks before the *effendi* left, the house's large yard had hummed with poor Arab laborers (*horanim*, to use my mother's term) who had originally come to Haifa to look for work.[36] Now, they sat in our yard, hoping for protection from the *effendi*. As he turned toward the street, she said, he waved his arm in a grand "come with me" gesture, and they followed him.

I remember well the opening in the fence where Mr. Azam's son stood, and I will also never forget the window in our bedroom. In the thick frame of that window, on the bottom left, was a big, ugly gash that exposed its stone innards. This was a scar from a bullet fired in 1948 during the war, when my mother was pregnant with me and snipers would sit on the roof of the Yavne Clinic and shoot down at the streets and houses. My father refused to fix the wall because it was thanks to its thickness that his wife and daughter survived.

After my pregnant mother's brush with death, my father's older brother, Chaim, grew worried about her and visited frequently. To avoid becoming a sniper's target on the wide, dangerous streets, Uncle Chaim had to sneak through backyards and alleyways to reach our house. And, indeed, a short time after our windowsill stopped that bullet, another bullet from the same snipers' nest on Yavne Street hit a pregnant woman who was trying to cross Ibn Sina. From inside our house, my mother heard her screams; grabbed a new, thick white towel; and ran into the street to help her. She stopped the flow of blood with the towel and waited with her until the ambulance arrived. My mother had no way of finding out what ultimately happened to the woman she tried to save. Telling the story years later, she would lament, "And there went my best towel."

≈ ✳ ≈

I heard an echo of my mother's stories decades later, when I was preparing to write my book on Yehuda Amichai, Israel's unofficial national poet.[37] One of the most important sources for my study were dozens of love letters that Amichai had written in Haifa, years before his star rose in the firmament of Hebrew literature.[38] He lived in the city between August 1947 and April 1948, the stormiest period in Haifa's history, as well as a formative one in his own life. During that time his beloved girlfriend, Ruth Hermann, was studying in New York City. She had intended to return after a year but wound up staying permanently. The letters he sent her weave an intimate story at whose center is a young man's desire to be a poet. At the same time, they coalesce to form a detailed historical document, rare in its vitality. These letters provide a firsthand testimony, from a Jewish-Zionist point of view, of the first months of the war, the shootings and violence that occurred on the streets of Haifa almost every day.

I discovered Amichai's letters in 2003. This finding revolutionized the scholarship on Amichai as a budding poet and also breathed life into the stories my mother told me of the war. In a letter from the middle of December 1947, for example, I read, "Here is a regular occurrence these days. Suddenly, shots from near and far, people run into buildings." In a letter that he sent less than two weeks later, Amichai told Ruth, "A woman was killed on Herzl Street while hanging up the diapers of her two-month-old baby to dry." And in another letter from December, he writes of his pupil's story of a bullet that entered the bathroom and broke the mirror.[39] The personal and artistic lens through which reality is examined in the letters also sheds light, of course, on the poet as a young man. In January Amichai interwove gallows humor with the fear of being shot by a sniper: "People walk in the cover of buildings, leisurely . . . shop, talk, until they either reach a street that rises from the lower level or an empty lot. There, you see a ridiculous scene. They cross that segment of the street running, bent double, with quick jumps, 'Thank God, we crossed!'"[40]

Amichai later translated his description of the pedestrians' strategy for dodging bullets into poetic lines that blend existential fear with the fear of abandonment. The words "empty lot," which he used matter-of-factly in the letter he wrote in January, became the metaphorical title and leitmotif of a bitter poem he composed around that time. (The poem refers to the winter month of Tevet — likely February — in the future tense: "and in Tevet, there will be winds." This suggests that the poem was written early in the winter.) Amichai finally copied "The Empty Lot" into an aerogram when the recognition that Ruth would not return began to sink in. On April 7, 1948, he gathered the courage to ask her directly in a poem: "The entire question is simple: / Will you *cross* the *empty lot* in order / To *reach* me, / Or are you afraid."[41] These poetic lines recall the vocabulary he used in his January letter — "empty lot," "cross," "reach." As we know, Ruth never "crossed the empty lot" to reach the man who waited for her. On April 7 her farewell letter, which would break Amichai's heart, had already been mailed. After receiving it, Amichai joined the elite units of the Palmach and was stationed far away from Haifa, at the raging warfront in the Negev. He would not publish the poem about the empty lot until 1958, and even then he would erase the traces of battle-ridden Haifa from its surface.

A Literary Refuge on Hassan Shukri Street

When the Iraqi-born Jewish author Sami Michael first arrived in Haifa in the early 1950s, there were no longer battles and the majority of the city's Arabs were already gone. A gifted journalist, communist and native Arabic speaker, Michael was invited by the Arab writer and editor Emil Habibi to join *Al-Ittihad*, the Arabic-language, communist newspaper published in Haifa. The young Michael fell in love with the city and never left. At first he made his home in Wadi Nisnas, where most of the Arabs who stayed in Haifa after the war were concentrated, and continued writing in

Arabic. It was not until the 1970s that he published the first of the fifteen
novels he would write in Hebrew (to date). Haifa serves as the setting for
five of them, and, of those five, three revolve closely around Jewish-Arab
relations.[42]

In these novels Michael creates ambiguous situations at whose center
are Haifaian protagonists who are simultaneously Jewish and Arab. Their
dual identity, so to speak, is often a product of their country of origin or
of a boundary-crossing love.[43] These "double" characters are a literary representation of the author's desire for a common Jewish-Arab existence, a
quest that determines the locality of the novels and draws their heroes to
Haifa's seamline. There, at the threshold between the Arab Wadi Nisnas
and the large Jewish neighborhood of Hadar, Michael gropes toward the
suppressed, pluralistic Haifaian subconscious as it is revealed in public
buildings, street names, and garden paths. His dual-identity protagonists
pass through the seamline. They arrive in its vicinity by foot and by car,
independently and together, voluntarily and unwillingly, by choice and
by chance. They climb up to the Solel Boneh Circle on the western tip
of Hassan Shukri Street, recoil from the police station, mingle with the
crowds in front of the May Cinema, and stop inadvertently in front of city
hall. The characters are not aware — at least not on the face of the page
— of the historical significance of Hassan Shukri Street and city hall and
their unique status in the chronicles of both the city and the land. Yet the
author who pulls the strings leads his actors to the seamline and directs
them in sometimes unbearable scenes that nonetheless contain flickers
of the shining story behind this setting. Moreover, the extreme precision
with which Michael details the routes his heroes take along the seamline
underscores his recognition of the alternate possibilities for Arab-Jewish
relationships that it represents.

Michael's first Haifaian novel, *Refuge* (*Hasut*), introduces the reader to
a gallery of characters with multifaceted identities, most of whom are connected to Israel's Communist Party. It is set in October 1973, during the
Yom Kippur War. At its center is the Jewish couple Shula and Marduch —
she is Israeli born, while he is from Iraq. Marduch is now serving in the Israeli army on the southern front, while Shula's childhood boyfriend, Rami,
is stationed on the northern one. The Communist Party has demanded
that Shula hide an Arab-Christian poet, Fatkhi, who might be wanted by

the police. She shelters him in her home, despite her trepidations. The novel also features Shula's friends, Shoshana and Fuad. Shoshana is an Israeli Jew, while her husband, Fuad, is an Arab Muslim from Haifa. Unavoidably, the war has heightened the tensions within their family.

One of the most intense scenes in *Refuge* takes place on Hassan Shukri Street on the second day of the Yom Kippur War. The author summons his cast of characters to the heart of this sensitive historical area: Shula, the Jewish communist; her mentally disabled son; the teenager Naim, whose ethnically mixed parents are Shula's friends; an old Holocaust survivor; a mostly Jewish crowd of passersby; and an Arab policeman. Michael exploits the close proximity of the seamline's landmarks to one another to heighten both the narrative and social tensions, creating a pressure cooker on the verge of explosion.

On that particular morning Shula had gone to visit her childhood home in the suburb of Kiryat Hayim, where she ran into Goldschmidt, her parents' neighbor. His son Rami, the first man she ever loved, was now fighting in the Golan Heights. Goldschmidt asked Shula to give him a ride to city hall, which was not far from where she lived. While driving into the city, however, she became distracted by memories of her former beloved and got lost. Goldschmidt offered to make his way to his destination on his own, but Shula insisted on bringing him to the door. The car climbed up Liberation Ascent Road — Ma'ale HaShihrur in Hebrew — toward Hassan Shukri, where Shula dropped off Goldschmidt at city hall.

She then tried to continue on her way home, but was halted when "across from the courthouse, at the edge of Memorial Park, the crowd blocked her way."[44] This is the place to note that in various interviews, Michael has confirmed that he writes only about the world that is familiar to him. Indeed, the Haifa map that he draws, so to speak, in his books is testimony to the areas where he has lived and wandered in Haifa over the decades during which he made this city his home. In the scene from *Refuge* at hand, Michael uses the markers that are so familiar to Haifaians to signal to his readers that Shula has barely moved along Hassan Shukri Street — only one hundred yards separate city hall, where she dropped off her passenger, and the courthouse, where she was stopped against her will. As Shula waited in her car for the road to clear, she caught a glimpse of the person at the center of the commotion blocking her way. It was

none other than Naim, the son of her friends from the Communist Party
— fellow protagonists of the book, Fuad and Shoshana.

Unlike Shula, Naim had arrived at the seamline with a premeditated
purpose. In the previous chapter Michael revealed Naim's fractured family
in all its pathos. The eldest son wanted to be Jewish, like his mother, while
Naim and his younger brother wanted to be Arab, like their father. Naim,
who had painted the Palestinian flag in gouache paints one day earlier to
signal his national identity, came to Memorial Park expecting to watch the
Arab airplanes as they finally bombed Israel. Michael, the veteran Haifaian
author, led Naim there because it is a great lookout point, using Haifa's
topography to satisfy the caprice of his conflicted adolescent hero. Memorial Park, planted to glorify those who fell in the 1948 war for Israel's
independence, was the place where the boy hoped to witness the defeat of
that state. Yet no airplanes arrived, and instead of fulfilling his nationalist
dreams, Naim found himself aiding an old Holocaust survivor who was
having difficulty reaching a bomb shelter when the air-raid sirens sounded.
Afterward the old man wanted to bless him for his kindness and asked
for his name. Instead of providing his real name, Naim goaded the old
man by telling him a common Muslim name. The old man panicked, and
the crowd — already tense due to the air raid — fell on Naim, under the
mistaken assumption that he had hurt the old man. At that very moment
Shula appeared, a kind of deus ex machina, and intervened in Naim's favor.

The novel's title, *Refuge*, reflects the humanist ideals held by its author.[45] Giving refuge to a guest is a core value for Michael, who grew up as
a member of a protected minority in Iraq, in the bosom of Middle Eastern
ethics. According to this principle, one must grant refuge — be it from en-
emies or natural disaster — to guests, no matter their religious, familial, or
tribal affiliations. Although the term *hasut* derives from the Hebrew root
het samekh heh (ה.ס.ה), which means "protect," and is close in meaning to
kaf samekh heh (ה.ס.כ.), which means "cover," another root reverberates in
it: *het vav samekh* (ס.ו.ה), "to have pity." The quintessential representation
of *hasut* in this novel is the refuge that Shula, the Jewish communist, offered Fatkhi, the Arab communist poet whom she hid in her house after
the war broke out. Another instance of refuge recalled in the novel occurs
with regard to Shula's Jewish husband, who had been granted refuge by
strangers while the authorities in his Arab homeland of Iraq were chasing

him. The last case of refuge, one more marginal to the plot of the novel, was that granted by Shula to Naim when she literally covered or protected him from the angry crowd with her body. Faced with the boy's dire situation, Shula "ignored" her son's "screams" and exited her car:

> The boy [Naim] was close to fainting. His shirt was torn, blood oozed from his lip, there was a swelling on his forehead. . . . Shula threw herself on him, crying, "Don't touch him!"
>
> Everyone was stupefied — even the old man fell silent. "You know him?" . . .
>
> "Of course. His mother's a friend of mine."
>
> "So he's a Jew."[46]

This episode reveals Shula in all her nobility. She offered refuge to the Arab poet, but only because the Communist Party expected her to do so; on the seamline, however, she physically protected the weak because of an irrepressible inner impulse. It is no coincidence that the empathy-filled meeting between the Jewish woman and the Arab-Jewish son of her friends, in the midst of an anti-Arab crowd, is set — where else — on Hassan Shukri Street at the edge of Memorial Park.

A few years after the events in the novel take place, a real monument, sculpted into black volcanic rock, would be laid on Memorial Park's southern border.[47] This rock was the work of the leftist artist Gershon Knispel, commissioned by the municipality to commemorate, as the words on the monument state, "The Liberation of Haifa: 1948."[48] In his wisdom Knispel forged a low monument whose sadness and symbols seem to lament Jews and Arabs alike — those who fell in the war but also those for whom Haifa had been home for decades, who had left and were unable to return.[49] A map of the routes that the fighters took in 1948 is carved into the black, unfinished stone, and above it hovers a figure that may be a dove or, perhaps, an angel with an amputated wing. It may be that in his piece of art, Knispel was implying that after the spring of 1948, Haifa, the city that lost half of its population — men, women, and children — was like a crippled dove that could not fly. On the other side of the black monument a dead soldier has been sculpted. A helmet on his head, a gun at his side, there is no indication to show whether he is Jewish or Arab.

Although the paths of the two former communists, the author and the

War Monument in Memorial Park *Courtesy of photographer Adi Silberstein*

sculptor, crossed but rarely, Knispel's work of art visually depicts humanist ideals similar to those Michael expresses in words.[50] In fact, the architect Waleed Karkabi, the son of one of the most deeply rooted, aristocratic Arab families in Haifa, wrote the following to me in 2015: "The truth is that for years after the establishment of the state, the only body that protected the broken Arab minority, organized it, and tried to include it in the life of the country was the Communist Party, which was a Jewish-Arab party!"[51] It seems that the fictional characters of *Refuge*, like the flesh-and-blood people who served as Michael's inspiration for them, behaved in this spirit.[52] They were members of the Haifa Communist Party who acted honorably despite the rifts that existed between them.

Refuge goes beyond city hall, Memorial Park, and the courthouse; it also resurrects a more ominous landmark on the seamline—the police station. The stone building that housed the police station was built as a residence for the family of Taufiq Bey el-Khalil, whose father was Mustafa Pasha el-Khalil, Haifa's mayor at the end of the nineteenth century (Taufiq was also Hassan Shukri's brother-in law).

This building's basic planning principle is that of an Arab *liwan* house,

with a central common inner space.[53] Indeed, it looks like a traditional
Middle Eastern home, except for its tall windows, which testify to Western influences.[54] The design details of this cubical structure attest to the
affluence of its original owners: a tall entrance archway resting atop columns, to which Carrara Italian marble steps lead; ornate lintels; an interior staircase with marble carvings; decorated stone walls; and a floor
of white marble inlaid with black patterns. The large garden surrounding
the structure, its high fence, and the inset wrought-iron gate separated
the house from the street, ensuring the privacy of its residents. When the
building became a police station during the British Mandate, this distance
between the building and the street made it more intimidating. In 1948 it
was turned into an Israeli police station and functioned as one through the
early 1970s, when the plot of *Refuge* unfolds.

On the same morning that Naim, *Refuge*'s young protagonist, set out to
watch for airplanes in Memorial Park, his father, Fuad, the Arab communist, went to register at the nearby police station, as he was mandated to
do twice a day. His Jewish wife, Shoshana, accompanied him from their
home in Wadi Nisnas almost all the way to the station but stopped at the
crossroad where Hadar HaCarmel meets the wadi—the Solel Boneh Circle on the seamline:

> Shoshana pressed quietly against his arm.... They stood in Haneviim
> Street.... Shoshana extricated her arm from his, and the sea breeze
> invaded [the space] between them. Behind her was Wadi Nisnas, in
> front of her, Fuad's solid body hiding Hassan Shukri Street and the
> police station....
>
>   "Shalom," she said, turning and walking away toward the melan-
> choly Wadi Nisnas. He stood for a long time with his back to the po-
> lice station, watching her as she crossed Solel Boneh Circle.[55]

Michael is meticulous in describing the exact spot at which the two
were standing. The sea breeze, usually welcome in his writings, now has
"invaded" (*palsha*), separating the man and woman who had been holding
onto each other tightly just a minute earlier. Nevertheless, Fuad tries to
shield Shoshana from the ominous sight of the police station. He blocks
her view of it with his burly body, as if he is strong enough to deal with
going there, but she is too weak to withstand the sorrow it causes. The two

stand on the seamline between Wadi Nisnas and Hassan Shukri Street in the space that is no one's and therefore everyone's, where their border-crossing love may survive.

The Solel Boneh Circle that Shoshana crossed, like its namesake, the modern marble headquarters of the construction company, declares its Zionist identity. The words "Solel" and "Boneh" mean "Paves" and "Builds." Solel Boneh was the first tall building in the city. It was designed by Shmuel Rozov and constructed at the tip of the slope at the end of Hassan Shukri Street in the 1950s. Abba Hushi, Haifa's ambitious mayor, wanted the headquarters of the largest construction company in Israel to be located in his city and initiated the project. But despite the Zionist associations of its name, the location of the circle in this intermediary space attracts those who live between the two worlds, such as the heroes of Michael's Haifa novels. This is why Huda, the anxious protagonist of his novel, *A Trumpet in the Wadi*, decides on Solel Boneh as the point of embarkation for her few, often frustrating, romantic outings from the wadi. For Huda, the Arab Christian who falls in love with a Jewish man over the course of the novel, as for others of Michael's characters, crossing the circle symbolizes the passage from one realm to another: from the safety of home to the uncertainty of the outside world. At the same time, this place's liminal status promises a measure of freedom and perhaps a chance for love.

Two of Solel Boneh's appearances in *A Trumpet in the Wadi* bookend the first romantic outing taken by Huda and Alex, her Jewish love interest. Huda asks him to pick her up there, instead of in the wadi where they both live, because she prefers a neutral space, one that is neither Jewish nor Arab: "We'll meet at Solel Boneh. I don't want us to be seen in the wadi. . . . At nine-thirty he waited for me in the pickup beside Solel Boneh's marble edifice. He was tense and drove wildly [to Mount Carmel]." A combination of Huda's hesitations, Alex's awareness of them, and a random intruder prevent the couple from embracing in the lovers' lane on the Carmel. It is only at the end of the truncated date, right before he drops her off at the neutral Solel Boneh Circle, that Huda and Alex finally kiss. Perhaps the seamline is the only place where the two can initiate their relationship:

I got out on Solel Boneh Circle and he drove off to return the pickup. . . . When Alex stopped the vehicle and leaned over to open the door for me he saw that I did not recoil from his arm which rubbed against my breasts, and stopped and looked into my eyes. His lips were on mine for a brief eternal moment. . . . My face still felt the bristles of his beard, the smell of tobacco, the touch of his nose.[56]

Not far from where Huda's love begins to flourish, Yosef, another of Michael's fictional heroes, meets his future wife for the first time. Yosef appears in *Waters Kissing Waters*, a novel published in 2001 but written in the 1950s, the period in which its plot unfurls. It focuses on marginalized groups other than Israeli Arabs, specifically, recent immigrants, some of whom are Jewish refugees from Arab countries (Mizrahi Jews). In the 1950s, and for decades later, Jews of European origin (Ashkenazi) often treated Mizrahi Jews as inferior. Yosef, an immigrant from Iraq, arrives at Solel Boneh Circle from Wadi Nisnas, where he lives with and feels protected by Arabs, whose customs he knows from his homeland. As with Shoshana, Fuad, Naim, and Huda — his emergence on the seamline is not a coincidence. Yosef's route from his rented room in the wadi toward the unfamiliar world of his Ashkenazi date passes through the "noisy Solel Boneh Circle."[57] He meets Ktina in front of the May Cinema that neighbors the circle and, as he has little money, is relieved when she declines his offer to see a film. Instead, he leads her for a stroll in Memorial Park.

The park spreads over a government lot on the mountain ledge where the Burj al-Salam fortress once stood.[58] At the observation point that overlooks the port on the northern tip of the park, a Turkish cannon, heavy and dark, used to aim its barrel at the bay. In the 1950s it served as a steed for the children of Hadar HaCarmel. Next to it stretched a stone pergola with long benches, waiting patiently for the ivy planted around it to entwine its columns and shelter it from the scorching sun. A half-circle stone stage neighbored the pergola, and the low wall that surrounded it bore a memorial inscription and an eternal light. Scattered across the lawns were small stone markers inscribed with the names of various military units that fought in Haifa and the north in 1948. During the day the park was the domain of children, but in the evenings it belonged to romantic couples who walked through its broad paths and, upon arriving at the lookout, stood breathless, facing the lights of the bay, the port, and the ships that sparkled like stars beneath them.

Cannon in Memorial Park
Photograph by Aviv Itzhaki

Yosef, the protagonist of *Waters Kissing Waters*, too, wants to stroll in Memorial Park on his first date, but when he and Ktina meander toward this famous lookout she shies away. Ktina is wary of walking through the dark paths of memory or, as they are portrayed in the novel, the hedged-in paths of Memorial Park:

> "Let's wander around Memorial Park a bit, you can see a beautiful view from there," he said.
>
> They strolled along a path exposed to the sky and fenced in by pruned hedges. Before the expanse of the spectacular bay and its lights . . . opened up before their eyes, Ktina stopped short as though she'd hit a wall: "You should know, I don't like dark places."[59]

Later in the novel the reader learns the true source of Ktina's fears, but that romantic evening walk through the park has an artistic purpose beyond framing her as a tragic character. The stroll, deliberately set in Memorial Park, is also testimony to the complex relationship that the novel's hero, or his creator, have with the Israeli space: the enchantment with its spectacular beauty, the awareness of the weight of memories, and the fear of them. Indeed, Michael does not deny the autobiographical layers at the foundation of this book, which he wrote as a young man; it is plausible that its landscape represents the early impressions and conflicts that imprinted themselves on him during his first years in Israel. The landmarks of Hassan Shukri Street — Memorial Park, city hall, the police station, and the courthouse — not only play a part in Haifa-based plots woven by the city's authors but also reflect the hidden regions of the soul.[60]

Facing the Courthouse

Although the minimalist poetics of the author Yoel Hoffmann are far removed from Michael's social realism and the profusion and intensity of emotions that typify his writing, the landmarks of Haifa amplify the inner world of his characters as well. This is especially true in *Ephraim*, Hoffmann's lyrical, fragmented work, which is both overtly and implicitly autobiographical.[61] While walking through Hadar HaCarmel, Ephraim, the eponymous hero, reaches the long-standing shopping center at Bet HaKranot, a few streets away from the seamline. He intends to buy himself a shirt, but as he is looking for one, someone asks him where the courthouse is. Instead of directing the stranger toward Hassan Shukri Street, Ephraim accompanies him to his destination:

> Ephraim walks
> with him up to the entrance of the courthouse and sees
> lawyers there.
> Now, he wants to die, but he doesn't have
> a rope and he doesn't have a revolver and he doesn't have bullets
> and his heart is full of memories.[62]

The sight of the governmental institution to which he had politely led the man profoundly disturbs Ephraim's mood. His peaceful day at once turns upside down after he is diverted from his route and reaches the seamline. The sudden, unexpected encounter with the courthouse there reminds him of the "crime" he had committed and makes him feel as though he were both the accused and the judge, and he sentences himself to death.

The grave offense that Ephraim had committed was abandoning his faithful wife of many decades for no apparent reason. On the last day of the second millennium, he took the suitcase he had packed in November, left his home in Tel Aviv, and moved into his friend's house in Haifa's Center Carmel neighborhood. A few weeks later, on a wintery January day, he decided to descend into Hadar HaCarmel, with which he is clearly very familiar. There, Ephraim is unexpectedly brought, so to speak, to court.

Hoffmann employs the historical, urban landmark of the district courthouse to shape both the novel's Odyssean quest and the complex subconscious of its hero. The courthouse abruptly cuts short Ephraim's wanderings in Hadar HaCarmel and sends him back to the home of his host higher up on the hill. Moreover, standing in front of the courthouse rattles him and makes it impossible for him to further suppress his feelings of guilt. This inner turmoil caused by the visit to the seamline and its institutions is expressed through the cityscape in Hoffmann's inimitable, lyrical language. Ephraim boards a bus that climbs up the mountain to Center Carmel:

> his heart is severed from its ties. Tears roll down
> his cheeks and wet his mouth with salt water.
> The ships in the bay sail inside the waters
> of the tear — just like fish in an aquarium.[63]

From this point on Hoffmann erases the separation between inside and out: the ships do not sail in the salty seawater but rather in the saltwater of Ephraim's tear; the mere sight of the courthouse building breaks his heart, releases it from its bonds, and becomes the inner voice of his conscience.

Ephraim's turbulent reaction to the courthouse is caused by more than the presence of lawyers at its entrance: the large structure itself is awe inspiring. It is humble but projects authority, as befits its role as the symbol of the law. This governmental, white, stone structure is one story tall, drawn with simple, clean lines; stairs lead up to its arched entrance, located in the center of a symmetrical Palladian façade.[64] Above the doorway's romantic frame of three arches, quarried one inside the other, bronze letters announce, "Law Courts."[65] By design these letters protrude from the face of the wall so that the shadow they cast underscores their prominence.[66] The severe letters and their dark shadows, together with the arches carved into the depths of the façade, grant the building its official bearing, which strikes anxiety into the heart of someone like Ephraim who has gone astray.[67] Even the colors that dominate the courthouse emphasize the

Courthouse entrance with judges
Courtesy of the Yeri Rimon Private Collection, Haifa

contrast between guilty and innocent: its outer walls are white, while its
doors are black. This juxtaposition continues indoors as well, with all the
woodwork painted black and the inner walls white.[68]

The dominant line of the courthouse is a horizontal one, and although
the building is "anchored in the colonial context," its overall design is one
of modernist restraint.[69] The modernist influence is most notable in the
continuous stripes of "ribbon" windows, shutters, and portholes. These
are set in recessed rows, whose finish is flawlessly smooth, while the rest
of the façade is clad with rougher stone (in the *musamsam* technique).[70]
The contrast of texture between the sleek indented lines of windows and
the subtle coarseness of the rest of the building's exterior contribute to the
sculptural three-dimensional impression of the mantle.[71] The horizontal
stripes along the building's walls, and their alternating play of polished
and rough stone, counter the courthouse's height, granting it an air of
modesty and impartiality.

Front view of the courthouse, 1930s
Courtesy of the Central Zionist Archives; photographer unknown

Natural light streams into the building through a clerestory. The design's point of departure is a tower-like unit that forms the entrance hall, from which three arms extend in the shape of a T.[72] The large formal courtroom is located in the long, central arm of the T, and the judge would sit in the entrance axis. The secondary halls are smaller, thereby emphasizing the hierarchy that the courthouse upheld.[73]

The Haifa courthouse was designed by Austen St. Barbe Harrison (1891–1976), the most important British architect to work in Mandatory Palestine.[74] It is one of only two buildings of his in which the inspiration of modernism and Erich Mendelsohn's work are recognizable.[75] Like his contemporaries, Harrison was educated in the neoclassical aesthetics of the École des Beaux-Arts and believed that a building's appearance ought to reflect its purpose and content. During his studies and service in Greece and Palestine, however, he was captivated by the charms of Eastern sensibilities.[76] He created an original style that merged local, Byzantine, Islamic, and Western characteristics in a manner that blurred their disparate origins, forging an aesthetic whole greater than the sum of its parts.[77] As the chief architect of public works in Palestine between 1923 and 1937, he left his mark on everything built in the country during that period.[78] The gesture Harrison made toward modernism was also a nod to regionalism, as modernism influenced the architecture of the Jewish settlement and became one of the hallmarks of the Palestinian landscape in the 1920s and 1930s.[79] According to Ron Fuchs, the architectural scholar who studied his work, Harrison "traveled in the superior spheres of the exalted ... like the forefathers of the *Beaux Arts*, his style is also worthy of the description 'sublime public.'"[80] In Haifa's courthouse, that transcendence is unmistakable.[81]

The Most Beautiful City Hall in the Land

Ten years after the elegant courthouse was completed, Haifa's city hall was inaugurated. It was the last building of its kind that was built in Haifa. Like the previously constructed courthouse and the Technion in its vicinity, classical European motifs dominate city hall's design even as it embraces local components.[82] All three buildings share a glorious, arched central entranceway, heralded by elegant stairs and bookended by two equal wings. If the courthouse is city hall's older sibling, the Technion, which overlooks them both from the mountain slope, is their parent of sorts, its spirit radiating across the entire city.

Approximately thirty years after the Technion was built, and fifteen years after it opened, city hall's conservative architect Benjamin Chaikin paid homage to both Harrison's nearby courthouse and Alexander Baerwald's temple to science farther up the hill: an arch hails an arch; rough stone answers rough stone; and a wide, generous plaza calls to its sister. Indeed, the western border of city hall is Baerwald Street, which continues the central axis of the Technion. Like Chaikin, Baerwald was an engineer in the Public Works Department of a large empire, a Jew loyal to his king or his kaiser who, in time of war, abandoned his drafting pencil to serve his country. Yet after fulfilling his duty, each man followed his heart and returned to Palestine.

Chaikin was a product of London aesthetics. Born in Saint Petersburg in 1883, a descendant of a rabbinic dynasty—his father served in London as *dayan*, a judge in the religious court, and the head of the association of synagogues—he arrived in England as a child. There he was educated and completed his architectural studies. During World War I, he served in the British Engineers Corps and so arrived in Palestine with Field Marshal Edmund Allenby. In 1920 Chaikin joined the office of the renowned architect Patrick Geddes in Jerusalem. There he planned many of the important government, public, and university buildings. During World War II he once again enlisted in His Highness's army. But when the British Mandate ended, Chaikin stayed in Israel. He died in 1950 and was buried in Jerusalem.

In British Mandatory Palestine, Chaikin was a Brit among Jews and a Jew among the British. He garnered respect and affection from the British, and the high commissioner in particular deeply appreciated his architectural talents. Chaikin, for his part, remained loyal to the English tradition in his architectural planning, an expression of his personal commitment to the British throne. His buildings are more similar in their design to those of other British architects in Palestine than to those built in the International Style by contemporary architects who came from the continent itself. At the same time, in Chaikin's buildings one can recognize his attempt to create a style that incorporates Eastern elements with biblical and archaeological connections side by side with influences from art deco and the International Style, all the while taking the history and geography of the place into consideration.[83]

At the end of the 1930s the municipality of Haifa forewent an architectural contest and appointed the Jerusalemite Chaikin to design its city hall. It may be that the affection the British — and specifically the commissioner — had for him factored into this decision. In any event, the city hall that Chaikin planned for Haifa is considered the most beautiful in the land to this day. Together with its historical relatives — the courthouse and the Technion — city hall creates a conservative, stylistic consistency, and, with them, it rules the urban landscape. Its architectural vicinity, however, is different, with small-scale houses representing an eclectic blend of styles. Some are residences in an urban Arab tradition, clad with stone or plaster, but many reflect the aesthetics of European modernism. These were constructed using the cheap, adaptable cement that surrendered to the whims of the architects, most of whom were graduates of German and Austrian schools of architecture.[84] They left Europe in the 1930s due to the rise of fascism. In the decade preceding city hall's construction, these architects made Hadar HaCarmel the main hub for avant-garde architectural works in the modernist International and Bauhaus Styles. The massive city hall, however, seemed to pledge a different allegiance. During World War II, in the eye of the storm, at a time of quick growth and often problematic changes in the population, a statement may have been hidden in city hall's traditional design: it was an immovable stalwart, a secure fortress of sanity that protected the status quo and announced its allegiance to colonialism.

On the cover of the most important book about Haifa architecture to date, the title, *Bauhaus on the Carmel*, is writ large. Beneath it, in a much smaller font, it continues, *and the Crossroads of Empire*.[85] In the case of city hall, the emphasis is reversed: the melody of the Bauhaus Style is a distant echo, while the voice of the empire is loud and clear.

Haifa's city hall is an architectural monument that has defied wars, victories, and defeats.[86] In planning this grand building, Chaikin synthesized English conservatism, a restrained neoclassicism, and indigenous elements. The perfect harmony of its design befits a municipal structure with regional importance. A vast tiled plaza — more than thirty-one yards wide and adorned with flowerbeds and trees — separates the front of city hall from Hassan Shukri Street and underscores its significance in the urban space. Memorial Park, which stretches across the street, becomes a continuation of this generous plaza and augments the view from the front of the five-story building.

City hall stands as its architect envisioned it — forever observing and observed: from the inside it observes Memorial Park and the sea through the giant window that Chaikin carved in its front northern wall; from the plaza outside it can be observed in its entirety, stately and regal. The main entryway captures the eye first — marble steps lead to an impressive door made of latticed steel and glasswork. Above it, a graded arch soars four stories high, as if quarried into the depth of the entrance. At the center of the arch is a long, sunken window that extends the glasswork of the door. And floating above the magnificent archway is the symbol of the city: a sailboat carved in stone, ruling the waves of the sea.

The panorama seen from its window, however, was almost obscured. Two years after the establishment of the state, Abba Hushi, a labor leader who had played no part in the city hall enterprise, became mayor. He intended to erect a massive commemoration center for the Jews who had

View of city hall
from Baerwald Street
*Courtesy of Haifa City
Archives*

fallen in the battles for Haifa directly across the street, which would have blocked city hall's view and diminished the impression it makes on onlookers.[87] Despite Hushi's legendary power as mayor, however, he was not successful.[88] The drawings were shelved. The monuments erected in Memorial Park lie close to the ground and the open view survives.

The design of city hall resembles the letter "U"—its short "bottom" faces north, toward the Haifa bay, while its two "arms" stretch southward. On either side of the taller edifice that houses the main entrance, two equal wings stand at attention like bodyguards.[89] The loftiness of the building does not dwarf the humans who enter it: the height of the central "body" broadcasts its status, but the fact that the two wings are nearly as tall softens and humanizes the structure as a whole. These wings are narrow in the front, inlaid with square windows, and their sides extend south along the green Haifaian streets that border the long arms of the "U": Bialik Street on the east and Baerwald Street on the west. Before new additions altered the building's symmetrical structure, a glorious frame of large ficus trees surrounded city hall, as it stood nobly, distinct from the neighboring buildings with its conservative English Style, substantial size, and unique position on the land.

Grandeur was not Chaikin's sole aim, however. Consideration of the climate was of primary importance to him and guided the shape of the building itself. The challenge he took upon himself was, as he wrote, "to plan the building so that the rooms, occupied by clerks or councilmembers, would derive the maximum benefit from the summer breezes."[90] Therefore, he arranged the side wings such that there were rooms on only one side of the corridor and chose a special glass for the windows that prevented the penetration of direct sunlight. The building's symmetrical U form created a back patio used for stylized inner gardens and parking, but Chaikin added a short middle arm to this basic U, creating a kind of W.[91] As a result of this center arm, the building gained the privilege of a larger surface area, which allowed for more air and natural light in all the parts of city hall.[92] To ensure that time spent in the building was a delight for employees and visitors alike, then, Chaikin's architectural plan enlisted the light of the sun and the northwest winds from the sea.

The entire building is made of concrete, clad with Carmel stone quarried in nearby Tira and chiseled to create a rough surface of bumps and crevices. The beauty of city hall, its endurance despite the ravages of time, and the rare integrity of its every detail are a testament to the superior quality of its construction, materials, and workmanship. The skill of its master stonecutters shines from the foundation to the window frames, cornices, and the glorious central archway. The symbol of the city, a boat flanked by two towers, which hovers over that arch, was carved by the local sculptor Israel Rubinstein.[93] The clocks high on each side of the building and the artfully wrought glass and metal lights that illuminate the side exits are but two of the details that intensify the profound impression that the building makes on all observers. The promise of grandeur and loyalty to the landscape, implied by the outside of city hall, is kept even after one enters the building and strolls through its corridors. The local stone that cloaks the façade is echoed on the inside through the patterned reddish-brown Hebron marble of the floors. The walls of the common spaces and staircases are also clad with local marble, while mosaic floors, incorporating a variety of decorative tiles, pave the upper stories. The large conference room of the city council, captured in countless photographs of meetings, is covered with wood from Turkey.

But the star of the inner space is, without a doubt, the regal double staircase — the creative product of master craftsmen in metal, wood, and stone, in the spirit of art deco. This staircase rises from the center of the lobby, alternately merging and splitting on each landing; its railings, carved from walnut, supported by steel bars wrought in Middle Eastern ironwork and painted black, meet in rare perfection with the marble curves of the stairs. Chaikin tamed the hard materials — marble, steel, and wood — and, for him, they became like clay in a potter's hands. They weave into

one another, sing in unison, and, without a trifle of vanity, bequeath the
building its nobility.

The glory of this staircase, however, lies in more than its magnificent
design and well-wrought materials — it shines in the way the architect
invited the landscape into the municipal temple he built: he placed this
perfect staircase directly behind the entrance arch. It climbs up four stories, accompanied by a giant glass window. As the citizens of Haifa walk
up the stairs on the way to the municipal offices, they bask in their city's
view of the sea. Thus, city hall makes the landscape part of its inner decor,
welcoming in the ships, the port, the bay, and the distant mountains on its
other side.

While Chaikin made an enormous investment in his architectural designs themselves, he was acutely aware that the symbolic message conveyed by a public building is determined not only by its appearance but
by its visual relationship with the buildings around it. He criticized the
low height of the newly inaugurated National Institution Building in
Jerusalem, arguing that an official Jewish structure ought not to appear
"hunched over" next to the taller buildings of other religions.[94] It is no
wonder, therefore, that when Chaikin planned Haifa's city hall, which
was supposed to embody a strong, influential urban authority, he created
a structure that broadcasts its unshakable status among its architectural
neighbors.

Even to my little girl eyes, there was no doubt that city hall was the most
important building in the neighborhood. I used to gaze at its magnificent
entrance while playing across from it in Memorial Park. When we walked
back home on Baerwald Street, the rows of windows along its western wall
accompanied us all the way to where Baerwald crossed Ibn Sina Street. At
that intersection stood the Zion Hotel, which would be immortalized a
few years later in the annals of cinema as well as in my own memory.

Stardust at the Zion Hotel

In April 1960 my mother, my brother, and I entered the Zion Hotel mere
mortals but left it covered with stardust. This was when Hollywood arrived in Haifa. . . .

In the spring of 1959 the famous American film director and producer,

Otto Preminger, decided to make a film about the birth of the State of Israel based on the 1958 Zionist novel *Exodus* by Leon Uris. Furthermore, he was determined to shoot it *on location* in the newly established state. This would be the first American film to be shot in Israel, and its production would ultimately be credited, among other things, for its unmatched contribution to the development of the Israeli film industry.[95] When he visited the country before shooting began, Preminger fell in love with its landscape and, scrapping his original plan, decided to film in color. He declared, "I want to show Israel, the real star of *Exodus*. . . . I can do this best in color." On January 26, 1960, he publicly announced that he had hired the blacklisted writer Dalton Trumbo to write the screenplay, becoming the first person who "broke the blacklist."[96]

Filming began on March 28, and the headquarters of the production was none other than the Zion Hotel in Haifa, which at the time was the fanciest hotel in the city. And so for a glorious three months Haifa became a film studio and shoot location all at once. The entire crew, about five hundred people, were housed in the Zion Hotel, which was specially refurbished and fitted for the production's needs and equipment; the entire building was exclusively at the crew's disposal, from its elegant halls to the basement, which was occupied by the costume department. Preminger stayed in the beautiful Room 116, which overlooked the bay and part of the port. He famously used the view of Haifa and its port as the setting for the unforgettable, stunning opening scene of the movie that features the refugees crowded on the ship's deck facing the unattainable shore. When a large boat anchored in the port during the shooting, threatening to ruin the shot, Preminger commanded his general manager, "Get that ship out of the ocean; take it away, Martin."[97]

Now, my mother's maiden name was "Preminger," and Otto was her father's cousin. When he arrived in Haifa, she contacted him, and he invited us to the hotel. Imagine me, not yet twelve years old, walking up the wide marble steps; entering the spacious lobby, tiled with black-speckled white marble; and sighting the divine Paul Newman with Eva Marie Saint at the bar. My mother carried a bouquet of flowers, and my brother and I were dressed in our "Saturday best." We rode the elevator, the first I had ever taken, to Otto Preminger's room, where we were treated to soft drinks and cakes, while my mother and the director chatted away in German. When I

The Zion Hotel *Courtesy of the Dresner family*

came to school the next day, all my classmates crowded around, trying to touch me. I told them how I'd seen Paul Newman and the other stars up close and about the glamour of the lobby and the bar, the likes of which we had seen only in movies, if at all.

While working on this book, I interviewed Michael Dresner, the son of Avraham Dresner, the courageous man who built the Zion Hotel in 1937. We sat in his office, in a building abutting the former hotel, which had long ago been swallowed by municipal offices. "My father was a Zionist," he told me, perhaps to interpret the name of the hotel. "In any event, at first there were 28 rooms, and about a decade later he added another wing until it reached 110 rooms." Mr. Dresner also recounted how, when his father bought the first lot on the corner of Ibn Sina and Baerwald in 1936, the Arab owner told him to throw a stone as far as he could, and the place where it fell would be the border of his lot. Only afterward did they calculate and determine the price: 1,000 pounds sterling. One detail he revealed was especially moving for me: his father had come from Chernovitz, my mother's hometown.

The new, grander structure that swallowed the original hotel boasted a lavish entrance. This expanded Zion Hotel was planned after 1948 by Heinz Fenchel, who, more than any other architect, introduced an element of glamour and luxury to the Israeli scene.[98] He had started his career in Berlin as a set designer, but, with the rise of the Nazis, chose to emigrate and went to Palestine instead of Hollywood. There he worked as an architect and interior designer. He was known as a "total architect," who dictated every detail of his buildings, down to the very doorknobs. Unlike his contemporaries, whose Spartan, minimalist International Style fit Israel's mood and its socialist bent (and dominated its construction), Fenchel's creations often hindered his career, for they brought an opulence, a kind of bourgeois culture to Palestine.[99] Indeed, many of the hotel lobbies he designed looked like movie sets. Perhaps Preminger was attracted to the Zion Hotel in part due to its quasi-cinematic design.

Thanks to *Exodus* and the director's decision to hold court at the Zion Hotel, glamour touched Ibn Sina Street briefly, in 1960. But by the time it did, we had already moved more than a mile away from my first home.

The Stone Houses of My Neighborhood

The house on 4 Ibn Sina Street, where I lived until 1954, was at the opposite end of the street from the Zion Hotel. Unlike the massive concrete hotel, my home was an unremarkable stone structure, but to me in those early years it was the prettiest in the world and its garden the most delightful. According to the hand-drawn blueprints that I found in the City Archives, a little over three yards separated the house from the stone fence encircling it. That space contained a flowerbed bordered by a low stoop with only a narrow path separating it from the building itself. The stoop was comfortable to sit on, and in an old photograph I am perched on it with the teenage daughter of our next-door neighbors. In the mornings before he went to work, my father would sit on that same stoop with Gadi, my brother, a cute toddler with golden curls who sucked two fingers and held the worn collar of a shirt to calm himself. Gadi, thin and sickly, barely ate anything, and

Author and neighbor on the front stoop *Family photo, photographer unknown*

my father would try to feed him a dish we dubbed *Ei veh Buch*. My mother would dissolve sugar in raw egg yolk in a little bowl, and, with stories from an illustrated book, my father would try to coax his young son to taste a spoonful. Later I understood that the name of our family dish meant "egg and book" — in our family's language the two German words, *Ei* (egg) and *Buch* (book), were connected by the Hebrew *veh* (and).

From the plans in the archive, one can also see that, due to the slope of the lot, the building had only ground-floor apartments in the front, while the upper floors had apartments in both the front and back. We lived in the eastern of the two ground-floor apartments. The Sasson family lived in the western one. On Saturdays Mr. Sasson would sit in his pajamas on the open porch and crack watermelon seeds. His voluptuous wife would sit with him and, sometimes, their daughters and their oldest son, Aaron. (Over a decade later, at his little print shop on Peretz Street, Mr. Sasson would print the invitations to Gadi's bar mitzvah for free.) There was a wide, paved pathway along the western side of 4 Ibn Sina that reached all the way to the back of the building, where a staircase led to the upper floors; a garden stretched next to the pathway, planted with a haphazard mixture of trees and shrubs.

The door to our ground-floor apartment was in the front of the building, and when it opened, one could see straight into our rectangular family room, one of whose long walls was actually a giant window. I sat next to it one spring, sick with chicken pox, watching the other children playing in the yard to the east. Once upon a time, this windowed-in room had been a spacious porch, but now it served as our entry hall, sitting room, and dining room. There, we ate and played and had Passover seders. Yet we always called it "the porch," preserving its prior life. A wooden trunk, where we stored blankets, stood near the wall and was one of the few items to accompany us when we moved to a new apartment before I began first grade.

At the end of the long porch was the door to the dimly lit kitchen, which had only one small window. I always loved to sit there and listen to my mother's spellbinding stories about the British and wartime in Haifa; her blithe days in Tel Aviv with Leeza, her beloved friend and roommate, who, betrayed by the man she loved, intentionally returned to war-torn Poland to die; and her hometown of Chernovitz, with gypsies telling fortunes on the banks of its Prut River. From Chernovitz, she remembered romantic German songs, delicious *cremeschnitte*, and an aunt who brought her one orange when she was sick, of which she gave each of her five siblings a wedge. When she arrived in Israel, she said, she ate oranges until she was sick of them.

To the right of the porch was a large, L-shaped room that served us all as a bedroom. Across its entrance yawned the wide-silled window that still bore the scar from the sniper's bullet. It had a lace curtain that moved lightly in the breeze but did not block the light. My father and mother slept in the alcove of the L. When I was three years and three months old, my brother was born. He was named for my mother's father, Gedalyahu, but we called him Gadi. When my mother and my new brother returned from the hospital, I moved to an iron folding bed; a pleated cloth was draped around it with a repeating pattern of a girl with curly, chestnut hair playing with a colorful ball. I had no idea, then, that we lived in terribly cramped quarters. I was a cheerful girl whose narrow world was limited to a few streets: Ibn Sina, of course, and Hassan Shukri, the bustling HaNeviim Street, and its two residential offshoots, HaNeviim Steps Street and Yavne Street.

The building at 3 Yavne Street was home to the clinic where we visited our pediatrician. This was the elaborately ornamented house on whose roof, my mother told me, the snipers had perched in 1948. Before the war Yavne had been a typical seamline street with pretty, Arab-owned houses, many of whose lessees were Jewish. The two houses close to the corner of Yavne and HaNeviim belonged to Taufiq Magdelani, an Arab of Lebanese descent who arrived in Haifa at the end of the nineteenth century; understood the city's potential; and, in the lower city, established Haifa's largest and most successful construction materials business. In 1923 he built a house for his family on 3 Yavne Street; at first he erected two stories, but in 1928 he added a third floor and magnificent terraces. These terraces, like those of the neighboring 1 Yavne, which Magdelani built as an investment in the 1930s, flaunted latticed railings from Magdelani's precast plaster workshop. The three arches that dominate the façade of 3 Yavne announce that this is a typical *liwan* house, with a common inner space. The house next door, constructed a decade later, is more "modern," influenced by the International Style, with a central staircase and two apartments on each floor.

Mrs. Magdelani (née Khouri) was the sister of the grandmother of architect Waleed Karkabi from the municipality of Haifa. When Karkabi's grandfather, the owner of a well-known porcelain and crystal store, wanted to build a house for his family, Mr. Magdelani, his rich brother-in-law, advised him to buy the nearby lot on Yavne Street. Thus, in 1926 a more modest house was built at 5 Yavne, belonging to Elias and Alice Toubi (also née Khouri).[100]

After she was prematurely widowed, Mrs. Toubi rented out her home's top floor to an Orthodox Jewish family to make ends meet. The relationship between both families was excellent. Karkabi recalled the story of how, in 1946, during the tense days between World War II and the 1948 war, "a few boys from the neighborhood taunted and harassed the father of the family as he returned home at dusk and offended him." When the courageous Arab landlady saw this, she went out to the street, defended her Jewish tenant, embarrassed the attackers, and chased them away — they never bothered the father of the family again. Mrs. Toubi and a few of her descendants remained in Haifa after 1948, but her sister and the rest of the Magdelani family left the city. Their home, like other Arab-owned houses, became *rekhush natush* (abandoned property).

The Magdelani House,
3 Yavne Street
Courtesy of photographer
Adi Silberstein

Some of these "abandoned" Arab stone houses — the ornate structures on the corner of Yavne, my garden-enclosed house on Ibn Sina, and the large buildings that accompanied me on the way to the synagogue with my father — are interwoven into the fabric of my childhood memories and became a part of my being. On Shabbat mornings, my father used to take me to Hadrat Kodesh, "his" synagogue. We would leave Ibn Sina for HaNeviim, turn right, and within two minutes, reach the end of that wide, flat street. There we suddenly saw the sea: the flat street stopped abruptly, and in front of us, like a carpet, rolled down wide, comfortable steps at whose sides stood large stone houses like broad-shouldered bodyguards. I would skip down the steps, and the sea would wink in and out of view: there, then gone; there, then gone. The wrought iron gates of the traditional Arab houses, their arches and balconies, watched us from the side.

These houses, which formed HaNeviim Steps Street, were the beginning of the Al Burj neighborhood, constructed in the first decades of the twentieth century by wealthy Arabs who wished to leave the lower city. At the forefront of this trend was the Greek Orthodox Touma family, who dealt in shipping and real estate. Gabriel Touma owned the large house that towers above the rest on the slope east of the stairs, and he passed it on to his son, Emil, a historian and intellectual, one of the prominent leaders of the Israeli Communist Party.[101] Its three tall arches, whose style is quintessentially Arab, are effortlessly combined with the enclosed, modernist staircase, which was added due to the fear of snipers when tensions grew. Likewise, the buildings below the Touma house charmingly merge local construction with the modern style that found a home in Haifa in the 1930s.

At the bottom of HaNeviim Steps Street stood Hadrat Kodesh itself, a fortress-like cubical structure, which rose upward as though trying to compensate for its low position on the slope. Its windows were colorful stained glass, and crystal chandeliers dangled downward from its high ceiling, filling it with an ethereal light.[102] This was the first Ashkenazi synagogue in Haifa, and its history intersects with some of the formative events in the life of the city.[103] In the 1930s the foundations of the current building were laid atop those of the earlier structure, in which, according to tradition, the holy Rabbi Nahman of Bratslav, the grandson of the Besht, prayed in 1798 after making the dangerous pilgrimage to the Holy Land.[104] A full 115 years later, this synagogue served as a stronghold for the Hebrew language during the historical "war of the languages." In 1913, the Ezra Association of German Jews, one of the founders of the newly built Hebrew Reali School, demanded that studies there be conducted in German: "On Hanukkah, all the students and teachers . . . left the [Reali] school building and marched until they reached the Hadrat Kodesh synagogue. There, they sat down on the synagogue's benches and without delay, continued their studies [in Hebrew] in high spirits."[105]

Thirty-five years went by, and in 1948 Hadrat Kodesh was forced to take part in a different war, in the early stages of which the synagogue was targeted by Arabs, and the Torah scrolls were heroically lifted out of the Holy Ark and rescued.[106] Furthermore, because of its location on the seamline, the building served as the lowest command post of the Hagana in Haifa at the front lines.[107] When the battles ended, the synagogue returned to functioning as an important place of worship. In fact, until Haifa's Central

Synagogue on Herzl Street was ready for use, Hadrat Kodesh functioned as the city's main Ashkenazi synagogue. The worshippers at Hadrat Kodesh were from Haifa's old Ashkenazi community, joined by Holocaust survivors. The renowned rabbi Joshua Kaniel, who had lived nearby since the 1920s, was among the synagogue's worshippers and served as its rabbi.[108] In the 1950s and 1960s, the services, which were led by both a legendary cantor and a superior reader, attracted masses to the synagogue. It was filled wall to wall, and on holidays people stood outside because the building could not contain them.[109]

The last time I went there with my father I was six years old, so I remember the synagogue mainly thanks to the descent down the stairs, my palm in my father's hand, each step bringing the sea closer to us. The interior of the synagogue and the walk back home have become blurry since then, but the pleasures that awaited me when we returned to 4 Ibn Sina are still fresh in my memory.

Wonders and Suspicions on Ibn Sina Street

After our traditional Shabbat lunch, the adults would retire for their coveted, ritual afternoon nap, known in the German Haifa milieu as *schlafstunde*. Then we, the children of 4 Ibn Sina, could play to our hearts' content. Mr. and Mrs. Amir lived in the back wing of the building and Rafi, Mr. Amir's son from a previous marriage, would come from the distant Abbas Street every Shabbat to visit his father. And so the Amirs' back porch became our playground — luckily for us, as we were not allowed to make any noise in our own homes on Shabbat afternoons. We were all in the Amirs' home: our upstairs neighbors Tsipi and her brother, Tsvika; my brother, Gadi, and I; and, of course, Rafi. We arranged the chairs in a row on the back porch to act as the train cars. Rafi was usually the locomotive at the head, and so we all rattled along on the train to Tel Aviv.

On weekdays we played primarily with Tsipi and Tsvika, who were a little older than us. In their house we hid under a tent made of sheets on the veranda; with them, we played "doctor and patient" until we were caught; with them, we dressed up on Purim; and, with them, we went to our very first movie in the Armon Movie Theater on HaNeviim Street: Cecil DeMille's movie about the circus, *The Greatest Show on Earth*. We grew up without television — it did not arrive in Israel until 1967 — so this was the very first time that we, the children of 4 Ibn Sina, saw moving photographs. Tsipi had braids, and Tsvika had a broken tooth and straight hair that always fell into his eyes. They were our first real friends, our best friends. When we moved to another neighborhood, saying good-bye to them was the hardest thing to do.

A few months after we moved to 85 Herzl Street we had one more opportunity to play with Tsipi and Tsvika — we did not know that it would be our last and that we would never again play in the garden of 4 Ibn Sina and go wild with our friends in their adventure-filled house. It was the week before our first Passover in our new home — as was the case every year, my mother had to help my father full-time at the store. Because Jewish custom is to change over all the dishes for the week of Passover, the week before it was the busiest of the year for housewares stores.[110] Schools in Israel are always closed that week, so my parents asked Tsipi and Tsvika's mother to take care of us during the workday. I was six and a half, and Gadi was three. We were playing in the garden on the western side of the building we knew so well. When lunchtime arrived, Tsipi, Tsvika, and Gadi all went upstairs, while I lingered downstairs, nibbling on the last sections of an orange that I had eaten earlier.

Suddenly a man emerged from Ibn Sina Street — young, tall, bearded. I had never seen him before. He crossed into the yard, walked down the paved path bordering the garden, and approached me. He asked if I wanted him to buy me candy at the kiosk on the corner. Despite the secure atmosphere that prevailed in Israel of that time and the fact that it was unusual for parents to warn their children against strangers, my mother had long before told me about child snatchers. The minute I saw the bearded man, I knew in my gut that I had to flee, but I also realized that if I ran, he would catch me. I had to trick him. So I told him that I really wanted the candy, but my hands were too sticky from the orange I had just eaten, and I had to go wash them. The bearded man tried to wipe my hands with his handkerchief, but I insisted that my hands were still sticky. "I'll just run up for one minute," I told him. "I'll come back right away to get the candy, and I won't tell anyone." He believed me. I ran upstairs, shaking, and told Tsipi and Tsvika's mother everything that had just happened. She sat me down to eat lunch, but first made me swear that I would not tell my mother. I assume that she did not want my mother to know that she had allowed me to stay alone outside without supervision.

For the next couple of days I walked around with this secret gnawing at the pit of my stomach, but I kept my word and did not mention anything to my mother. Then, a few days later, when my mother picked up Gadi and me, as she did every evening, the three of us walked together to the bus stop to return to our new home on 85 Herzl. And there, near the bus stop, the bearded man reappeared. I grabbed my mother's sleeve and whispered, "Mommy, there is the man who tried to kidnap me!" My mother, of course, had no idea what I was talking about. By the time I managed to explain, the bearded man had noticed us. I vividly remember that he threw open the door of a taxi and slammed it before he had even sat down or straightened his long legs. The taxi tore away. The bearded man disappeared forever.

After that day I stopped eating oranges, and I never played on Ibn Sina, the street of my childhood, again.

But the incident with the bearded man occurred after a full six enchanted years on Ibn Sina Street. This was a street that offered everything a child's heart desires: an empty lot, a palace, and even its very own magician, Mr. Alterman. The lot across the street from our house was the perfect place to play. The palace was the small, old, beautiful Shalom Hotel. And the magician was the most amiable man on the street. We thought that he had supernatural powers because he created hats, boats, and little sparkly people from discarded materials, like chocolate wrappers made of "silver" paper, that he collected. The little dolls that he sculpted, he gave to us, the children of Ibn Sina Street.

Ibn Sina was also home to the Taubers (house number 6), my parents' friends; the Rosenfelds (12), our relatives; and the charming, magnetic couple Mr. and Mrs. Sturm (20). At the time I had no idea what bonds of pain tied them together, all those people who assembled on Saturday afternoons or evenings. They were a part of the mysterious network of "acquaintances," "relatives," or "friends" whose specific connection to my parents was hidden beneath a thick fog.

The tragic truth did not rise to the surface until after my father died, but when it did, that truth answered many of the nebulous questions that had accumulated inside me over time.

My Father's Story

My father died when I was ten years old, with little warning. Suddenly, we were lost, the ground shaking under our feet, left without protection. My mother tried her best to keep us afloat, but for me the void was excruciating. Two years later a girl, a relative from kibbutz Tel Yosef, was taunting me — she told me that my mother was actually my stepmother, not my real mother. I was about twelve years old and now believed that I had no father or mother. The revelation was so threatening that I did not share it with anyone. But a few weeks later, when my mother would not allow me to visit some cousins, I threw it at her, furiously: "You're only forbidding me from going because you're not my mother. You're my stepmother!" To my surprise, she was not angry. She sat me down across from her, closed the door, and said, "Who told you that?" And when I answered, she responded, "That girl? She heard bells ringing, but didn't know what church they were from.[111] Yes, I have something to tell you, but don't worry, I am your real mother." She revealed that my father had been married in the past, in Vienna, to Ola (Olga) Fishhof, a woman of Czech-Jewish origin. They had a little daughter named Hannah'le, who was born in 1934. My father had owned a multistory china and crystal store. On the day of the Anschluss — March 13, 1938, when the German fascists entered Vienna — my father's Austrian head manager said, *"Herr Scharf, jetzt bin ich der Herr"* —Mister Scharf, now I am the "Mister." I will never forget this sentence. My mother quoted it to me in German, as if she had memorized it. She must have heard it from my father when he told her the story.

My father was taken to Dachau — before the war, Dachau was "only" a work camp in Germany. Eventually Ola transferred the ownership of their store "of her own free will" to the head manager, who became the "Mister."[112] At that time it was still possible to free prisoners from Dachau, and she succeeded in obtaining an exit visa for my father. He was banned from returning to Vienna, so they were set to meet at the port and sail to Palestine. To her distress, Ola was told that no children were allowed on the boat. So she decided to leave the four-and-a-half-year-old Hannah'le with relatives. She hoped that the girl would be able to leave Austria on one of the *Kindertransports*, the children's groups that were sent from Reich-controlled countries to England. Ola could not possibly have imagined the magnitude of the horror that was to come. She and my father reunited and left for Palestine on an illegal migrant boat. They did not have entry visas, and intended to smuggle themselves into the land, then a common practice for Jewish refugees. As the boat neared Palestine, all the passengers were ordered to throw every identifying document and object overboard, so that if they were captured, the British would not know where they came from and thus could not return them to Europe, as was their protocol. On that rickety boat, they met and befriended the Taubers. Luckily, the vessel managed to escape the British police, and my father and Ola arrived in Haifa, where my father's brother, my Uncle Chaim, lived. Like the Taubers, they rented a small apartment on Ibn Sina Street, where other friends from their Vienna days lived—the Sturms, as well as Ola's cousin, Robert Rosenfeld, who had come to Palestine with his wife in the early 1930s. Thanks to him, my father found work at the local German newspaper, *Yediot Hadashot*.

Ola and my father spent the war years in terrible fear for their daughter's fate—it turned out that Hannah'le was too young to board a *Kindertransport*. At first, they received letters through the Red Cross, which informed them that before their relatives had been sent to a concentration camp, they had successfully transferred the little girl to Czechoslovakia to live with her grandmother, Ola's mother. But after a while, there were no more letters—only silence. In 1945, after the war, an acquaintance came to their house, a survivor from Auschwitz, who told them that he had seen little Hannah'le and her grandmother there. The desperate searches and hopes ended in nothing. Ola died of a broken heart a short time later and asked to be buried in Tel Yosef, where her uncle Friedrich Lederer, who had arrived from Czechoslovakia before the war, lived. I know nothing of my father's torment when he heard of his daughter's fate and shortly after became a widower. I only know that my father met my mother a few months after Ola died and fell in love with her. They were allotted a mere twelve years of happiness together.

My parents were married in August 1946, in the offices of Haifa's chief rabbinate, by the good Rabbi Kaniel.[113] In the autumn of 2014, as I climbed through a newly built neighborhood on the mountain slope, I stumbled upon a sign that read, "Rabbi Kaniel Street." I was overwhelmed with warmth, as if I had again heard my mother's voice speaking fondly of

him, as she always did. Suddenly, I made the connection: I had recently
discovered that Rabbi Kaniel used to pray at Hadrat Kodesh, my father's
old synagogue.[114] This must have been where my father and the rabbi met.
I will never know what the rabbi said to the man who arrived in Haifa from
Vienna with a flaming sword turning in his heart. Did the rabbi know Ola?
Did he try to comfort my father after she died? What did he say to the
new couple whom he married in the spacious house that Baerwald had
designed high on Arlozorov Street?

After my parents' honeymoon on Mount Canaan, my mother moved
into the apartment where my father had lived with his first wife — 4 Ibn
Sina, the stone house I remember from my childhood. I was born on Tuesday, July 20, 1948, in the Bether Hospital. My father brought my mother
dark red dahlias and said, "You gave me Hannah'le back." Afterward he
rode the bus for an hour to announce my birth to those closest to him —
Paula (née Lederer) and Alfred Hahn — who lived in the suburb of Kiryat
Motzkin. When he arrived, however, their daughter refused to wake her
parents in the middle of their traditional *schlafstunde*. When my mother
told me the story, I learned that Paula and Alfred, whom I loved with all
my heart, were Ola's cousins. In fact, years later Paula provided me with
additional details of this story. But as long as he lived, my father never revealed his secrets to me. In the evenings, when I had stayed awake, waiting
for him to come home from the store, he told me of Vienna and the blue
Donau that runs through it (the Danube River); the snowballs; the giant
Ferris wheel, the *Riesenrad*; a streetcar called *Tramvai*; and the Schoen-
brunn Palace with its endless gardens, but he left out the little girl whom
he had charmed with these attractions. Years later my mother told me that
my father swore that he would never set foot on Austrian soil again.

Once, before I had heard the story, I found a photograph of him with
his lost family and asked my mother about who the woman and the little
girl were in the picture with my father. She told me that they were relatives.
When I investigated our exact relationship with the Fishhof, Lederer, Rosenfeld, and Hahn families, I never got a straight answer. Now that I knew
the story, all the pieces of the puzzle fell into place, but my father was no
longer alive to expand on them, and my mother knew only some of the
answers to my questions. In 1995 I finally summoned the courage to break
my father's vow and traveled to Vienna. I found Hannah'le's German name

—Edith Scharf—written in orderly gothic handwriting in the Jewish community's records: "Daughter of Jakob and Olga Scharf, Glassergasse 14, Vienna." In Yad Vashem, there is a Page of Testimony with the name Hannah Scharf, written in my father's trembling hand. With an atypical stubbornness, this otherwise tender and accommodating man furiously refused to submit a request for reparations from the Nazis.

During the years of splendor on Ibn Sina Street, I knew many of the characters in my father's sad story, but their parts in the story itself were actively hidden from me. On Saturday afternoons we went to the Taubers for coffee and cake. Mr. Tauber was bald, and Mrs. Tauber had gray hair separated by a side part, one curl falling over her forehead, and an eternal smile on her face. Their daughter, Lily, used to join us, along with her husband and son. Lily was glamorous and seemed as though she had come from another world: she wore dark red lipstick, cat-eye glasses with a tortoise shell frame, high heels, and elegantly fitted dresses with flared skirts. Many years later I understood why she seemed so different. Like Hannah'le, she was born in Vienna, but unlike Hannah'le, she was one of those lucky girls who left on the *Kindertransport* to England. After the war the Taubers reunited with their daughter, but she was already more British than Viennese.

On Saturday nights we used to visit the Rosenfelds on the first floor of a stone house with a long, roofed porch. The jokester cousin, Dolf Fishhof, and his wife completed the gatherings. The Rosenfelds were Orthodox Jews, and at the end of Shabbat, they performed the *havdala* service, separating the Sabbath from the rest of the week with candles, spices, and wine. Then Mr. Rosenfeld, Dolf, and the other men would sing in German in canon *Ach wie wohl ist mir am Abend / Wenn die Glocken Laeuten bim bam* (Oh how pleasant it is for me in the evening / When the bells ring ding dong).

We went to the Sturms less frequently. They lived in one of the last and most impressive houses on Ibn Sina Street. There, unlike at the homes of the Taubers and Rosenfelds, we, the children, were the guests of honor. Joyfully, we would climb the grand white marble stairs, straight to the apartment on the top floor. Herr Sturm would open the door with his shiny, bald head and his big, kindhearted smile. The spacious salon looked as though it had been transplanted from abroad: the furniture they had brought from Vienna was heavy; the chairs, deep; and the rug, thick and soft. Their manners were European and the language, as in all the houses we visited, was purely German, but here it was spoken in softer tones. Frau Sturm was older than my parents, always impeccably made-up, and her blue coiffure, perfect. With manicured hands, she would delicately pour coffee for the guests and serve cake on thin porcelain dishes. Their enchanting salon opened onto a balcony that overlooked Ibn Sina Street and beyond to Hassan Shukri, Memorial Park, and even the bay and its ships.

On one of the first Independence Days, in 1953, we were guests at the Sturms' and looked down on the masses celebrating on Hassan Shukri Street and in Memorial Park. In the skies fireworks exploded over Memorial Park in a variety of colors — the first fireworks I had seen in my life.[115] On the balcony my parents stood with all the other guests of the radiant-faced Sturms. The joy was total — the joy of those who had escaped the sword and had finally found a place to rest their feet, former illegal immigrants to whom, just a few years earlier, a blue State of Israel identification card had been issued with the now-privileged inscription: "Jew." On November 8, 1948, the minister of the interior had imposed an administrative curfew to enable government workers to go door-to-door and issue these cards.[116] My parents' ID numbers were 0633671 and 0633670. And we, the only children on that balcony, were almost five and two years old — children who had been born into freedom. We did not yet understand the importance of the day — Independence Day — and we did not know that there were those nearby who were not celebrating. Likewise, the meaning of Memorial Park's name and what, exactly, it memorialized remained a mystery.

The Towers Stood Silent

While Memorial Park memorializes Jews who fell in 1948, it ignores the Arab inhabitants who lived in Haifa before the establishment of the State of Israel.[117] Across the street from the park, however, a symbol of the prewar city still survives, watching over all who enter city hall. It is the original emblem of Haifa, carved in stone in 1942 above the building's entrance archway by the artist Israel Rubinstein. Nothing about it has been changed.

A scroll inscribed with three languages unfurls at the bottom of this

Original emblem of Haifa, as carved on city hall
Courtesy of photographer Adi Silberstein

emblem; in its center the city's name is written in the Latin alphabet; on the right, in the Arabic alphabet; and on the left, in Hebrew. The language of the British Mandate held the position of power in the center, but Hebrew and Arabic, which represented the two main populations in the city, were given equal status. After the establishment of the state, the writing on the emblem's scroll was changed on most official signs and documents: English was pushed to the side, Arabic remained on the right, while Hebrew took prominence at the center. Nevertheless, at the height of the majestic city hall, the equality of Hebrew and Arabic is maintained.[118] Above the scroll, at the heart of the symbol, a regal sailboat floats on the waves; behind it, two towers or lighthouses stand guard at either end of a breakwater, marking the nautical entrance to the port.

In 1936 the city's fathers selected the artist Esther Berlin to design a symbol that would express the true spirit of the city. She did so by alluding to the quintessential elements of a port city: a ship, breakwaters, and towers. At that time Haifa's port was the biggest in the land, a source of pride for the city's inhabitants, Arabs and Jews alike. It was not only economically significant — it also symbolized the cosmopolitan character of the city and its connections with the world across the sea.

A similar backdrop of the Haifa bay and port can be excavated from beneath a dense metaphorical layer in a few of Yehuda Amichai's well-known yet misunderstood poems. On his beloved girlfriend's final day in the country, August 31, 1947, Amichai accompanied her to the Haifa port, where she boarded a ship to America. He waved good-bye to her from the dock and stood there until her yellow straw hat disappeared over the horizon. Although he thought that Ruth would return to him, the separation seared his heart. Over the following months he yearned for her and wrote her three letters a week, but in April 1948 she severed the relationship. Camouflaged shrapnel from that terrible explosion is scattered throughout Amichai's poems.

A sonnet in his now-canonic cycle *Ahavnu Kan* (We loved here), which he would publish eight years after their farewell at the port, subtly hints at that personal trauma. The sonnet's lines obliquely describe a vista with images similar to those on the city's symbol:

> The tall *towers* are still silent
> and the *broken one* does not yet know about the *breaker*.
> He who enlarges *waters from waters*
> will separate us without bridges[119]

The silent towers, the word *breaker*, and the waters recall the quintessential Haifa landscape. The *tall towers* may be seen as lighthouses (in Hebrew, "light *towers*"), while the word *breaker* suggests a *breakwater*, both staples of any port city.[120] The differentiation of *waters from waters* evokes the way breakwaters separate the waters of the bay from the waters of the open sea.

When lighthouses "speak," they do so through light beams or sirens, directing ships into the port and preventing them from smashing against rocks or a breakwater. "Silent" lighthouses, on the other hand, fail to warn the ships of a coming catastrophe. Amichai sets the scene of his heartbreak against the landscape where his emotional crash occurred: the port is the place of pain, the locus of the separation from Ruth.[121] The *towers* were silent that summer day when Amichai and his beloved Ruth said good-bye at the port. That silence continued for the many long months afterward. No siren or light beam warned the man in love that he would soon become the *broken one* while his beloved would become the *breaker*.

The power of a classic poem is that it can hold multiple, sometimes unintended meanings. In an alternate political reading of this sonnet one could say that the towers/lighthouses on Haifa's symbol were *silent* when a joint committee of Jews and Arabs met to discuss the design of the city's emblem in 1936. Nobody knew then — certainly not the Arabs whose lives would be shattered in 1948—that twelve years after choosing this unifying symbol, both they and their city would be *broken*. Indeed, Haifa has never recovered from that breaking.

A city's architectural structures and parks, intersections and harbors, become semiotic signs in the minds, memories, and emotions of its inhabitants and writers. They carry meaning and convey information through their presence, the texture of their designs, and the materials of their construction. They are the words and sentences that make up the language of the city, dictating its rhythm and its music. In Haifa the public buildings on its seamline preserve the municipal memory of cooperation, the morals that forged Haifa's unique character. The city's people and structures are in an eternal, evolving conversation with the mountain and the sea, as echoed in the classic symbol of Haifa.

And perhaps, a well-wrought symbol, like a well-wrought poem, has prophetic powers. At the top of the emblem — above the scroll, the boat, and the port — hovers an elliptical stone crown, interwoven with an olive branch. Some say it is a depiction of Dahir al-Umar's strong fortress; others argue that it is a visual representation of that structure's name, Burj al-Salam, Fortress of Peace. City hall, with Haifa's sculptured symbol at its head, stands facing the fortress's former grounds, and it too bears an olive branch. Perhaps peace will come and Arabs and Jews will once again work together to improve the fate of their city; perhaps the gospel of peace will one day emerge from Haifa.[122]

2

THE TECHnION

The Genesis of Hadar HaCarmel

According to the chronicles of modern Hebrew Haifa, the district of Hadar HaCarmel was brought into the world by "the wondrous deed of erecting a technical school in a desolate, thorn-strewn place on the Carmel, far from the city's settlement."[1] These words were written in 1958, the year of the tenth anniversary of the State of Israel and almost fifty years after the construction of that very technical school, the Technion.[2] At that time it still seemed that the neighborhood born of this "wondrous deed" would keep growing; the Technion would continue to shower it with light and warmth; and Haifa as a whole would retain its status as a flourishing metropolis.

Completed in 1914, the Technion — the Technological Institute of Israel — stood alone on the middle of the northern slope of Mount Carmel, between its peak and the sea, and served as the foundation of the most important Jewish neighborhood in Haifa. Hadar HaCarmel—literally, "the splendor of the Carmel" and simply "Hadar" to locals—was initially planned as a "garden city." In the 1920s it grew around the Technion building, which had been standing there for a decade. From its inception, Hadar gradually spread down the slope, its streets ultimately forming a grid. The grid's horizontal avenues are wide and straight and run parallel to the coastline; they are intersected by winding vertical streets, stairs, and narrow alleys that weave their way down the mountain toward the bay.[3] The area around the Technion was the center of commerce, culture, and entertainment for Jewish Haifa.[4] There, many of the inhabitants of Hadar, immigrants and refugees from the other side of the sea, struggled to build the life they had dreamt of in their newly adopted city. Some tried to recreate their former world, and some tried to forget it, but the legacies of their other homelands subtly shaped the sites of their new city. They longed for the European milieu they left behind—the cafés, the music, and their mother tongues. They spun the stories of their newfound loves and passed them on to their children. They passed on tastes and scents and raised children imprinted with the traces of their parents' worlds. They taught them the old rituals and languages that gradually became irrelevant to the younger generation. This was the site of tug-of-wars between parents and children, the biological and the spiritual, teachers and students, the culture of the past and the sensibilities of the future.

Even before I understood the forces that shaped the quarter in which I was born and raised, even before I grasped its structure and design, the Technion area at the heart of Hadar seeped into my consciousness. It was as if a mysterious hand led me along the paths of the history of Haifa, taking pains to show me early in my life the monumental work of the architect Alexander Baerwald and the venerable area adjacent to it. The Technion's round dome and symmetrical lines accompanied me as I grew, while the triangles decorating its roof and the tall stairway leading to its huge entrance archways were etched in my heart. My nursery school dwelt nearby, and, at the end of each day, my mother and I would pass by the Technion and often sit in the garden nestled in front of that broad-armed building between the rows of tall trees.

The western border of the Technion complex, the one closest to that garden, was Shmaryahu Levin Street, which I passed daily. It gently descends toward the sea and, on the way, crosses Herzl Street, the northern border of the complex and the main thoroughfare in Hadar. I always feel warmth toward this little intersection of Shmaryahu Levin and Herzl: on its corner was one of the many coffee houses that characterized Haifa, the Viennese Café Krips, where my parents met for the first time.

As Herzl Street passes by the Technion, it meets the vertical Balfour Street, the institute's eastern border. This crossroads is unique in its topography: Balfour Street soars up Mount Carmel at a dramatic angle from the broad Herzl Street. In fact, it is the only "vertical" street in the city that rises straight toward the peak of the Carmel uninterrupted. Balfour is also the steepest street that has ever been paved in Israel — its angle is the maximum incline allowed by Israel's Planning and Construction Law. The histories of the buildings that stand at this intersection are a microcosm of the city's development as a whole and, specifically, of Hadar HaCarmel. This space has continued to evolve in the memory of those who have lived in Haifa and of the authors who have written about it.

In the 1950s, when my daily route touched the Technion, Hadar had been bustling around it for over two decades, and the school had earned an international reputation as a prestigious institute for applied sciences.[5] It had also already garnered a glorious national history that included its service as a home to each of Hadar's public institutions in their infancy; the neighborhood's sole source of water in its fledgling years; a communal site for performances and celebrations; a shelter for Jewish refugees in times of danger; a provider of technological assistance to the British against the Nazis; and a major player in the national struggle during Israel's War of Independence. Furthermore, the building itself was one of the fundamental architectural symbols of the Zionist movement. Photographs of it adorn every encyclopedia entry on the history of the Jewish settlement in Palestine, and it is described as embodying the new Hebrew Style, an architectural aesthetic with parallels in both literature and art.[6]

The Edifice and Its Architect

The designer of the Technion, Alexander Baerwald, lived a life made of the stuff of Hollywood. This talented architect, a graduate of the Institute

of Technology in Berlin, played cello in a chamber music group, wrote poetry, and occasionally painted. Born in 1877 to an assimilated Jewish family, he held the respected post of architect of the Prussian Public Works
Department in Berlin. When he was only thirty-two years old, he was invited by the Jewish leaders who were planning the Technion to participate
in its construction, mainly because he was Jewish. To prepare, he took an
instructional journey to Palestine that determined his development as an
architect. He decoded the region's indigenous style, the Heimatstil, and
envisioned a palace, or shrine, to higher education on a long and narrow
stretch of rocky land on the Carmel slope facing the sea.

    When he began the construction in 1911, he lived on the Carmel and
would ride a donkey down the Donkey Path to the construction site. An
illustrated story he wrote in rhyme that was found in his estate humor-
ously relates the adventures of Baerwald, the son of Europe, on the mountain in the Middle East.[7] He struggled with the hard rocks, the aridity, the
conflicting opinions of the Jewish leaders, the Turkish police, and a lack of
skilled workers and machinery — yet he continued building. All the while
he was also working in Germany and was even decorated with a medal
from the kaiser for the Prussian Royal Library in Berlin. In the midst of the
Great War, he joined the German navy and fought for his homeland, but
even on the front he dreamt about the educational complex he had been
forced to leave behind. After the war he returned to that remote Palestinian
town and began designing more buildings in the style that he had created.
However, the man who planned the shrine to education died prematurely,
after completing only a portion of what he had intended. Thankfully, he
finished the dream castle of the Technion and a few additional works, but
many of his other designs went unfulfilled. He fell while still holding his
drafting pencil, leaving his students and colleagues to fight over his legacy.
In 1932, approximately two years after he died, there was an exhibition in
his hometown of Berlin, dedicated to the "loyal" architect "to whom the
Professional Society of Architects and Engineers in Berlin owes a great
debt."[8] In Haifa his touch is recognizable throughout the city, not only in
the buildings that he himself designed but also in those constructed after
he died, which still pay homage to his genius.

    In planning the Technion Baerwald fully embraced a new architectural
language, which used the characteristics of indigenous architecture that

he had identified on his initial trip to Palestine.[9] He valued the influence of the local culture and internalized it.[10] He avoided both conspicuous colonialist features and decorative orientalism. His work combined his Prussian professionalism, European classicism, and updated construction techniques with Islamic morphology, the local Arab style, and ancient Jewish symbology.

Baerwald's Technion gazes north over Hadar and Haifa's lower city toward the Mediterranean. Its design displays both ancient and contemporary Middle Eastern motifs and classical European forms in a modern spatial order.[11] A wide bank of external steps ascends toward its elevated main entrance, rising up from ceremonial gardens that unfold along a palm tree–lined boulevard. The front façade has a symmetrical composition, comprised of five parts, that brings to mind an ancient temple: the central, domed mass is bookended by two main wings, with a secondary body at the end of each wing. Each individual part is symmetrical within itself: the two main wings have evenly spaced quartets of rectangular windows. Above each window is a ventilation aperture. The arches beneath, on the basement floor, correspond precisely to each group of four windows. The unforgettable deep-set entrance in the central mass stands out due to its dome and the strict symmetry on either side. Its depth is accentuated by the flat plane of the side wings' façades. A giant vault shelters the entrance, casting its authority over the entire composition.[12]

From a distance it almost seems as if the low building is a part of the stony mountain, but, close up, it is impossible not to be awestruck by the intricate work of the arches that form its entrance: three nesting arches, one inside another. In the wall behind them, three tall, sculpted arches frame the arched doors and the arched windows above them, making it difficult for an onlooker to know how many arches there are altogether; each arch seems to be a reflection of another arch, as in a hall of mirrors.

A Star of David is showcased high above the entrance doors, as though the entrance's glory is there solely to frame it and, by extension, the Technion's unbreakable bond with the Jewish people. Thus, the architectural, decorative, and topographical mechanisms channel the eye toward the symbol of Zionist ideology, a testament to the architect's identification with the Technion's national mission. All five parts of the façade are clad in limestone from the nearby shore of Atlit and carved with details of traditional

The Technion *Courtesy of Haifa City Archives; photographer W. Loewenheim*

stonework. Baerwald wanted to remain faithful to the ancient style and so asked the stonemasons "not to fix imperfections in the stone" so as to preserve their natural, rough texture.[13] Ornaments, pointed arches, and hexagonal and circular portholes decorate the façade; an Assyrian-style row of sharp teeth marches on the roof above it, while the polygonic dome at the center of the structure is taken from a reconstructed model of King Solomon's temple. All these echo the architect's desire to draw from the glorious construction tradition of the Middle East in its entirety.

The central, inner space has a very different aesthetic. Light streams into it from the dome and the large window above the entrance. A main staircase with a magnificently crafted wooden railing ascends from the lobby to the large hall above, breaking the symmetry. It is a modern, open, dynamic space that blurs the lines between inside and out. For example, its walls are made of smooth, plastered chalkstone, but select architectural details, such as the inner doorposts, are made of the façade's rough limestone.[14]

The corridors that branch out from either side of the lobby also break the
boundary between inside and out: on one of their sides is a series of open
archways similar to the arcade of a well-ventilated mosque designed to accommodate the climate. Each corridor leads to a graded lecture hall. High
on the back wall of the lobby, a window rises, shaped like the two tablets
inscribed with the Ten Commandments, and above it, a hollow Star of
David. The marble floor is paved in a magnificent pattern. While the inner
space showcases Baerwald's contemporary aspirations, the design of the
façade is more conservative and Middle Eastern in style to match the environment. When viewed from outside, the building looks like a massive,
terraced structure that is preventing the mountain from sliding into the
sea. Baerwald succeeded, then, in navigating the balancing act presented
by the assignment he had taken upon himself. He designed a monumental
building that proudly announced its cultural and national mission, all the
while creating the impression that the Technion had grown naturally out
of its landscape.

Technion inner staircase
Courtesy of Haifa City Archives; photographer W. Loewenheim

To complement his masterpiece Baerwald also conceived of a garden that would continue the building's design. He consulted the artist and garden aficionado, Hermann Struck, his friend from Berlin, on the garden's design: straight lines of trees on either side of a palm tree boulevard that served as the middle axis. In 1923 Albert Einstein visited and symbolically planted two palm trees as a sign of support for the Technion. The gardener, Abraham Ginzburg, who lived with his family in the water tower on the highest point of the complex, also planted grass and flowers. Surrounded by a stone fence ornate with the purple flowers of thick bougainvillea, the lovely garden spread down the entire expanse in front of the building. Years later the gardener's assistant would remember it in detail: "The garden was divided into four. In the western part, near the entrance gate, was a round pool, a column inlaid with pebbles at its center, water trickling into the pond. . . . Around the pool there were concrete benches . . . and behind them, trees that provided shade, which was particularly pleasant in the hot summer. In the second quarter of the garden rose trees with which the land was blessed: palm, fig, pomegranate, plum, carob, and vines."[15]

From my early childhood I remember the garden that emerges from this description—its greenery, its bubbling waters, and the feeling of secluded, protected serenity that it bestowed on all its visitors. Many little children, like me, played among the tall trees, chasing butterflies and enjoying themselves, while their mothers sat and chatted, supervising and feeding the children or tending to little babies in their carriages. A few heartwarming lines in a letter that the then fledgling poet Yehuda Amichai wrote in 1947 confirm my memory of the garden's denizens: "The sun is shining and in the little garden near the Technion babysitters and young mothers come with their children in carriages. . . . That green garden is filled with life."[16] Both my nursery school and kindergarten were located nearby, making the garden an inseparable part of the landscape of my childhood. I used to visit it almost every day with my mother and my baby brother on the way home, especially from Sonya's Nursery, my nursery school on Ahad Ha'am Street. That street, located west of the Technion, was filled with trees and old houses, remnants of the Technikum neighborhood that had been absorbed into Hadar HaCarmel. The house where Sonya's Nursery resided still stands, the remains of old playground equipment hidden in its backyard.

Author as the white butterfly
Photograph by Alexander Jakobovitch,
Photo Alexander Studio, Haifa

In that yard the three butterflies from Levin Kipnis's story played and frol-
icked in the sun — a white butterfly, a yellow butterfly, and a red butterfly.[17]
Each wore a long dress in a different color, a pair of paper and wire antennae,
and two gorgeous wings. In the class play at the end of the school year, these
three butterflies appeared alongside the sun, the rain, and all the garden's col-
orful flowers, and I, the white butterfly, proudly addressed the audience: "Dear
parents, thank you for coming to Sonya Nursery School's celebration."

In my nursery school days, it seemed to me, as to generations of Haifa
children who grew up in the area, that the Technion and its garden had
been on the slope since the beginning of time. Of course, colossal buildings don't spontaneously spring up, especially not in a small town on the
periphery of the Ottoman Empire over a century ago. Nevertheless, the
relatively short time that elapsed between the conception and execution
of the Technion's edifice is part of what makes its erection a miracle.

As early as 1901 the Fifth Zionist Congress decided to build a Jewish
university that emphasized technological subjects. In 1902 the great Zionist dreamer, Theodor Herzl, published the utopian novel *Altneuland*, in
which he dubbed Haifa "the city of the future" and predicted it would play

a leading role in industry and technology. But the Technion itself was actually the product of the initiative of a non-Zionist organization.

In 1907 Paul Nathan, the leader of the relief organization Ezra Association of German Jews, visited Palestine and started working toward building an institution for technological studies, a "Technikum," the likes of which were found nowhere in the vast reaches of the Ottoman Empire. His initiative won the support of the German kaiser, who, like other major European powers, was invested in spreading his country's culture and benefiting its economy. Nathan chose Haifa to fulfill his vision, even though at the time, it was still relatively small, with a population of twenty thousand, only 10 percent of whom were Jewish. Nevertheless, he was convinced of the city's potential as a future center of industry and a transportational hub (the Hejaz Railway had been inaugurated there in 1905). In 1908 a lot was purchased with the funding of German, Russian, and American Jews.[18] Arthur Ruppin, the father of Jewish settlement in Palestine who founded the Palestine Land Development Company, foresaw the urban development that would follow the Technion and bought the surrounding land, which would become the Hadar HaCarmel neighborhood less than two decades later.

In 1909 the lot was encircled by a fence to ensure ownership, according to Ottoman law. Meanwhile, Jewish experts in Germany had already designed the curriculum for the Technion and decided to create a preparatory school for it, which ultimately became the Hebrew Reali School. Baerwald was invited to plan the entire complex, and in 1910 he opened an office in Haifa. In 1911, even before receiving a permit, the construction materials had been collected and hauled to the site on camels and in carts. The project faced many obstacles, however: Ottoman bureaucratic procedures, an inadequate and technologically unskilled workforce, a lack of modern machinery, and stubborn land that rejected the foundation.[19] Despite all this, the cornerstone was laid in April 1912. In 1913 the main Technion building was almost finished, its workshops had been completed, and its well—at the time the deepest in the country—had been dug. The high school building had also been finished. With its small dome and toothed roof, the Hebrew Reali School was a diminutive reflection of the main Technion building. Unlike its bigger brother, however, its structure was charmingly asymmetrical. In its design Baerwald allowed himself to surrender more to local, vernacular architectural elements than he did in the Technion's.

As construction progressed, the Zionists and the non-Zionists on the board of trustees engaged in a series of power struggles. The peak of these conflicts was the fight over the language of instruction, eventually known as the "war of the languages." The non-Zionists wanted German, while the Zionists believed that teaching in Hebrew was tantamount. Due to the "discord," those who championed Hebrew, led by the high school's principal, Arthur Biram, were forced to conduct studies outside the premises, even though the high school building was ready for use. The echoes of this dispute even reached the *New York Times* in a 1914 article titled "Zionist Outbreaks Due to Language."[20] That year studies at the technological institute were about to begin. However, in August 1914 Germany declared war on Russia. In 1916 the complex housed the German army and in 1917 became a Turkish military hospital, which spared it from the bombings. In 1918, when the British entered the city, they erected a military tent camp there. It was not until 1920 that the Technion was transferred into the hands of the World Zionist Organization. But it took three more years to return the building to its former glory. The Technion, intended to be the sole technical academic institution in the Ottoman Empire, opened its doors only after that empire's downfall. Ten years passed between 1914, when classes were supposed to begin under the Ottoman sultan, to its actual opening under the British Crown. The Technion was officially inaugurated in February 1925 and finally started to fulfill its original mission. Baerwald was appointed professor of architecture and, ironically, began teaching in German.

Twenty-five years later, in the abnormally snowy Haifa winter of 1950, the Technion celebrated its silver jubilee in the independent State of Israel. One of its first visionaries, the Zionist leader and scientist Chaim Weizmann, then the first president of the young state, participated in the ceremony. The Technion's director enumerated its achievements: it had graduated more than one thousand engineers and quadrupled the number of its laboratories. The quick growth of Haifa's Jewish population also contributed to the Technion's expansion and the thriving of its urban surroundings. Joining the veteran Reali, schools around the Technion multiplied, among them, my kindergarten.

Coffee Houses as Landmarks

"Milka's" school, my kindergarten, was in the area of the Technion, not far from the lovely Sonya's Nursery, where we were all carefree butterflies.

In Milka's kindergarten on Ben Yehuda Street, however, we did not flit from flower to flower. Instead, we learned to behave, to wait patiently for our turn, whether for lunch or a ride on the carousel in the front yard. Milka's school was affiliated with the Organization for Working Mothers, which meant that it included an afternoon nap and a four o'clock snack: a light-blue Bakelite cup filled to the brim with nauseating cocoa and dark bread smeared with jelly. But on Fridays school ended early, and, instead of the afternoon nap, we all eagerly awaited the man with the panas kesem, *or magic lantern. That lantern was housed in a large, wooden box, on whose front was affixed an illustrated scroll. The schoolroom was darkened midday, and we sat entranced while the man stood next to the box, slowly turning the scroll as he told the story. Lit from behind, the colorful pictures were revealed in front of our eyes, one after the other, and the tale, every week the same, was etched in our hearts: "Hannah'le and her Shabbat Dress." First, the picture of Hannah'le in her beautiful white dress; then, Hannah'le taking care of a dirty kitten; next, Hannah'le helping an elderly coal porter carry his heavy sack; and, finally, Hannah'le weeping and distraught after realizing that her dress was stained with mud and coal dust. The stars saw her tears, however, and, in reward for her kind heart, turned every stain into a star so that the dress was even prettier than it had been at first.*[21]

But Fridays held another magic: my father. By law, businesses and schools had to close early that day in honor of Shabbat, so he was able to pick me up from school on his way back from work. My father and I marched home hand in hand: I was in heaven. We walked down Ben Yehuda Street, and every week, or so it seemed, just before we turned toward the Technion, we would pass the same girl on the same corner, calling up to a high balcony for her mom (*ima*) to come out. At the top of her lungs, she would scream "Iiiiimaaaa!" And we, giggling, imitated her tone, calling out a random rhyme we had made up: "Kadiiiimaaa" (which means "forward"). From that corner we continued past the wall around the Reali School. In the spaces between the cypress trunks that hid the schoolyard, we could see only the running feet of the children playing. Here we would chant "this school Re'*ali* is not norm*ali*!" a popular local joke about the exclusive snobby institution. Then we turned onto Shmaryahu Levin Street, crossed Herzl, and from there, onward.

When I walked home with my father on Fridays, we never stopped on the enchanting Herzl Street and did not reach the large Herzl/Balfour intersection, but I knew the pleasures it held from my many strolls with my mother. Our stated destination was usually Meyer Coffee, where she bought quality ground coffee, but when the spirit came over my mother, we would go to Café Snir, the café and ice cream parlor in the Clock House on the bustling Herzl/Balfour intersection. We would sit next to the window, overlooking the street's sharp decline. My mother, Dora, would order café au lait for her and ice cream for me in a shiny silver goblet: three scoops, one white, one pink, and one chocolate, with a triangle wafer. Was it here that she first drew me the map of their love, hers and my father's? This map was dotted with the European establishments around the Technion complex. First was Café Krips at the corner of Herzl and Shmaryahu Levin. In front of it was a small plaza and inside, between walls inlaid with black tiles, one could climb the two steps to a gallery area encircled by a shiny metal railing. My mother told me that when she first moved to Haifa from Tel Aviv in 1940, she became friends with a woman named Frau Sturm. To this day I can remember her silvery-blue hair, arranged in a tall, structured coiffure of curls, and her beautiful hands, even though I never learned her first name (the way I was brought up, children never addressed unrelated adults by their first name). In fact, it was because of Frau Sturm that my mother met my father. My mother was sitting with her in Café Krips when suddenly a man entered and approached the table. He was an acquaintance of Frau Sturm's from when they both lived in Vienna. His name was Jakob Scharf. Frau Sturm introduced my mother to him, saying, "This is Dora Preminger. She's originally from Chernovitz."

"Chernovitz?" the man verified. "My sister lived in Chernovitz."

"My sister lived in Chernovitz" is the only fragment from that conversation that reached me verbatim. And what else did my father tell my mother about his older sister, Haya, who had moved to Chernovitz when she got married? Did he tell the woman he had just met about his only visit to Chernovitz in 1927? Many years later I would meet Haya's son, Joseph, and he would tell me about that visit from the point of view of the six-year-old child he was then. That was the year that Joseph began first grade, but because of the family's limited means, he did not have a school bag. My father, the uncle who had just arrived from Vienna, gave his little nephew his own expensive leather briefcase. Joseph kept that bag until he escaped Chernovitz at the beginning of World War II. And my father? Did he know that his sister Haya had already perished when the name Chernovitz reverberated in Café Krips?

Later I learned that Café Krips had been established by the Viennese pastry chef Walter Krips. I found out that he was among the first to bring whipped cream to Haifa, a fact that perhaps explains why my father went there so often. He used to tell us wonders about the superior *schlagsahne* served in Vienna.[22]

My father proposed three months after they met at Krips. He took my mother to Balfour Keller, the most expensive Viennese restaurant in town. Its name hinted at its location in the subterranean floor of the building — the cellar (*Keller* in German). The image of the painted chef who welcomed them with his white hat and handlebar moustache continued smiling from the top of the menu that stood outside the restaurant for many years afterward. That evening my father gave my mother a square, golden watch as an engagement present, which she wore until the day she died. The landmarks in my mother's story were all clustered in the same area, and I could identify them easily. I passed Krips every day on my way to and from preschool, while Balfour Cellar sat near the Herzl/Balfour intersection, diagonally across from the Clock House, where Café Snir served me ice cream balls in chilled silver dishes.

Coffee houses were an important part of my life, not only as the backdrop of my parents' romance. When I was a little older than a kindergartner, my mother used to take me slightly farther afield, to Café Ritz. There she taught me how to read German because, like many of Hadar's cafés, Ritz didn't have magazines in any other language. Viennese culture inspired much of Hadar HaCarmel, since many of its residents were central European immigrants. The spirit of European capitals continued to hover over my city throughout my youth. Earlier newspaper ads from the time of Hadar's swift growth in the 1930s showed the importance of its cafés. In Café Vienna on Nordau Street, just south of Herzl near the Technion, they served homemade "Viennese ice cream" in the summer, and in Café Sternheim next door they danced to imported Austrian music.

The author Yehoshua Kenaz moved to Haifa with his family at a young age because his father worked for the British during World War II. Although he lived some distance from Hadar HaCarmel, his close friend Nili Friedlander recalled during our conversation that he knew it well — he even gave her a walking tour of his childhood Haifa.[23] In the story "Musical Moment" Kenaz's narrator visited Hadar HaCarmel twice a week because Mrs. Chanina, his "first violin teacher," lived in a stone house on the elegant Yerushalayim Street or, as Kenaz calls it, "one of those quiet streets near the Institute of Technology." After the frustrating and anxiety-provoking violin lessons, his mother would take him to a "German café" in the neighborhood.[24]

Kenaz's autobiographical stories paint the city and his life there with the sensitivity and talent for observing detail that are his trademark. The reader of the story "Henrik's Secret" is able to follow the footsteps of the narrator and his new friend, Henrik, just as the two boys follow Wanda, Henrik's beautiful sister. Behind the stone fence surrounding the café at the corner of Nordau and Balfour, they watch Wanda dancing with an English soldier. Indeed, these cafés, with their European dance bands, attracted many of the British Mandate's officers. In the eyes of the adolescent boys spying on these European leisure spots, they were the peak of glamor and intrigue.

Unlike the nameless cafés in Kenaz's stories, which are recalled by the child narrator only through their cultural affiliation — "a German café" — one long-lived popular establishment has been preserved in literature by name: Café Atara.[25] It was joined at the hip to Balfour Cellar in the same building. Atara did not star in my mother's stories, but it has the privilege of appearing in important Haifa literary works. Among the regulars of that café was the twenty-three-year-old Yehuda Amichai, who lived in Haifa in 1947–48 and would emerge as one of the revolutionaries of Hebrew literature within a decade.

"We sat in Café Atara / in Hadar HaCarmel," says the speaker in one of the moving tributes Amichai wrote for his father. "A Meeting with My Father" is a poem he wrote late in his life, over thirty years after the period it depicts. It is the only place in his oeuvre where he openly confronts the difficult months during which he lived in Haifa. Upon reading this poem in 1980, when it first appeared in *The Great Tranquility: Questions and Answers*, I rejoiced at both the unexpected connection between my hometown and my beloved poet and the fact that the most elevated figure in Amichai's poetry, his father, was eternalized in a Haifa-centric poem.[26] I understood the fatefulness of the time of their meeting and the gap between the poem's dramatic circumstances and the intimate, everyday language with which it describes them. Yet at the time neither I nor almost any other reader could have known the poem's full background.[27] Twenty-three years passed between the publication of "A Meeting with My Father" and the day when I learned the full story behind it:

A MEETING WITH MY FATHER

My father came to me in one of the intermissions
Between two wars or between two loves
As if to an actor resting backstage in half-darkness.
We sat in the Café Atara
In Hadar HaCarmel. He asked me about my small room
And if I was coping on my modest teacher's pay.

Daddy, daddy, before me you must have begot
Cherries that you loved,
Black with so much redness!
My brothers, sweet cherries
From that world.

The time was the time of evening prayer.
My father knew I no longer prayed
And said, let's play chess
The way I taught you as a child.

The time was October 1947,
Before the fateful days and the first shots.
And we didn't know then I'd be called the generation of '48
And I played chess with my father, checkmate '48.[28]

The speaker's father comes to visit his son "between two wars or between two loves." As the last stanza explicitly states the date, "October 1947," the "two wars" are those in which Amichai served as a soldier: World War II, which ended in 1945, and Israel's War of Independence, which erupted in 1948. The phrase "between two loves," however, is more ambiguous. Who were the two loves? Amichai married his first wife, Tamar, in 1949, but what was the love that preceded it and who was the beloved?

After Amichai's death I met Ruth née Hermann, the woman he had loved in those days, and discovered a treasure trove of love letters that she, their addressee, had preserved for sixty years. It so happens that the meeting between young Amichai and his father described in the poem occurred approximately one year before he fell in love with Tamar and two months after August 1947, when Ruth, his girlfriend at the time, sailed to the United States. The father, who traveled from Jerusalem to Haifa, knew that his son's heart was broken and tried to comfort him in his quiet, understated way — by playing chess with him the way he would when the poet was a child. The religious father did not scold his son for no longer reciting his prayers and instead simply tried to lighten his burden. The threads of intimacy woven throughout the poem, however, are severed due to "the time," and the tender language of the father-son conversation gives way to the lexicon of speeches and newspapers: "first shots" and "the generation of '48."[29] The second stanza of the poem departs from both vocabularies and becomes an emotional cry. The "cherries" in its second line express longing for Europe, the birthplace of those sweet fruits, but also the birthplace of the poet as well as his father, who might have secretly wished that his children were European, like him.

"A Meeting with My Father" was written decades after the 1948 war had ended and the poet's father had died. From the distance of time, the speaker dubs himself and those who fought in that war "the checkmate generation": the generation that went to die but also the generation that "checkmated" the enemy and won the war. The emotional second stanza of the poem evokes the story of the binding of Isaac: the poem's syntactical construction of "cherries *that you loved*" is similar to the biblical verse, "the only son *that you loved*." The story of the binding of Isaac and God's demand that the father sacrifice his beloved son has long been a symbol of that bloody war and the sacrifice of sons on the altar of the nation. Within the short poem, then, there is a summary of both the personal — the father's worry and the son's loss of the woman he loves — and the national experiences. These were the days of autumn 1947 in Haifa's Hadar HaCarmel neighborhood, a few weeks before the United Nations vote on the Partition Plan, on the threshold of the war. Amichai and his father felt the looming "mate" of the checkmate, knew the love affair was over but did not talk about it, and together longed for the bygone time when the son was a European child who could buy sweet cherry cake in a German café.

The link between the father and Café Atara recurs in another poem in the same collection, albeit without explicitly mentioning Haifa. "A Second Meeting with My Father" opens, "Again, I met my father in Café Atara / This time he was already dead." This jarring line undoes the power of death, for the fact that the father "was already dead" does not prevent him from meeting with his son. Moreover, the second meeting takes place in the same coffee house as the first. For Amichai, then, as for many citizens of Hadar, the milieu of the European café was like a "holding environment" — a womb, or a loving father — a means of visiting the sweet past, even for a minute:

> Happy are those
> Who have a patisserie next door to a coffee house,
> You can call inside: "Another cake, more
> Sweetness, let's have more!"
>
> Happy is he whose dead father is next door to him
> And he can call him always.[30]

As in its twin Café Atara poem, Amichai uses the syntax to convey meaning when he speaks about the coffee house and his father: "Happy are those" and then "Happy is he." The Hebrew word *ashrei* ("happy are" and "happy is") recalls the long *ashrei* prayer, which is composed of three different psalms and is recited thrice daily during synagogue services: *ashrei yoshvei veitekha.* ("Happy are those who dwell in Your home.") Through the syntax and linguistic allusions, the poet connects the warmth and sweetness imbued by the café with memories of his childhood synagogue and his father's love and faith. One may even suggest that Amichai has substituted the coffee house (*bet café*) for the house of worship (*bet knesset*).

In a letter from October 15, 1947, Amichai wrote to Ruth: "Last night I came back to my room and behold, my father was sitting there. . . . He . . .

brought ready-made sandwiches with him, and we ate together. . . . I was very, very happy."[31] The 1980 poem, "A meeting with my father," then, is an autobiographical one in which most of the details are accurate: Amichai's father did visit him in Haifa in the autumn of 1947. While Atara is not explicitly mentioned in that letter, its importance to Amichai is evident. Three earlier letters from the first month after Ruth's departure mention Café Atara.[32] According to them, the poet used to sit there when writing his long aerograms to her. A letter he wrote in the first week after she left sheds light on his frequent visits to the café: "for some reason, it is still hard for me to write the letters in my room. I go up to the Carmel or sit in Atara."[33] Amichai implies that it is easier to write love letters in a noisy café than in a quiet, lonely room.

But the poet had a more substantial reason for sitting in the café. The letters reveal that in the last months of 1947, Amichai was certain that poetry was his calling. Furthermore, before that autumn he had begun to forge what would ultimately become his unique contribution to Hebrew literature, that is, a poetic style that draws from everyday life. He wanted to absorb the mundane, to jot down his impressions on paper and hone his writing process. Atara, then, was an ideal place from which he could observe the lives of passersby. The café sat on the slope of the mountain, and its terrace and windows provided an excellent lookout over the neighborhood. In some of the letters, Amichai specifically refers to the morning tide of people flooding down the mountain to work and the evening ebb as they returned home. It is likely that he first noticed the power of this daily flux of people from his seat in Atara on the slope. Indeed, early on Amichai sent romantic letters dense with musings on the craft of poetry and the power of the quotidian, but as the United Nations vote on the Partition Plan approached, the echoes of the period and its trepidations grew louder and louder.

The letters also reveal the geographic outlines of Amichai's life in Haifa. During that period he lived west of the Technion. It is likely that he would leave his home, cross the Technion's garden, glimpse the toddlers playing there, and continue eastward to Café Atara. After the United Nations vote on November 29, 1947, however, his focus began to shift. In a letter written on December 21, Amichai particularly noted the young men, the students running up and down the Technion's steps "with agile and hard footsteps . . . in their stride that wondrous mixture of harsh, heavy-footed masculinity and the agility of a Greek youth in the Olympic Games." His words are not a mere expression of admiration of young men but rather a code for the escalating situation in Haifa at the end of 1947: "And especially in days like these, they [the men on the steps] have justification and good reason to walk erect and grow moustaches of all kinds and be a little vain."[34] Inside this epistolary description, the young man hides a patriotic message that he wished to convey to his addressee, hinting to her about the unstable security situation at the time. The unique national role that the Technion was filling, secretly preparing for war, lies between the lines. Furthermore, he indirectly reveals to her that although he detests war, the day is near when he, too, will climb the Technion's steps on his way, not to class, but to military and weapons training.

It was an open secret in British Mandatory Haifa that the Technion was the city's headquarters of the Hagana, the Jewish paramilitary organization. The Technion was the only academic institution in Palestine located at the heart of a Jewish settlement, and it made its various facilities available to serve the Jewish people during the Mandate years (1922–48). It also sheltered Jewish refugees during the Arab riots of 1929 and 1936. Throughout the Mandate period the Technion's workshops met the munitions needs of the Hagana, and training sessions were conducted at night in its cellars, halls, and classrooms. A sophisticated system of buzzers warned of approaching British police. Furthermore, one of the Hagana's central arms caches in Haifa was housed in the depths of the Technion's well, and starting in the 1920s guns and ammunition were stored, weapons repaired, and hand grenades loaded in its basements. During World War II, when most of the *yishuv*, the Jewish settlement in Palestine, joined the British fight against the Nazis, the manpower of the Technion was recruited to conduct missions for the British army, and many junior and senior faculty built airplane engines and developed explosives in the Technion's laboratories and workshops. In the winter of 1947 the Technion became command central for the Hagana units that were on call, preparing for the fateful confrontation over Haifa. In 1948 studies were cancelled for a year when hundreds of students enlisted in the Carmeli Brigade and other units.[35] After the 1948 war, classes resumed, and students once again flooded the Technion to study.

The Architectural Crossroads of Herzl and Balfour

Throughout the next decade the Technion building, weary of war and hardship, watched the Hadar neighborhood from its vantage point high on the slope. In its aging, stone heart, it reflected on the people who had brought it into the world and who now were memorialized in the names of surrounding streets: the road that would have continued its palm boulevard was named for Baerwald, its true father; on its west were Shmaryahu Levin and Ahad Ha'am Streets, named for the two Zionist leaders who raised funds for its construction, headed its board of directors, and oversaw its foundation.[36] And yes, the elegant Herzl Street to its north was appropriately named for the prophet of political Zionism, whose vision inspired the choice of Haifa as the Technion's home. The steep street that rises majestically up from Herzl is named for Lord Arthur Balfour, the British foreign secretary who declared his government's support for a Jewish national home in Palestine in 1917 and graced the Technion with a visit a month after its inauguration.

If Baerwald were still alive in the 1950s, standing at the entrance of his masterpiece and looking down onto the Herzl/Balfour intersection, he would see the beautiful Ginzburg Flower Shop nearby and perhaps fondly remember Abraham Ginzburg, the gardener who cared for the Technion's gardens so devotedly. He might proudly contemplate how this intersection near the Technion became the first in the city to have a traffic light due to the masses of people and vehicles that flowed through it.[37] He might even be impressed by the pedestrian underpass that the city excavated beneath the street. And perhaps, Baerwald, the architect, would wish that someone would tell the full saga of the Technion as well as the tales of the neighboring houses and the people who roamed their interiors. Perhaps he would listen to the stories of the Technion's architectural descendants on the Herzl/Balfour intersection; these are the buildings whose designs it nourished, so to speak, but that frequently rebelled against its style.

Indeed, thin threads tie all four buildings in the intersection to Baerwald: on the southeast a three-story residential house; on the northeast the Business Center; on the northwest the white, photogenic Clock House; and on the southwest the mammoth Bet HaKranot.

The three-story residential house that sits on the southeast corner was

probably the first house built in the intersection. A few scattered memories and photographs support its claim to primogeniture, but the available
archival material is scant, and the fog of time obscures the details of its beginnings. Its literary fate, however, is striking and more illustrious than that
of its three neighbors. An enchanting bookstore called Ein HaKore (The
Reader's Eye) occupied its horizontal façade facing Herzl for many years.
It had been a bibliophile's oasis at the heart of the bustling Herzl Street.
I would frequent Ein HaKore in high school, leafing through the newest
poetry collections on display, drinking in lines that had not reached our
literature curriculum. My gifted classmate at the Alliance School, Itamar,
recalled that when he was an engineering student at the Technion and
the textbooks he needed were sold out, he could always find them at Ein
HaKore . . . in French. In her semiautobiographical novel, *Corner People*,
the author Esty G. Hayim resurrects this bookstore and portrays her visit
there as a turning point in her life.[38]

But this old corner building is tightly bound to Hebrew literature in
hidden ways as well: the house's builders and former owners were the
Levin family, the great-grandparents of noted Haifa author Yehudit Katzir.
The fictional descendants of her family roam the pages of her early stories.
They dine at Balfour Cellar and frequent Café Atara, run through the underpass, and skip along Herzl Street. Twenty-five years after the publication of her first story, Katzir revealed her characters' Haifaian pedigree in
the family saga she wrote, *Zillah*. This epic novel preserves the Levins' tradition of the house's primacy in the Herzl/Balfour intersection: in *Zillah*
Katzir transcribes the words of her grandfather, Aminadav Levin, as they
were recorded on a cassette tape: "When the house, the fourth in Hadar
HaCarmel, was built, and my family . . . moved into it, they rented out a
room to the painter, Professor Hermann Struck, and his wife, Malka, who
had just emigrated from Germany." He recalled that the artist "used to sit
on the balcony and sketch the landscape of the bay in charcoal for long
hours." He added that the Strucks stayed "in the room and then moved
to the nice, comfortable stone house up the mountain that the architect
Baerwald designed for them."[39] Indeed, the designer of the Technion
not only planned the painter's permanent home but also was a close, old
friend of Struck's, one of the first tenants of the intersection. In fact, Struck
drew a striking portrait of the goateed Baerwald. And as for the claim of

The Business Center
and the intersection
Courtesy of Haifa
City Archives

primacy, since Struck immigrated to Palestine in 1922, we can deduce that
this house was already standing by that year.

The planning of the second-eldest building in the intersection, the
Business Center, began in the midst of the violence of 1929, when attacks
on Jews — which had been wreaking havoc throughout the country —
reached Haifa. Before the center was built, all of Haifa's commercial hubs
were located in the Arab-dominated lower city, as Hadar was viewed as a
garden city, a quasi suburb without commercial infrastructure.[40] One of
the motivations behind erecting a business center in Hadar HaCarmel was
the need for established stores in the Jewish neighborhood, should the
district once again be cut off from its usual suppliers. The style and building materials of Hadar HaCarmel's Business Center reflect the shift in
local architecture that stemmed from both economic and political factors.
The cement factory Nesher had started production a couple of years prior,
creating pressure to change the British law requiring stone façades. The
center was made entirely from cement, which was cheap and lessened the
need to rely on Arab stoneworkers. The modern design of the building,

which was so different from the Technion, was completed in 1933. It signaled the beginning of a cultural and political move away from Baerwald's original architectural, and perhaps ideological, dream of becoming a part of the existing Middle Eastern space. The Business Center building is shaped like an "L." The lines that stretch through the openings of its windows and balconies give its façade a horizontal emphasis in the International (or Bauhaus) Style, a feature that foreshadowed the style that would become prevalent in the neighborhood within the next two decades.[41] Yet behind the center's concrete walls and quintessentially modern design lies part of the tragic story of Baerwald. The year he began planning the center was also the last year of his life. He had submitted a proposal at the beginning of 1930 and promised to revise it, but died of cancer in October of that year. The completion of the project was entrusted to the architect Leon Vamos, and Baerwald's plans were lost. As a result, the architects' respective contributions to the final design remain unknown to this day.[42]

To the west of the Business Center on Herzl Street stands the third tenant of the intersection: the first office building in Hadar, Bet HaSha'on, the Clock House, erected between 1934 and 1936. Its designer, Gideon Kaminka, was sent to Palestine to build it in 1933 by one of his clients in Vienna. When Kaminka was nineteen years old, he went to Berlin to consult with none other than Baerwald himself about his professional future. Inspired by their meeting, he began studying architecture in the Technische Hochschule in Vienna, which was known for its tempered modernism. Kaminka arrived in Haifa when he was thirty years old. In the ensuing decades he contributed to the city's public life, primarily in the realms of construction and planning, and represented the Viennese modernist tradition there.[43] Like him, many of Hadar HaCarmel's residents were from central Europe, and he ultimately acted on their behalf as an elected official in the Histadrut (the workers' union).[44] The Clock House that Kaminka designed is composed of three simple bodies, two of which hug the corner where it stands. One lies flat, along Herzl, and the other faces down the slope. The third body stands above, straight and tall, creating the "tower" whose head boasts the famous clock. Although the building does not follow the International Style to the letter, its square terraces with their horizontal iron railings and the two-story-tall glass window near the staircase signal the architect's tendencies in that direction.[45] The aesthetic cleanliness of

The Clock House *Courtesy of Haifa City Archives*

Kaminka's design of the Clock House fits the intersection beautifully. Its clock has become an urban landmark that adorns many postcards.[46]

The fourth and last building to be erected on the Herzl/Balfour intersection is the majestic Bet HaKranot, the closest to the Technion. It remained the true focus of Haifa's business and fashion industry for a long time. The very first pair of high-heel stylish shoes that I owned came from Bet HaKranot's elegant Dan Gavrieli store. My mother took me there before my high school graduation, and I picked them, a shiny, deep maroon color and very pretty. Shopping at Bet HaKranot was reserved for special occasions, and its prestigious status was a source of pride for the city's people for decades. In the 1961 deluxe edition of *Altneuland*, published in honor of Herzl's hundredth birthday, the municipality of Haifa promoted Bet HaKranot as a commercial flagship, including a nighttime photograph of its shining stores to demonstrate the fulfillment of Herzl's prophecy of Haifa as "the city of the future." But the circumstances under which Bet HaKranot was built are darker than the book in honor of Herzl suggests and are connected to the tensions that dominated that period.

In 1934–35 the commercial development of Herzl Street accelerated due to the surge of immigrants from Europe fleeing the Nazi threat. Worried that the stores would overrun the Technion's tranquil garden, the board of trustees instigated the construction of Bet HaKranot to serve, among other things, as a barrier protecting the northern border of the garden.[47] The construction was sponsored by two national funds, Keren HaYesod (United Israel Appeal) and Keren Kayemet (Jewish National Fund). The plural of *keren* (fund) in Hebrew is *kranot*; the building was therefore named Bet HaKranot, literally, "House of the Funds." The architect Joseph Klarwein won second place in the competition. During that period he also planned the Dagon Silos in the lower city, and in subsequent decades he would build historical projects on a national scale. The jewel in his crown is the column-encircled Israeli parliament building, the Knesset, in Jerusalem. It is possible that planning Bet HaKranot, which was inspired by the Technion, the symbol of Zionist Haifa, prepared him for designing the monumental symbol of Israeli democracy. Regardless, to the delight of the board of trustees, Klarwein designed the block-long Bet HaKranot in homage to the Technion, cladding its façade with the same stone that Baerwald used.[48]

Bet HaKranot stretches along Herzl Street across the entire northern border of the Technion complex between Shmaryahu Levin and Balfour. The end on Shmaryahu Levin is rounded to reflect that street's soft decline, while the portion that borders Balfour seems aware of its status at the city's heart, and the spacious plaza in front of it broadcasts authority. This is how *Bauhaus on the Carmel* describes this last major landmark to arrive on the intersection: "He [Klarwein] . . . aligned the new building parallel to the main Technion façade and not with Herzl Street, which stood at an angle to it . . . not only strengthening the visual relationship of his building with Baerwald's monumental edifice, but also opening up . . . an interesting triangular urban space. . . . It was simple and dignified, with a regular series of columns marching in rhythm down Herzl Street."[49] The rare combination of simplicity and dignity remained a part of Klarwein's architectural vocabulary throughout his career.

Indeed, Bet HaKranot bolstered the commercial development of its vicinity. Herzl Street quickly changed from a residential street to the main thoroughfare in all of Haifa, and the Herzl/Balfour intersection grew so thick with traffic that an underground passage was dug beneath Balfour Street so pedestrians could cross it safely. This underpass was decorated

Balfour Street and part of Bet HaKranot rising toward the Technion
Permission from PalPhot; photographer Yehuda Dorfzaun

with public artwork in the collective optimistic and patriotic spirit of the 1950s.[50] Heading each of its two entryways is a mosaic whose subject is biblical, its style ancient, and its scenery local. Mordechai Gumpel, the artist who created them in collaboration with his wife, Miriam, developed an artistic method that was exclusively manual, used the naturally varied shades of local stones, and created the illusion of movement through the way the small stones were carved. He believed that the ancient medium of the mosaic, which had been found in archaeological digs in Israel, would radiate the spirit of the ancient Middle East onto the Israeli identity, connecting it to the ethos of nation building.

The Tunnel and the Intersection of Fantasy and Fate

Adorned with colorful tableaus, its walls clad in marble, the underpass was absorbed naturally into the neighborhood's landscape.[51] It was affectionately nicknamed "the tunnel," even though "tunnel is too big a word for this small underpass."[52] Who could have predicted that this passageway would star in the stories and fantasies of the children who had passed through it over the years? But it was mostly the darkness beneath the earth that ignited their imagination, not the beautiful art. Regardless, the underpass was not the only denizen of the intersection to imprint itself in memory. The corner of Herzl and Balfour was a magnet for adults and children alike. Its array of stores and sparkling display windows, cafés, and effervescent life were powerful attractors — and there was more. When parades passed through town, they would stop in the intersection to the joy of the masses watching from the sidewalks, the balconies of the Clock House, and the surrounding buildings. On Independence Day the intersection was closed to traffic, and many of the city's Jewish residents danced there in joyous, raucous circles.

The lives of many Haifaians crossed the intersection, and its rhythm penetrated their blood. For many Haifa children, it was one of the landmarks that symbolized their maturation; some of them became writers, others — scholars. The vivid images of the place continue to live between the pages of their works, which revolve around this focal point of their city. The dimensions of the intersection and its meaning transformed with me as I grew. When crossing it as a little girl, I held my mother's hand tightly; it felt enormous yet it was so near to the calm and sweetness of our shared ice cream at Café Snir, my feet dangling from the tall stool. The crossroad shrunk a bit in my teens — I would reach it on my own and dive into the crisp volumes of poetry at my favorite bookstore.

Three heroines of three separate Haifa literary works metabolize the intersection within their consciousness. Although each one of them is depicted with great artistry and represents an intimate experience, they demonstrate three distinct sensibilities in the relationship between a person and her hometown. Two of the writers of these works were born in 1963, and they remember the area as it was in their childhood. Unfortunately, authors born in the city in the 1960s and their contemporaries may be the last witnesses to Hadar as it was in its heyday, and their work preserves what is no longer there.

In Hadar HaCarmel's days of glory, as it was being built and expanded, the Herzl/Balfour intersection stood out not only in the great investment the city's founders made in its development but also in the names they selected for its streets: Theodor Herzl was the father of modern Zionism, while the British Lord Balfour provided external, international confirmation of the movement's aspirations. These national allusions imprinted on the intersection did not escape the pens of the city's authors. Sami Michael, for example, confronted the intersection's Zionist message in his famous novel *A Trumpet in the Wadi*, which highlights the tensions between Israeli Arabs and Jews. The confessional narrative of the novel's Arab protagonist, Huda, focuses on her neighborhood, Wadi Nisnas, and turns to the Jewish Hadar HaCarmel in only a few snapshots. Yet it preserves the perpetual ascent and descent inherent to Haifa. Indeed, this topography is branded in the consciousness of every Haifa resident, woman and man, Arab and Jew. In Haifa of the 1980s, as it is reflected in Michael's work, however, there is a recognizable difference between the emotional attitudes of different ethnic groups toward the very same sites. When Huda is driven through Hadar by the Jewish man who has just entered her life, the couple's trepidations merge with the obstacles presented by the city's mountainous terrain: "On steep Balfour Street the engine groaned aloud and [Alex] slapped the wheel and grumbled, 'Not pulling, not pulling. Shitty car.' I looked down and even my dress looked faded in the passing lights. The thrill of expectation dispelled and my spirits fell. I wanted to go home."[53]

Huda is a traditional Arab girl, and her fear of becoming intimate with a man is exacerbated by her fear of the unknown Jewish neighborhood. Huda, who freely travels by foot in the vicinity of her neighborhood, the Arab Wadi Nisnas, arrives in the heart of the Jewish Hadar only as a passenger in a car. Her footsteps up and down Haifa's steep slopes are limited to the Arab wadi and its surroundings. Furthermore, the landmark Herzl/Balfour crossing has an almost "castrating" effect on her. The feminine, colorful dress that Huda wore for her date fades in the lights of the "Zionist" intersection. Her sexual anticipations wilt as the car groans on the steep Balfour ascent. She feels like a stranger and longs to escape, to return home. The emotional and physical experiences of the Christian-Arab woman in the heart of Hadar are in sharp contrast to those of her Jewish counterparts. The heroines of Esty G. Hayim and Yehudit Katzir roam freely around the intersection on foot, trying to fulfill the dreams it promises.

Esty G. Hayim, who grew up in Haifa, published five novels before she wrote *Corner People*, a quasi autobiography that takes place in the author's hometown and fleshes out its public and personal landmarks. Dvori, the novel's main character, knows the intersection well, and her visits in its vicinity are the formative events of her childhood. Each encounter in that location is awarded a detailed description whose aftershocks echo throughout the work. Set in the late 1960s, the book is a nightmarish bildungsroman that is told, for the most part, from the point of view of a young girl. With remarkable precision, she documents her life and the lives of those she loves, a family of Holocaust survivors from Hungary struggling to survive under the shadow of the mother's mental illness. Dvori's daily routine is confined mostly within the narrow borders of the Neve Sha'anan neighborhood, but a few specific peaks in her loaded narrative are tied to Hadar HaCarmel and its heart.

The intersection's debut in the book is connected to Dvori's recollection of a painful journey that took place when she was only five years old. At the corner of Nordau Street, near the intersection, she and her family were supposed to embark on an enchanted trip to the Sea of Galilee. The memory of the little girl's odyssey is interwoven with the landscape of Haifa: boarding a bus in Neve Sha'anan; crossing a bridge; passing soot-covered houses alternating with fragments of seascape; running through narrow streets with her father, mother, and brother from the bus stop in Hadar all the way to the intersection; entering the underpass; and climbing up Balfour on the other side to reach the meeting point of the tour. The descent into the underpass and the ascent out of it were seared in Dvori's mind. Crossing through its dark depths, she was frightened by a crippled beggar who reached out his calloused palm for change. When she emerged into the light of day, however, her fear evaporated because of a Barbie doll in the display window of the toy store Pinocchio at the corner of Balfour. Finally, the family boarded the tour bus. But as the bus wheeled away, the memory of the poor beggar in the tunnel haunted Dvori, and in her imagination his misfortune merged with the Holocaust stories she heard at home. Moreover, at the end of the odyssey, there was no reward: Dvori, her brother and her parents never reached the Sea of Galilee.[54]

The five-year-old's trip through the intersection is described at the beginning of *Corner People* in a childish, unmediated form, but when the narrative nears its end, this crossroads reappears, this time, from the point of view of the adult Dvori, as she returns to the path of her childhood odyssey. Now the glamour has vanished from the intersection, and every station in the reconstructed route is a disappointment. The only emotion that time does not dull is the fear of the tunnel, and the threat that dwells in it invades the subconscious of the mature heroine: "I dreamt a terrible dream, and in it I . . . chop off my left shin. . . . Suddenly, I find myself in the underground passage on the corner of Herzl and Balfour. The stump is exposed and I hold out a charred aluminum pot for change."[55]

In her dream Dvori herself becomes the maimed beggar whom she first encountered when she was five. He has evolved into a symbol in her psyche, merged with the fears from her childhood home, and years later has returned as a nightmare. Her descents into the tunnel, then, represent diving into the depth of her soul. But while the tunnel is a world of darkness and nightmares, the urban space above it abounds with magic. In this very site, the heroine discovered her calling. For her, the corner of Herzl and Balfour is the place where fear, fantasy, and fate meet.

Three years after her initial journey to the intersection, Dvori returns, this time accompanied by her aunt Esther, or, as she is called in Hungarian, Esther Neini. This is the happiest moment in the novel. Dvori is eight, and her glamorous aunt, who has appeared suddenly from Hungary, treats her to an adventurous shopping trip in Hadar. This expedition triggers the process of turning Dvori into a writer. The two visit the Ein HaKore bookstore at the corner of Herzl and Balfour. There, the aunt buys grown-up books like *Anna Karenina* for the little girl. In one of the many neighboring cafés, Dvori confesses to her aunt that, for her, words have "color and smell and taste," and Esther Neini admits that she too has always had a love affair with the written word.[56] The revelation of their common secret becomes a rite of consecration: from now on Dvori knows that she is destined to be a writer. The apex of this second trip to the intersection is the purchase of two typewriters: one in Hungarian, for Esther Neini, and one in Hebrew, for her little niece. The protagonist's future is determined, then, within the boundaries of that beloved, familiar urban space.

Unavoidably, this fateful outing ends with Esther Neini and Dvori crossing through the tunnel. Unlike the sprint to the tour bus with her parents when she was five, this time the eight-year-old girl notices every detail, especially regarding the beggar: "I examined his palm, stretched out for the next donor. Four fingers were missing. . . . Perhaps, it was those same Nazis who shot Aunt Olga in the foot?" Dvori is still projecting her family's terrifying Holocaust stories onto the figure of the beggar, and even the strength of Esther Neini cannot overcome them. Furthermore, this descent into the dark tunnel foreshadows the fact that the period of ultimate bliss with her aunt will not last. The next trip to Hadar with Esther Neini marks Dvori's separation from her. When the two walk down the treasure-lined path that encircles the intersection for the last time, each detail on their way subverts its initial, happy parallel: "In the intervals between shopping, an inexplicable heaviness crept over me, as if something important had been lost. . . . The hour grew late. . . . Only the lights of the port promised their worthless promises."[57] The place where Dvori was anointed as an author is also the place where her short hope for happiness would be cut off. Throughout *Corner People*, this public space in the heart of Hadar becomes the center of the world, where the narrator examines the potential for human happiness and suffering.

Not so, in Yehudit Katzir's first story, "Disneyel." Here, Katzir's Haifaian voice is that of a ten-year-old girl who sees the world through a child's prism. Her hometown is dominated by the Carmel ridge, the omnipresence of the sea, and the urban landmarks nestled within them. It is a city that exists in an eternal up or down motion, its condition dependent on the whims of nature. The memories of the story's narrator caress the Herzl/Balfour intersection with an eternal romantic light. Through them this space becomes the language in which the author reconstructs the pivotal moments of her young life, which were spent in a tight orbit around the three-story house built by her ancestors in the early 1920s.

When I first read the author's debut collection of stories, it deeply resonated with me — Katzir's portrayal of the core of Hadar preserved "my" Balfour Cellar along with other secret corners of my childhood. While the threads she wove together were of different colors than mine, the way she used cityscapes to delineate the routes of the heart rang true, and her stories gently led me to my own.

For Katzir, the steep Balfour Street, the trafficked Herzl Street, the tunnel, and the intersection are words in a private language; in "Disneyel" the city's sites are the components of the erotic urban idiom in which she describes the dangerous balancing act performed by her female protagonists and forges the symbiotic connection between a mother and daughter.

The plot of the story itself is simple, almost banal, and is told in Katzir's trademark address in the second-person feminine: *att*, or "you," the "you" being the narrator's mother. A beautiful and delicate woman from Haifa, a mother of two, is married to a man who, in her eyes, is too coarse. She has a suitor, a quasi family friend, Michael, who visits twice a year.

The title "Disneyel" is a combination of "Disney" and "Israel" but also hints at the name Michael (pronounced Mee-CHA-EL in Hebrew). He is a handsome but fickle man who used to burst into the lives of the mother and daughter twice a year when he visited the country for his real (or perhaps imaginary) businesses. The ostensible goal of his trips was to finalize grandiose plans for a Disneyland in Israel — Disneyel. Ever since the girl was four years old, she and her mother performed a set ritual before Michael's visits. They would take a taxi from the Carmel to Hadar, get off near the Herzl/Balfour intersection, cross through the tunnel, hear the music of the violinist playing there, and toss him a coin. They would then continue to the exit of the tunnel toward Bet HaKranot, where a cluster of exclusive women's clothing shops lay. The heroines of "Disneyel" would then buy a fancy dress for the mother and finish off with a celebratory ice cream on Balfour in Café Atara. When the magic password that ushers in this cherished ceremony, *yordim lehadar* (going down to Hadar), is uttered in the story for the first time, it is accompanied by a slow description, suffused with pleasure, of the biannual preparatory outing in the vicinity of the intersection that holds the treasures necessary for welcoming the guest.

In the eyes of the daughter, who reconstructs it, the ritual is shared by her and her mother, as if Michael were not only the object of the mother's romantic fantasies but also those of her little girl. As in a sacred religious ritual, every detail must be performed with the greatest precision. A flaw in the integrity of the preparations might harm or even prevent the fulfillment of the yearned-for goal. This ritual is described twice in the text. The first version is based on the daughter's cumulative knowledge, gained by repeating the ritual from the time she was four years old. It is stylized and general, as if in an imaginary Passover Haggadah that enumerates the rules of the holiday for the practitioners as they must be performed each year. What is reported in the narrative may be read as a guide for what to do before the hero or Prince Charming arrives.

The second depiction of the ritual, quoted here, is a painstaking reconstruction of the final, frenzied time as it was performed by the mother and her daughter. The rhythm of the text reflects the accelerated pace of this last performance of the ritual, in which there are more digressions than prescribed actions. These deviations might have contributed to the catastrophic ending.

> On that winter afternoon . . . when you suddenly said, We're going down to Hadar today, I looked at you without understanding, so you said again We're going down to Hadar today, and at five we took an umbrella, and we went out, and the wind with a long whistle swept us up . . . to a taxi, and then from the taxi all the way down to the corner of Herzl and Balfour. We passed through the violinist's tunnel, and . . . water flowed inside. He wasn't playing, he was sleeping . . . and the case was open. . . . You took out a whole lira and put it on the red velvet. . . . Then we came out the other side of the tunnel right in front of the store . . . and Mrs. Mueller . . . disappeared for a moment and returned, a hanger in her hand, on which a green velvet dress hung.[58]

This sad scene of the final performance of the ritual appears around the midway point of the narrative, and it triggers the crescendo that leads to the catastrophe at its end. The whistling wind and the speeding taxi from the Carmel to Hadar signal the beginning of the tragic fall. The narrator's language reflects the Haifaian topography that is etched in her body, as she depicts the chain of actions that foreshadows the descent into the abyss.[59] The language of loss in this story is the same as the language of pleasure; it is the vocabulary of Haifa: the verb *yordim* (going down) hints at the uncontrollable movement downward, while the rhythm of the sentences and the textual detailing of the route radiate the power of the motion that is an inextricable part of traveling on the steep roads of Haifa. The ritual described here includes most of the familiar components, but its core lies in the deviations from the regular sequence. The taxi ride, the Herzl/Balfour intersection, passing through the tunnel, and the visit to the clothing store all remain, but this time they occur in the winter and the pouring rain. The tunnel is flooded, the beggar violin player is asleep, and even the abnormally large offering the mother leaves in his case does not appease fate. In the clothing store the mother snatches a dress without the necessary alterations, and the ice cream at Café Atara is totally omitted. Instead, the mother and daughter leave the area of the intersection and run through the rain to the opposite side of Herzl Street. As each digression is noted, it amplifies the terror of the girl who foresees the calamity.

Despite all the pain, however, the tight bond between Katzir's speaker and the landscape of her city is not affected. Her swift, direct ride with her mother in a taxi down Balfour to the intersection also marks her intimate connection to the place. When she arrives at her destination, Katzir's young narrator feels the sidewalks and roads of late 1960s and early 1970s Hadar under her feet and, by walking up and down on them, claims them as her own.

The heroine and her ownership of the neighborhood may reflect her creator's biography. As Yehudit Katzir told me, she frequently visited the Herzl/Balfour intersection in her childhood, especially the southeast corner building owned by her family.[60] The business headquarters of her beloved grandfather, Aminadav Levin, was located in that house, while her mother's law office was on the nearby Shmaryahu Levin Street. When Katzir began her literary career in the late 1980s, her dying mother informed her, "you will write the novel about my grandmother."[61] Katzir obeyed this command twenty-five years later. Her 2013 family saga follows Zillah, the author's great-grandmother, throughout the twentieth century. Ultimately, it weaves together all of its disparate threads near Tel Aviv. Yet interwoven in its fabric are Haifa's tender landscapes, beneath which the narrator warms herself. Like a lover who soothes her longing for her beloved by interjecting oblique references to him into her conversations, so does Katzir embroider Haifaian moments throughout the long and winding plot of *Zillah*. At the heart of the book, she surrenders to her heart's desire, digresses from the plot, and dedicates an entire chapter to the romance of her mother's parents in Haifa. She titles the chapter "Love." The descriptions of the perfect love affair between Yehudit Levin (née Margolin) and Aminadav Levin may also be read as a map of little Haifa between 1931 and 1933, at whose center is the budding Hadar HaCarmel neighborhood: a dark window on Nordau Street, the view of the sea, the bay that was still visible from the balcony, and, yes, the house where their love blossomed, on the corner of Herzl and Balfour.

The direct, natural relationship of Katzir's Jewish heroines with the Herzl/Balfour intersection contrasts with the attitude of Huda, the Arab protagonist of *A Trumpet in the Wadi*. For Huda in the 1980s, the intersection and its Zionist street names symbolize Jewish dominance in Haifa. On a hypothetical continuum of a sense of belonging to the urban space and the intersection, Dvori from *Corner People* is located between Huda and the heroine of "Disneyel." She emerges into Hadar in a slow city bus that makes its way between varied landscapes and different neighborhoods. This tiring route illustrates the large distance between her and the heart of the city. While walking in the area of the intersection, she is devoid of the feeling of ownership that radiates from Katzir's heroine in "Disneyel." Dvori remains an outsider, even when she descends by foot (albeit not by car like Huda) to the depths of the underground passage. Haifa may be her home, but she still feels uprooted, always afraid of another Holocaust, even in her hometown.

The Symbol of Hadar HaCarmel

Before the establishment of the State of Israel, when Hadar HaCarmel was an autonomous entity, its leaders held a competition to design the emblem of their neighborhood. The design, selected by the artist Hermann Struck and two other judges, is crowned with a detailed drawing of the Technion's façade. Beneath it, houses descend on a diagonal slope, separated from the waves of the sea by a neat row of trees.[62] In a concise visual manner, this emblem captures the relationship between the Technion building and the buildings that it birthed and sheltered beneath its broad wings. It also preserved the city's quintessential feature, the decline of the mountain and the distance between the neighborhood and the sea.

Hadar HaCarmel is set on the slope, which is depicted in the emblem by the diagonal line. The entire area that stretched downward northeast of the Technion and reached the intersection of Herzl and Balfour would further grow to become the beating heart of Hadar for many years. From an urban history perspective, the buildings of the intersection are the descendants of the Technion. Architecturally, however, one can see the

unavoidable rift between parents and their children as well as the remnants of the struggle between loyalty to Baerwald's memory and status
and the modernist direction adopted later by Hadar's architects. While
Bet HaKranot looks up at the Technion with affection and respect, the
Clock House and the Business Center turn their backs to it, foreshadow-
ing the future aesthetic of the city. Both the planning of the area and its
buildings embody this combination of ideas and conflicts, great hopes for
integrating into the Middle Eastern landscape, and visions of an international, modern city. The tunnel, too, the latecomer to the intersection, witnessed the grand dreams of those who dug it, who envisioned thousands
of people crossing underground, shopping, and sitting in cafés.

The topography informed not only the creation of the urban space,
the design of the Technion, and its surrounding neighborhood but also
the souls of those who walked Haifa's streets and the heroes of its stories.
Most people who passed through the vicinity of the Herzl/Balfour intersection over the years did not know its history, but their consciousness
still absorbed something of the dramatic meeting place between the ambition of architects, the stubbornness of the mountain, and the hope for a
peaceful existence. The Technion and its garden, the slope, the tunnel, and
the intersection and its buildings all penetrated the souls of Haifa's children. They ran between the rows of trees in the Technion garden, played
near the bubbling pool, raced their bikes down Balfour, hurried through
the intersection to the neighboring schools, licked ice cream at Snir, went
with their mothers to buy shoes or a dress at Bet HaKranot, crossed the
busy streets ruled by Haifa's first traffic light, and passed the violin player.
The cool, dark tunnel; the sudden ascent of Balfour; the columns of Bet
HaKranot; and the plaza at its front were a kind of a liminal space for the
daughters and sons of Haifa through which they had to pass to mature and
grow. And, from above, the Technion looked at each of them affectionately and promised that things would stay like this forever.

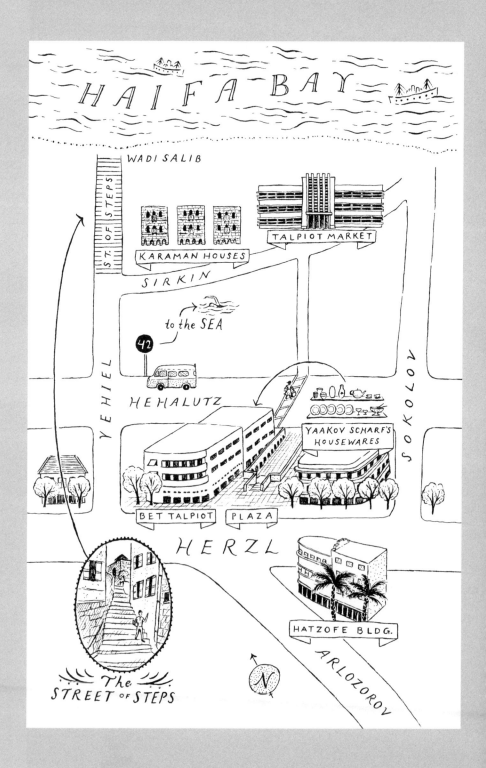

3

DOWN THE STEPS

Fragments of Sea and Sky

The architecture and urban planning of Hadar HaCarmel, which was the largest and most important Jewish neighborhood in Haifa for half a century (roughly 1925–75), are inextricably linked to its political and socioeconomic history, as well as, of course, its mountainous topography and geographic location. This meeting of human and mountain is especially palpable in the area below Herzl Street, in the vicinity of the Talpiot Market. There, the geography takes on a quasi-emotional quality that is physically felt with every stair and interval down the slope. The crossroad of the straight, horizontal Herzl and the diagonally ascending Arlozorov marks the beginning of this route. Overlooking it sits a building shaped like a wedge with a rounded tip, designed by Benjamin Orell and Ezekiel Zohar in the International Style. One of its sides faces Arlozorov, the important traffic artery; the other faces Herzl, the neighborhood's main thoroughfare. From its crown, a large sign announces *HaTzofe* (which means "the observer"). The sign refers not to the building's strategic position at the heart of this urban juncture but rather to the simple fact that the headquarters of the religious newspaper *HaTzofe* sat there until it folded.

This crossroads is where the different sections of the Hadar HaCarmel district meet. Here Arlozorov begins its slow, winding climb up the mountainside, while buses breathe heavily on their way to the top of the Carmel. Across, on Herzl Street, a wide plaza (today known as Shmuel Itzkovitz Plaza, after one of the founders of the neighborhood) stretches between two rounded buildings and looks downward toward the sea. From this kinetic intersection, one can climb up to the heights of Hadar HaCarmel or descend to the neighborhood's lower segments through stairs and narrow streets. Anyone who chooses the second option — that is, turning to Itzkovitz Plaza on Herzl and going straight down — will embark on an enthralling journey into the depths of the history of the district, the city, and perhaps even the entire country.

I call this lower area Talpiot, or "Gerstel Town."[1] In Haifa "Talpiot" automatically means Shuk Talpiot (Talpiot Market), but the name "Gerstel" is largely unknown. However, the architect Moshe Gerstel is one of the heroes in the story of Haifa, in general, and of Hadar HaCarmel, in particular. His stylistic fingerprints are especially evident in this area, where traditional stone Arab houses and modernist buildings stand side by side, interspersed with structures that combine both styles. Here Gerstel began to interweave his local architectural dream and his humanist worldview with Hajj Tahir Karaman, an important leader of the city's Arab community. A stone's throw away is the Street of Steps, whose tip touches the lowest edge of Hadar, the formerly Muslim neighborhood with the Christian name Wadi Salib (Salib means "cross" in Arabic). The name Wadi Salib is etched deeply in the memory of the Arab-Israeli conflict as well as in the memory of the social and ethnic struggle in Israel. The Street of Steps, however, has a pedigree of its own as the subject of the first Israeli urban novel, Yehudit Hendel's *The Street of Steps*. In that novel the author renders the mountainous structure of the city in the flesh and blood of its residents, inextricably weaving their fates with elements of the landscape.

Although I was not a resident of the Street of Steps, the slope was etched in me as well. My father's housewares store was situated not too far from there, a little higher up, near the Herzl/Arlozorov intersection. My memories of that area are rose-tinted because of our store. The store was the center of my universe. The lot that sprawled next to it was the first "mountain" whose rocks I climbed and whose yellow mustard flowers I picked in the winter. On Yehiel Street, which passed near the store, I accompanied my mother when she bought fresh ground coffee. The 42 bus stop across the way was where we all embarked on trips to the Bat Galim swimming pool by the sea. Down the lane in front of it, we would run toward the Talpiot Market with my father to purchase watermelons when they were in season.

The Architectural Marvel of the Talpiot Market

Indeed, it is an easy trip from this crossroads to the market. A pair of comfortable, shallow staircases lead downward from the plaza on Herzl Street; from their west end one can continue through a roofed underpass to He-Halutz Street. From there, a short footpath stretches down to Sirkin Street, where the Talpiot Market is situated. Because of this street's narrowness and meandering path, the main façade of the market is revealed to the pedestrian temptingly, piece by piece. This gradual revelation, combined with the odd angle at which it stands, adds to the drama that the structure creates. Nevertheless, this is only one facet of this breathtaking building, arguably the largest Bauhaus structure in the world. From its façade on Sirkin Street, an angular entrance protrudes with straight, vertical, phallic lines above it, while the rounded curve of its feminine rear faces the sea. Photographs taken from myriad perspectives during its heyday secure its reputation as an architectural wonder.

The circumstances that surrounded the construction of the market and the urgency that motivated its completion are no less dramatic than the structure itself. A mere two months after it was inaugurated with great fanfare in April 1940, with Haifa's mayor thanking the architect who, "with imagination and ingenious creativity, gave this city of the future a structure in which she can take pride," Italy joined the war on Germany's side.[2] One month later, in July, Italy began bombing Haifa.

In 1937 all of Palestine was in the throes of what Arabs dubbed "The Arab Revolt" and Jews called "the events"—a series of violent riots primarily calling on the British to halt Jewish immigration. In Haifa Jewish residents of the predominantly Arab lower city fled to Hadar. Jews from other parts of the city were afraid to frequent the Arab produce markets in the lower city, which had, until then, supplied most of their food. Consequently, the Committee for Hadar HaCarmel (Va'ad) decided to initiate a mammoth undertaking to build the "ultimate" market in the heart of the Jewish neighborhood. Similar circumstances led to the 1929 construction of the Business Center at the intersection of Herzl and Balfour.[3] The Talpiot Market would serve the Jews of the city so they would not have to endanger themselves when buying fresh produce and dairy products. The perfect location was clear: a spontaneous peddler "market" had already emerged on Sirkin Street as a result of the volatile situation.[4] It was also where Tnuva, the chief co-op for dairy products, maintained storage facilities for products that it collected from the villages and kibbutzim.[5]

This perfectly situated lot of land, however, lay on ground that was almost impossible to build on. The slope was steep, and the ground itself was rocky and stubborn. As Hayim Aharonovitch recalls in his comprehensive book on Hadar HaCarmel, "The disadvantages of the place were plain to see . . . but in all, it was the only place that suited the purpose."[6] The Va'ad launched a competition for the market's design, "limited to architects living in Palestine. . . . It drew ninety-six entries."[7] The first prize was unanimously awarded to the plan designed by Gerstel and the engineer C. Cohen. It was selected in large part because it offered the most efficient solution to the issues of accessibility and topography; it also required only local materials.

Many decades later the memoirist Nissim Levi (aka Nassuma), who was born, as he says, "with the market" in 1940 and lived nearby, would remember the effervescent life that hummed around it in the 1940s and 1950s:

> I close my eyes and imagine the shuk in its days of glory. . . . This
> was the biggest and fanciest shopping center in the Middle East. . . .
> The central structure was roofed with a brilliant glass ceiling, and
> the sunlight that seeped inside glittered on the fresh fruits and veg-
> etables and created a colorful celebration that the eye can never get

enough of. . . . *Indeed, he* [Gerstel] *was a man of vision.* There were stores for selling beans, spices, herrings, cheeses, sweets, a plethora of colors and smells. Added to it was a symphony of the voices of the sellers in the stores, who improvised songs and funny lines in order to attract the attention of the shoppers.[8]

Nassuma's recollections appear in his 2009 book, *Nassuma from Pajamas Street*, but one can also hear them firsthand in the tours that Nassuma periodically leads around the market, "the playground of his childhood," where he "learned what makes a good eggplant . . . how to choose a radish, beet, and turnip . . . that a light cabbage is good for stuffing and a heavy one, . . . for salad."[9] Ya'akov Weiss, another neighbor of Shuk Talpiot, who used to live on 27 Sirkin, close to where Nassuma grew up, remembered "the small hours of the night, [when] the vendors went to the wholesale market on the bottom floor of the building and brought fresh produce. Later they transferred it to their stalls. . . . The market had a way of life and order of its own, and one could see people from every echelon of society, rubbing shoulders with one another."[10]

In her novel *Corner People*, Esty G. Hayim wrote about a swollen-legged grandmother, a Holocaust survivor who rules her family with the power of the meals that she prepares. In the 1970s this grandmother climbed from the stalls of Talpiot Market as she carried her loaded baskets "to the bus stop on Herzl Street."[11] Through the 1990s the market provided fresh and cheap food to people like the grandmother, who carefully counted their money and shopped there weekly to put food on the table.

Indeed, for half a century the market proved the wisdom of the competition judges who chose Gerstel's plan in 1937. When the decision was made to construct the market, Solel Boneh, the oldest construction company in Israel, committed itself to completing the building within ten months.[12] But despite the urgency, given the political and security issues, the work dragged on for two years. Even so, the Talpiot Market was one of the very few buildings whose construction continued and was completed during the tumultuous period after World War II broke out, when most construction materials were reserved for British military needs.

Even seventy years after it was built, leading architects Ada Karmi-Melamede and Dan Price describe the shuk with awe:

The Talpiot Market, north façade *Courtesy of Haifa City Archives*

The building . . . has three floors and merchant stalls organized around a central sky-lit atrium. [It] is situated on a sloping site and composed of two distinct parts. A rectangular building at the front, which is parallel to the street, and a circular market hall at the rear. The horizontal ribbon windows, which wrap around both parts, establish a datum line relative to the sloping street. From within the building, these ribbon windows open expansive views of Haifa and the bay. . . . The vertical articulation of the central entry anchors the building to the site and has a substantial presence on the street.

The skin of the building, a continuous horizontal wrapper, stretches like fabric over the structural grid. The envelope mimics the horizon and the sea, both of which are revealed through the ribbon windows as one moves from level to level. . . . The atrium . . . rises toward the translucent glass-brick ceiling and seems to extend beyond the roof level.[13]

It is no coincidence that the book's authors resort to poetic metaphors in their description, such as "the skin of the building . . . stretches like fabric" or "the envelope mimics the horizon and the sea." Despite Gerstel's devotion to modernism — using pure geometric forms and avoiding

The Talpiot Market,
the main entrance on
Sirkin Street
*Courtesy of Haifa
City Archives*

decoration for its own sake — his lyricism is impossible to overlook. The market's large northern face is rounded and soft beneath the erect, masculine tower to which it is attached. The long, vertical windows in this tower protrude, embraced throughout by horizontal ribbon windows that continue into infinity. And there is more. When the building was new, it was covered in pink and the vertical lines were emphasized in light green. For me, the building's geometric forms imitate the physical intimacy of a man and a woman in a sort of Rodin kiss. Indeed, to my joy, in a discussion about a different building, Leopold Gerstel — the son of the architect — confirmed that Rodin's work did indeed serve as inspiration to his father.

The recognition of the building's architectural achievement was instantaneous. The press of the period praised it profusely: "The structure that was built as a covered market is one of the most impressive International Style structures that has been erected in the land," raves the important Palestinian newspaper *Davar*. It continues and remarks on the "roof of glass bricks" and praises the main entrance, where "the strips of concrete become columns that create a monumental front." The *Palestine Post*, meanwhile, emphasized the influence of the works of Erich Mendelsohn on the market's curved, dynamic form. The structure became a symbol for the country's creative output, and its picture was displayed in a New York industrial exhibition of Palestinian products in the summer of 1947.[14]

One of the wonders of the new building was the spectacular roof — innovative in 1940 — which still evokes the admiration of great architects from subsequent generations. Fifty years after it was built, the authors of *Bauhaus on the Carmel* describe it as a "flat, glass-block roof of concentric rings, a structural and architectural tour-de-force for provincial Haifa."[15] Another twenty years later Karmi-Melamede and Price second their veneration and speak of it in spiritual language: "its ceiling is covered with a glass-block roof through which natural light washes over the interior of the building. The unique light from above . . . is like a hollow, transparent core."[16] The light from above shone on the entire space, and the glimpses of the sea through the windows made the experience of shopping in the market a pleasant one. In *White City*, the Tel Aviv Museum architectural photo exhibition about the Israeli International Style, two out of ten Haifa photographs are dedicated to the market, one of them solely to its roof.

The Lifelong Bond between an Arab Businessman and a Jewish Architect

It defies belief that the creator of this astonishing masterpiece has been forgotten and that the building on 35 Sirkin, once a "symbolic and literal bastion of Hadar" and an emblem of the International Style in Israeli architecture, has fallen into ruin.[17] Yet anyone who walks through the area I call "Gerstel Town" will discover more of Gerstel's wonders even today. Stone houses still stand along Sirkin Street, serving as testimony to Gerstel's idiosyncratic architectural aesthetic and perhaps also to his personality. I am speaking of the Karaman Houses, on 27 and 34 Sirkin Street, mute witnesses to the exceptional friendship of the rich Arab developer Hajj Tahir Karaman and the Vienna-educated Jewish architect Moshe Gerstel.

They first met in the eastern margins of Hadar — in other words, around Sirkin Street. Karaman, who lived in the area with his family, turned to Gerstel in 1937 and hired him to design rental residences for him nearby. Eventually, the partnership between the two grew into a deep personal bond. Karaman was a self-made manufacturer and businessman whose star shone brightly in the 1930s.[18] He was a nationalist Arab who was not opposed to cooperating with Jews and was considered one of the foremost leaders of the Arab community. In the 1940s he was appointed as one of Haifa's two Arab deputy mayors.[19] Karaman convinced his friends to invest in real estate and hire Gerstel as their architect; a few years later, when Gerstel faced financial difficulty, Karaman housed his family for four years in the rooms he built for Gerstel in his house on Sirkin Street.[20] The

Portrait of Hajj Tahir Karaman,
by Moshe Gerstel
*Courtesy of the artist's grandson,
Moshe Gerstel*

architect's grandson told me that during the 1948 war, Gerstel's son was
guarding caravans bringing food to Jerusalem and was captured.[21] Gerstel turned to his friend Karaman, and together they negotiated a prisoner
exchange, after which his son was freed. The 2013 architectural exhibition
Haifa Encounters in the city's Munio Gitai Weinraub Architecture Museum
featured a portrait of Karaman next to drawings and building plans.[22] He
is wearing a Western suit and tie with a red tarbush on his head; his eyes
are kind and there is a half smile playing on his lips under his moustache.
A label below the affectionate painting identifies it as the work of Moshe
Gerstel. Thus, in addition to their architectural collaboration, this beautiful painting remains a tribute to their rare friendship.

The tourist guidebook *Sur les traces du modernism*, published by the
International Center for City Architecture and Landscape, leads visitors
to one of Karaman's houses, 27 Sirkin, a concrete structure overlaid with
stone that was built on relatively steep, eastern-sloping ground. The authors of the guide skip over the connection between the landowner and
his designer, emphasizing instead the modernist characteristics of the
building and Gerstel's affinity for Mendelsohn, one of modernism's first
architects: "The most forward plane of the house contains three bands
of ribbon windows. The feeling of continuity in the façade is achieved

through thin stone stripes that serve, even today, as window seals."[23] They also pause to comment on the "rounded terraces with iron railings in the form of horizontal stripes that evoke modern details inspired by Erich Mendelsohn." This building is also captured in the aforementioned memoir by Ya'akov Weiss, *Forgotten Childhood*. Weiss describes the house's unique qualities from the point of view of a child in awe of the design of his home: "The shape of the building was like the Hebrew letter ב.... If one of the tenants wanted to go from one wing to another, he could go through the [connecting] terraces.... In the yard, there was a little pond with tall rims and, in it, goldfish. Above the pond, there was a lion made of porcelain, and the water came out of its mouth into the pond."[24]

Although the building at 27 Sirkin has deteriorated, and the stone lion no longer spouts water into the pond, its modernist qualities are evident and, along with them, the signature of the future creator of the Talpiot Market. It seems that, in planning the striking market, Gerstel used elements from the modernist architectural vocabulary he had drawn on while planning the Karaman Houses. Moreover, it may be that his familiarity with the immediate vicinity and its specific terrain — made possible by Karaman — ultimately contributed to his ability to overcome the challenges of building the market.

Gerstel's style cannot be defined exclusively in the modernist context. In the residential homes as well as the public structures he built, he tried to ensure that his buildings were in harmony with the landscape. He thus created an idiosyncratic European Modernist Style inspired by Mendelsohn that takes the surroundings into consideration and offers a less rigid narrative than that of orthodox modernism. As in the Karaman Houses, his work embraces local characteristics and vernacular motifs, including the incorporation of stone with various finishes, which he was a virtuoso at implementing. Although he was much admired, there are those who find fault with his unique, sometimes heterogeneous, aesthetic. Architect and modernism scholar Michael Levin, for example, argues that Gerstel's work is uneven, vacillating between modernism and eclecticism.[25] The interpretation of architect Waleed Karkabi, the head of the Department of Conservation in the Haifa Municipality, is more favorable. According to him, Gerstel's style is "an International Style that treats the surrounding space with respect." Karkabi, who has conducted in-depth research and curated an exhibition at the Munio Gitai Weinraub Museum of Architecture about architectural activity during the British Mandate, views the Karaman Houses as an example of "urban Haifaian architecture that combines elements from both the East and the West, the usage of local materials with traditional elements alongside modernist details."[26] Karkabi, then, sees in Gerstel a kind of architectural prophet of Jewish-Arab coexistence.

Gerstel himself was born in Lemberg, Galicia (in the former Austro-Hungarian Empire), in 1887; his mother tongue was German, and he finished his architectural studies in 1914 at the Technische Hochschule in Vienna. He moved to Romania in 1922, but after thirteen productive years in Bucharest, he left due to antisemitic legislation and growing violence against Jews. He immigrated to Palestine, settled in Haifa, and continued to work as an architect until his death in 1961. He designed many buildings for prominent Arab families, among others.[27] After the establishment of the State of Israel, however, his star faded but he continued to design for the Karaman family even after they left Haifa.

My Father's Store in a Gerstel Masterpiece

The area that I dubbed "Gerstel Town" at the beginning of this chapter includes the Karaman Houses, together with the Talpiot Market. As described earlier, these buildings create an architectural-historical cluster, the tour of which is recommended by the authors of *Sur les traces du modernisme*. These buildings are recognized as Gerstel's work, celebrated as landmarks and praised in architecture books, but, as far as I am concerned, the jewel in the crown is not among them. Very close by, almost directly above Sirkin Street and the Talpiot Market on the slope, lies a large building. This is Bet Talpiot (Talpiot House). Bet Talpiot borders Itzkovitz Plaza, and its address is 61 Herzl on its top level and, on its lower one, 62 HeHalutz. The latter was the address of my father's store. As a child, I was proud that the store was located in Bet Talpiot. Unbeknownst to me at the time, the days of glory of both my family and the building overlapped. Our short time of joy was eternalized by the legendary Photo Studio Talpiot on Bet Talpiot's second floor. There we were, the four of us, in 1953: me, almost five years old; my baby brother, Gadi, sucking two fingers; and our parents, a tentative smile on their faces, looking straight ahead.

Author's family: Ya'akov, Dora, Nili, and Gadi Scharf, 1953
Courtesy of Studio Gavra Tel Aviv; photographers Moshe and Ella Mandil,
Photo Studio Talpiot

Recently, I tried to learn more about the building called Bet Talpiot. The municipal workers and the activists at the Haifa History Society, with whom I consulted, attributed its design to the firm Sternberg-Givoni. One document in the archive hinted that Gerstel might have been involved. Truth be told, there was no rational explanation for my overwhelming desire to prove that Gerstel designed Bet Talpiot. Yet it felt as though if that illustrious man were its architect, a lost honor would be restored; it would repair the insult I feel every time I see the dilapidated state of this landmark of my childhood—my father's store. Intensive detective work eventually led me to the joyous discovery that Moshe Gerstel is, in fact, the architect who planned the original design of Bet Talpiot.

I must first explain that while Bet Talpiot still exists, its original beauty is mostly obscured. The building was specifically built for offices and retail businesses and is made up of two rectangular bodies that lie, one on top of the other, on the slope, partially overlapping. Most of the larger top structure sits on Herzl Street and the bottom, one story lower, on HeHalutz Street. The two bodies that make up the building are neither symmetrical nor identical in shape. The narrow façades of their shorter ends face Herzl (in the south) and HeHalutz (in the north), respectively. Bet Talpiot's long sides stretch between the two streets, creating a stylized façade on the building's eastern side (facing the hills of Neve Sha'anan), while the western side looks toward a backyard. A lovely pattern of office windows over storefront windows recurs in the same proportions across the three visible façades (northern, southern, and eastern).

Although the building as a whole is asymmetrical — in keeping with its modernist sensibilities — within this asymmetry Gerstel adheres to pleasing aesthetic principals. He believed that a structure's outside must reflect its inner function (a philosophy called organic architecture) and that it must be forged with integrity and simplicity, together with personal expression. And, indeed, one can see clearly that the building is divided into two floors of retail and two floors of offices. The height of the office stories is standard, while the commercial ground floors stand a story and a half tall. The extra half story serves as a storage gallery above the shops, taking advantage of the mountain slope and the differences in elevation between Herzl and HeHalutz Streets. As one of the great architects of Haifa, Gerstel knew not only how to deal with the difficult topography but also how to exploit it for the benefit of his clients. As a little girl visiting my father's store, I was seldom allowed to go up to the gallery — it was a secret domain known only to my father. And now I have discovered that its very existence is an example of Gerstel's consideration of the building's purpose. He thought of the benefits to the storekeepers and so provided all the shops, facing every direction on both levels throughout the build-ing, an additional half story of storage space.[28]

When we look at Bet Talpiot from Herzl Street or the plaza, the build-ing seems to defy the expectations of the observer, the Haifaian incline, and even symmetry itself. The southern façade facing Herzl is narrow with rounded terraces and seems to look at the street askance, as if to pro-claim that the building does not exist for Herzl Street alone. The north-ern façade that faces HeHalutz Street on the lower level is as narrow as its Herzl Street sister, but it does not echo her roundness — its lines are straight and angular. The eastern façade is much longer and looks con-siderably more important than the one that faces the main street, Herzl. When I was growing up, beautiful stores lined its entire length. I especially remember the children's clothing store because of the pleated, light blue skirt and white sweater that I got there. In front of these stores was a wide sidewalk that created a sort of terrace — open to the sky, facing the sea, and overlooking the streets below it. This sidewalk terrace stretches from the horizontal Herzl northward toward HeHalutz and seems to be suspended in the air above HeHalutz Street due to the topography. On the eastern façade of the HeHalutz level is a long roofed passage, quite different in character and style from the terrace above it. This passage is an arcade that flaunts tall arches and onto which storefronts open. When looking at the building at a distance, the entire eastern façade is revealed: on the lower level, the curved arches of the arcade, and above them the large rectangle inlaid with neatly arrayed windows on the upper level.

The exciting discovery that Gerstel had designed this gorgeous structure began when my diligent research assistant, Adi Silberstein, located a document in the City Archives with the heading "Haifa Town Planning Area" that referred to 61 Herzl. In square, carefully etched English letters that have faded over time, it reads, "Architect: M. Gerstel." The date on the document is April 11, 1949, but in its margins there are scribbled notes from 1968 in Hebrew. It reawakened my hope that I could link the design of my precious Bet Talpiot to the important architect. It seemed logical, as Gerstel Town, whose apex is the Talpiot Market and the neighboring Karaman Houses, is less than half a kilometer from Bet Talpiot. Additionally, I had already done much research and could see architectural similarities between the buildings. In both structures Gerstel's functional thinking is pronounced (in the Talpiot Market building, for example, he placed the windows very high up to allow the stall owners to display their merchandise on the shelves beneath them, while in Bet Talpiot it took the form of the aforementioned extra storage space). Moreover, in the design of both, there is a dialogue between sharp forms and round ones. Yet Gerstel's name on this document that Adi found was not sufficient proof that he had designed Bet Talpiot. Gerstel's grandson hinted that he had blueprints his grandfather had drawn for the building, but the city architects with whom I spoke thought that Gerstel might have been responsible for some construction improvements, but not the original plan.[29] I needed more definitive evidence, which only the original plan could provide. But it was nowhere to be found.

The curve of Bet Talpiot on tree-lined Herzl Street, 1955
Courtesy of Gabriel Laufer; photographer Dr. Dov Laufer

The *gramoshka*—the original architectural plan that's folded like an accordion—for 61 Herzl was filed away in deep storage in the City Archives and impossible for me to access on my own. It was only after a long, drawn-out process and entirely thanks to Waleed Karkabi that I succeeded in obtaining the building file from the archives. The top of the page displayed the name Sternberg-Givoni. I sat, disappointed, in the office in the municipal building, looking through the papers in the file again and again. I kept going through the documents and . . . suddenly I realized that the address was incorrect. I am not an architect, but as I was looking at the blueprints, I noticed something was wrong. The curve of the building in the design that was supposedly 61 Herzl turned westward, while the curve of the building that is etched in my memory turns eastward. It became clear that the document in front of me was the plan for 63 Herzl, which was indeed by Sternberg-Givoni and had been designed later to mirror 61 Herzl. Karkabi himself became curious and decided to persevere. He returned to deep storage and found out that there had been a mistake in the filing. On November 17, 2014, he called to say, "the file on Bet Talpiot was not on the computer. I had to enter through the back door and I saw that the building was indeed built in 1947, and 'Gerstel' is signed on the original plans. In the file I found, there are the original permits and a cover page from Gerstel." The building at 61 Herzl, then, was planned and built by Moshe Gerstel during the last year of the British Mandate, a year during which almost no new buildings were constructed in the city.[30]

For me, this discovery was proof that the building had monumental status, not only a personal nostalgic significance. From a broader cultural perspective, because it is indeed a Gerstel, the building will be added to the official portfolio of his works and will likely be designated for preservation. It will continue to stand on this ground in reality, not only in my memories. Moreover, from the stories I have heard about Gerstel, I had begun to like the man and felt an affinity for him — the architect with rare talents who never received the status he deserved. After 1948, when his Arab customers left the city, his career faltered and he was shunted aside. His fate touched me, as I associated it with those of so many people I knew from his generation, whom history had hurled from one place to another and turned their luck upside down. Gerstel was born in Galicia, not far from my father's birthplace. Like my father, he arrived in Vienna at a young age. But unlike him, Gerstel escaped the jaws of Europe before they bit him. Haifa and the Middle Eastern environment became, for him, a new homeland. He expressed the profound connection that he created with the city and its people through his architectural designs. Gerstel internalized Haifa's landscape and created buildings that embraced the slope and would never turn their backs to the sea.

Adjacent to Bet Talpiot, Gerstel planned twin staircases that stand, one facing the other, with each flight of stairs ending in an open landing, as though inducing passersby to pause and enjoy the sea vista. These symmetrical stairways connect the building's upper and lower levels — Herzl and HeHalutz Streets — and also follow the internal logic of Hadar HaCarmel's layout and the beat of steps that pulse through it. As described earlier, Hadar HaCarmel is arranged such that the pattern of the streets corresponds to the topography. This layout leads to comfortable, wide, horizontal streets intersected by steep vertical streets and pedestrian step paths. The system of steps in Bet Talpiot functions similarly to other step paths, and its urban location is well calculated: Bet Talpiot faces the intersection of Arlozorov and Herzl, and its staircases funnel the flow of people descending the mountain. Thanks to these steps, the traffic coming down the mountain does not halt at Herzl Street but continues down toward the foot of the Carmel. The passage from Herzl to HeHalutz does not end at the bottom of the stairs, however. From the final landing, one must walk through the arcade to reach HeHalutz Street. On one side of the arcade are deep, dark stores; on the other, a view of the outside through an elegant frame of tall arches and their columns. Although the building is modern in terms of its materials and aesthetics, Gerstel's connection to the Mediterranean milieu is imprinted in the design, especially in these archways.

More than anything else, I remember the steps that lead to the arcade. They were the steps that took me from 61 Herzl to 62 HeHalutz, and the store: *wide steps, ten and another ten and another ten, and I'm downstairs, and there's the long arcade. To my left a few dark wholesale stores; to my right the tall arches through which I can see the sky. At the end a large archway opens to HeHalutz Street. I go through it, turn left, and I'm there. This is the store. "For the Homemaker." Housewares. Dishes and kitchenware. Ya'akov Scharf.*

There he is, in a photograph an American relative took some sixty years ago. Wearing khaki shorts and woolen khaki socks stretched tight to just below his knees. With an open shirt, he stands in front of the store. His hair is wavy, all black and silver threads, and, as always, scrupulously combed back.

The display window is impeccably and artfully arrayed. China plates decorated with delicate flowers and crystalware that shatter the light into all the colors of the rainbow. When you enter, there is a narrow passage on your right, and, from there, you can climb wooden steps, very carefully, to the second floor. But it is better to go forward: a long counter and, behind it, my father. Thin tea glasses at his back in boxes, arranged by size on shelves stretching all the way to the ceiling. Across from the counter, more shelves full of merchandise. And all along the wall that welcomes those entering the store is a display case with glass doors, behind which the rare and precious articles dwell: china princesses in long, pink, fluffy dresses, adorned with white porcelain lace, their faces small and their features precise. Princes with tailcoats of blue porcelain and brown porcelain hats. Above them all, a splendid pentagonal decanter presides. On its head, an angular crystal crown that I covet. All these, it is forbidden to touch — only look. When I come to the store, I know to sit quietly and not disturb anything. My father receives the German-speaking customers with "Gnaedige Frau," which means "gracious lady," but I think it means "royal lady." It seems to me that he tries too hard to please the customers, and it makes me angry. Sometimes the shoppers bargain, and sometimes he is forced to lower the price. In Vienna, he tells us, a price was a price and no one ever disputed it.

On one side of our store there were two competing shoe stores and, on the other, Mr. Marcus's store. In the fall of 1956 we all crisscrossed the display window with packing tape. On the other three display windows of 62 HeHalutz, and all over Haifa, the glass panes were latticed with packing tape from fear of the bombings that might accompany the approaching battles, later known as the Sinai campaign. *Mr. Marcus is bald and sells gym shoes by HaMegaper and plaid slippers with a zipper. Rubber pipes too. Everything that's made of rubber. Every day my father and Mr. Marcus close their stores together at seven in the evening and on Fridays at one in the afternoon. With a long, hooked metal pole, they pull the rolling gate down over the glass of the display window. At the bottom are locks that secure it to the ground.* I remember the short conversations Mr. Marcus and my father conducted as they lowered the rolling gate. Once — now I know that it was on Friday September 23, 1955 — they spoke with excitement about that day's discovery of crude oil in the Negev. Together they dreamt about the great wealth that had befallen the little State of Israel, at long last.

The Bat Galim Pool by the Sea

But there is nothing like summer Fridays. My mother packs sandwiches in a large, plastic basket, and in the second bag, bathing suits and towels for all of us, and we go to the store to meet my father. At exactly one o'clock he will close the store, and together we will cross HeHalutz Street and wait for bus 42, which goes to the sea, meaning, Bat Galim! In a short time we'll be there; we'll get off the bus in the round square and then walk the entire length of Bat Galim Boulevard. The baskets in our hands, the palm trees rustling above us — perhaps we'll stop for a minute and buy cold, sweet, spiky sabres (cactus fruit) from the boys wearing gloves on the sidewalk. Right now there is no one happier than us in the world. Far away, at the other end of the boulevard, stands the tall, rounded building, awaiting us. In just a little bit we'll be there. Once we are, my father and my mother buy tickets, and together we cross the entrance gate to paradise. My mother and I enter the women's changing room, while my father and Gadi enter the men's. We meet outside afterward and, impatient, gallop toward the pool.

The pool. The pool. The grown-ups find a place to sit, perhaps on the wooden benches, the "tribunes" — the raised stands that overlook the water — and we wade in the shallow children's pool. The sun is blinding, but who cares? The water is warm and salty and wonderful, and soon they will take us to the large pool. My father and mother are excellent swimmers, and we ride on their backs and hold tight, I, to my father's neck, and Gadi, to my mother's. This way, we "swim" to the deep waters, look up at the three-story diving tower, and marvel at those who jump from it, especially those who dive from the top level, headfirst. Like all the children of Haifa, we heard the horror story that had infinite variations, but each one ended with the death of the jumper. There was once a courageous, adventurous teenager whom someone provoked into jumping headfirst from the third floor. He did so and jumped to his death, and the water of the pool grew red from the blood from his open head. In another version it was the British who bet him a large sum of money to jump, but in my mother's version the important point was that we should never dare jump, never. . . . Since then I have learned how to swim very well, but I never jump into the water. I will always wade down into the pool on the steps.

After swimming we are, of course, very hungry, and it is time for the sandwiches and the fruits and, afterward, playing in the sand on the beach on the other end of the pool. The salt is on our lips and dries on our skin, the sand is hot, the bottoms of our feet burn a little, and the sea and its mossy rocks and the half bridge that enters the water but does not lead anywhere. . . . And it is Friday, and tomorrow we'll all be together, and soon we will get dressed in the changing rooms and return home, tired and full of bliss.

Over the years Bat Galim — literally, "daughter of the waves" — and the pool have become the symbol of a lost childhood in the literary and memorial writings of poets and authors from Haifa. Generations of Haifa children long for it and bemoan its bitter fate. For a few decades the concrete skeleton of the rounded building has stood at the end of Bat Galim Boulevard. They called it the "Casino," even though it was never used for gambling. The Casino building and its connected pool were famous for their evening dances with live orchestras, performances, and a café-restaurant, which attracted many visitors, including officers of the British Mandate. The title of Natan Zach's poem, "Casino in Bat Galim, April 1983," is used as a heart-wrenching code that can be deciphered by those who were children in Haifa between the 1930s and the 1970s. A "pissed-in

The Bat Galim Pool,
with the sea in the
background
*Courtesy of photographer
Gabriel Laufer*

stairwell," "colonies of brown algae," and "yellowing mold" serve the old, despondent Zach as the language of the present. When he looks to the past, however, he needs only simple words: "whole" and "beautiful."

> What once was whole here, repaired and beautiful and fit
> For youth in a seaside city on a beach, a facility, in today's language,
> Where people laughed and swam . . .
>
> . . . would no longer be possible to reconstruct . . .
>
> What is fated to be lost, not even pain will help endure[31]

Zach's words merge longing for the good times with the recognition that even if the Casino is rebuilt, he will never again hear "the music of that orchestra" that he heard in his youth.

The Bat Galim neighborhood, in whose heart the Casino lies, kisses the shore on the western side of the city, where the sea and the mountain meet. One of the only *flat* neighborhoods in Haifa, Bat Galim was planned by the landscape architect Richard Kauffmann and built in the 1920s as a garden neighborhood. Its streets are arranged as a warp and woof, but most are perpendicular to the shore. The neighborhood is studded with architectural pearls from the 1920s and 1930s, but when we were children "Bat Galim" had only one meaning: the pool. The Casino building, which was an integral part of the pool experience for us, was built in 1934 by the imaginative architect Alfred Goldberger, who had emigrated from Vienna only one year prior. He created a structure of two parts that liken it to an anchored ship tied to the pier on the shore. The part that turned toward

The Casino at the
end of Bat Galim
Boulevard
Courtesy of the Matson
(G. Eric and Edith)
Photograph Collection,
Library of Congress

the sea, the "ship," was shaped like a ferry with a roofed terrace supported by concrete columns that had been poured inside the sea with what was then an original engineering innovation. The part that turned toward the street was a rounded, tall "drum" that protruded from a rectangular structure and represented the "pier" to which the "ship" was tied. The main boulevard of the Bat Galim neighborhood is perpendicular to the shore, and it meets the Casino exactly at the middle of the drum, dividing it in perfect symmetry. The ticket window and the entrance to the site were located inside that "drum," and those who entered it discovered a floor partially made of glass bricks, through which they could see the waves crashing against the rocks. Inside the Casino complex was a salt-water pool that was the first Olympic-sized pool in Israel; in its heyday it hosted official competitions. The structure and the pool functioned until 1972.[32]

The bittersweet stories of Yitzhak Kronzon, a cardiologist who lives in New York City but grew up in Haifa, cling to the past with longing and humor. In one of those stories, a kibbutz pool that he visited with his father in the forties triggers a description of the pool that was second to none—the one and only Bat Galim pool. Kronzon places the long paragraph dedicated to Bat Galim inside parentheses. While this seems to be appropriate, as Bat Galim is simply not connected to the plot of the story, there is, in fact, an inner motivation to this punctuation. Suspending the Bat Galim swimming pool in an island of parentheses is the only way the author can preserve it just as it was—whole and beautiful—without reference to its present state:

I liked pools very much. (The pool in Bat Galim is very large and sunny. Along its two sides are wooden stands that are weathered by the salt water and the hot sun, where families sit to sun themselves and eat sandwiches and fruit they bring from home. From the stands you can see the bathers in the water and the divers on the diving towers.... Next to the big pool is a little kiddie pool. It is so shallow that you can lie in the water and use your hands to hold yourself up, and make as if you're really swimming....) The Givat Brenner pool was completely different.[33]

Like every child of Haifa, Kronzon had heard about the youth who dove from the highest section of the tower. And like so many others, he too intertwines his version of the fateful dive with the description of the pool.[34] On Ge'ula Street, where Kronzon grew up, they used to say that before the boy jumped to his death, he had eaten watermelon, and when his stomach burst on impact the entire pool filled with its sections. But this piece of Haifa folklore did not prevent anyone from enjoying the salty, balmy sea water that filled the pool and the faucets that were placed in the wall and sprayed water on those standing next to them; sitting way up high on the tribunes; and watching the gold of the sun shimmering in the water. The light, azure, and salt continued to delight my summer days as long as my father was alive — that is, until I was ten years old. After that, times changed and the trips to Bat Galim ended.

The Wadi Salib Riots and the Novel That Foretold Them

Out of necessity, at age eleven, I was allowed to roam freely between my house on 85 Herzl and Bet Talpiot. My mother was forced to tend the store after my father's death, and I became more independent. While no one forbade me from wandering farther along Herzl Street, the plaza in front of Bet Talpiot became a kind of unmarked border of my childhood, a not-to-be-crossed-by-myself border. Each building on the route between home and the plaza had a personal, intimate meaning for me. At 85 Herzl: going down from the third floor; glancing left toward the sometimes-blossoming pomegranate tree in the lower yard; climbing up the front steps to Herzl

Street; and turning right. The first of the stores on the façade of 85 Herzl was HaMa'apil, an unglamorous family-owned eatery. The name was a remnant from the days when the *ma'apilim*—illegal immigrants—used to eat there for cheap. When the owners turned it into a chocolate store (which, for us, meant an eagerly anticipated bag of sweets every Friday), we continued calling the man and his wife HaMa'apil. To this day I don't know their names.

Next was Kahanovitch, the book and newspaper store, home to the only telephone in 85 Herzl. Everything about the world that existed beyond 85 Herzl, I learned from the newspapers and journals that the Kahanovitches displayed on the pillar next to their store, attached with wooden laundry pins. There, I saw the issues of *Ha'Olam HaZe* (This world)—scantily clad women on one side and, on the other, the piercing eyes of Rudolph Kastner awaiting a trial; the spy, Yisrael Ber; or the twists and turns of the "Lavon affair." Mr. and Mrs. Kahanovitch were educated people, we all knew; they had learned Hebrew when still in their famed Lithuanian high school, Tarbut.

After their store was the grocery store and, then, separate from 85 Herzl but nearby, stood "the kiosk," which is how we referred to both the little structure and its owner, a man with a disabled right hand, who sold carrot juice and, in the summer, hot corn. In the next building there was a dark bar, tiled with black tiles, and right next to it, a linen store. Only then did I cross Bilu Street. In the morning I looked left, right and left, and ran to school, but on the way back I would put my schoolbag on the pavement and chat with my friends on that corner, one eye drifting north to the blue bay. Two hundred footsteps and a few storefronts away from Bilu Street stood the gate of the Alliance School, my Alliance School. And then, more stores—books and buttons—while I carefully crossed Sokolov Street, which was more dangerous than Bilu and a little farther from home. I glanced toward the blue sea on the right, quickly stepping past the Sheleg ice cream store and the narrow alcove of the watchmaker Vang. . . . I was almost at the plaza. I had internalized the rhythm of the buildings, spaced evenly three meters apart, and the music of the downward sloping streets facing the sea. It was the language of my neighborhood, which penetrated my subconscious. Later I learned that this architectural rhythm was the concept of Sir Patrick Geddes, the urban planner and ecologist invited by

Hadar HaCarmel's founders to design the district. He envisioned Hadar as a garden city and thought that in the Levant, unlike the crowded European cities, large spaces between houses were necessary for air.[35]

One time, when I was walking along Herzl Street and had almost reached the plaza, a great mass of people appeared. Some marched in the street, not on the sidewalk, screaming loudly and holding up posters. Suddenly, out of nowhere, Mrs. Kahanovitch sprung up and said, "Go home, Nili, run home! This is no time for children to be outside. Return home quickly!" This happened the first summer after my father died. I don't remember why I was there, alone on Herzl Street, why I had wanted to go to our store right then. It was not until I grew up that I understood that the people screaming on the street that day — Thursday, July 9, 1959 — had been part of the Wadi Salib events that signaled the protest of the residents of the poor neighborhood on the lower boundary of Hadar HaCarmel. Back then, in my childhood, the wadi had seemed very far away, and I knew nothing about it, but like a river it rose beyond its banks and flooded the slopes above it; climbed the Street of Steps; and split, running through Sokolov and Yehiel Streets, where it rose and spilled onto my Herzl Street.

The Wadi Salib neighborhood, abandoned by most of its Arab residents during the 1948 war, filled up with new immigrants afterward. About a third of them came from North Africa, an oft-neglected group, many of whom suffered from unemployment and poor, inadequate housing. On Wednesday night of July 8, 1959, police clashed with a few of the neighborhood's residents and shot one of them. The next day some of the wadi's inhabitants protested in their neighborhood and, later, continued to wreak havoc outside of it. In light of the gravity of the situation, a National Investigative Committee for the Events of Wadi Salib was immediately established. To this committee, the deputy mayor, Zvi Barzilai, submitted a memorandum surprising in its sensitivity: "Anyone who tours the neighborhood and sees the dark crannies without air, without water and plumbing, can imagine the amount of bitterness, disappointment, and despair that the destitute family eats every day."[36] The committee's conclusions led, among other things, to the transfer of the residents to neighborhoods with better housing. Today, the Wadi Salib events are seen as the first social revolt in Israel against ethnic discrimination.

The demonstrators targeted Hadar HaCarmel because of its prosperous Ashkenazi image, as well as its proximity to the wadi. The committee's report from 1959, as well as recent studies, detail the route of the demonstrators through Hadar: "Two groups emerged from Wadi Salib toward Hadar HaCarmel, one running through Sokolov Street up to Herzl Street and back through Yehiel Street, and the second . . . to Sirkin. . . . They smashed display windows, damaged property, and quickly escaped."[37]

In this reconstruction, I recognize, of course, the segment between the corner of Sokolov and the plaza on Herzl, where I bumped into Mrs. Kahanovitch. Yehiel Street, which is so close to the store, also stands out from between the lines. In ordinary days Yehiel Street would be bustling with shoppers: in its upper corner, there was Ilka, the exclusive women's fashion store; and across the street and a little below on the slope, pleasant aromas wafted from the coffee store Schreiber, which I often visited with my mother. Lower yet was the Duchovni Bakery — *its name printed on the paper stickers that we peeled off the loaves of bread, and, on its windowsills, glass containers filled with rolls — the smell of fresh bread, two kinds, black and white, and sometimes caraway as well and challah on Fridays.* But the enraged people from the wadi didn't stop to smell the intoxicating aromas. They also didn't know that some five years before they marched up Yehiel Street, a perceptive author used to take that very path down to the wadi, sensing, even then, that something would boil over.

Yehudit Hendel, the young, adoring wife of the painter Zvi Meirovitch, used to walk down the slope of Yehiel Street in the early 1950s. She would come from the established and respected Yerushalayim Street, continue down the busy Yehiel Street, and from there head to the Street of Steps, which skips between the stone houses and overlooks Wadi Salib. She crossed the wadi until she reached the lower city to meet her husband, who painted posters for the neighborhood movie theater to provide for their growing family.

In 2010 Hendel told me, "Five years before the riots, I felt that they were going to erupt."[38] And, in truth, the book that she wrote then, her first novel, *The Street of Steps*, is a testament to her foresight. It won the prestigious Barasch Prize in 1954 and quickly became a bestseller. The critics welcomed it warmly, noting especially the courage that the author showed in writing about the ethnic conflict.[39]

The Street of Steps is a love story between a man and a woman from different ethnic and socioeconomic backgrounds. The time: early 1950s, when the scars of the 1948 war had not yet healed, but the decades that preceded that war are also recalled. The place: Haifa with all its layers, both topographical and social, and at the book's center, the Street of Steps and its residents. The first of these is the main protagonist, Avram, a native of the street, a veteran and war hero who worked as a sailor but is now unemployed. His mother died when he was a child, and he currently lives in the house where he grew up, along with his father and his desperate, war-disabled brother. In proximity live other characters who typify the dismal fates of the street's inhabitants, including Avram's drunk, ne'er-do-well uncle, Ovadya; and Malka, the poor neighbor whose husband was killed by Arabs many years earlier and whose only son was killed in the 1948 war. Next door to Avram's dark abode lives the family of a store owner. Their daughter, Rivka, is the girl Avram had loved in the past.

The other main character in the novel is Erella, Avram's current beloved, the beautiful, golden-haired daughter of a rich Ashkenazi contractor, who also lost her mother at a young age. Avram and Erella met during the 1948 war, shortly after the battle in which Erella's boyfriend was killed. While the two are in love and want to marry, Erella's widowed father furiously and openly objects to their union. He uses bigoted, prejudiced arguments against Avram, who comes from a lower socioeconomic class. The wealthy Erella lives with her father in a pine tree-lined street on the Carmel, while Avram lives in the poor, crowded Street of Steps.

Because of the disparity in their social status, the fate of Haifa's own Romeo and Juliet is determined before the story even begins. The steps in the book's title are not only a geographic marker of a street but also an expression of its author's social consciousness and an implicit recognition of the unique Haifaian conflation of topography and social status. In the 1950s those who lived higher up on the Carmel belonged to a higher socioeconomic class than those who lived toward the bottom, and this gap became even more pronounced in later years. This Haifaian feature is underscored in both the 1959 committee's memorandum and in a book written fifty years later by a Haifa historian and politician, Eli Nachmias. The memorandum states, "Every layer on the slope of the mountain is superior to the one beneath it, from both a topographical and a social point of view."[40] And, written in the 2009 book: "Rising in the ladder of life and society paralleled the topographical condition of the city; immigrants who established themselves moved to Hadar HaCarmel. . . . An additional rise meant climbing higher on Mount Carmel."[41] A similar perception is expressed through Avram, the novel's protagonist, who climbs from the lower part of the slope to Erella's house on the heights of the Carmel: "This side of the mountain was not badly crowded, and the air was laden with the fragrance of the fir groves. . . . Beyond the lights and the cozy, domestic houses something warm and tender emanated. . . . How strange it is, how different we in the valley are from the people up here."[42] The topographic layer at which the novel's hero lives is not a mere external element but a part of his personality. Even as a child, Avram grasped the social significance of the construction of his city. Hendel uses his consciousness to foreshadow the upcoming social protests that would threaten Haifa: "Above the Street of Steps, up on the Mountain, are shops featuring toys and fancy chocolates. At night, lights are turned on. There are lights in the display windows. . . . People's lives within their houses are locked, and not on the filthy pavements, or on the ground crawling with worms" (74; 82–83).

It is hard not to be impressed by the similarity between the words of Hendel's fictional hero, who calls Hadar HaCarmel "up on the Mountain," and the testimonies following the events of Wadi Salib five years later: "I wanted to build a bar in our neighborhood in Wadi Salib. . . . There is no modern café around us and I thought of creating something beautiful, the kind of thing that exists in Hadar above, with an espresso machine." This is what the leader of the revolt said to the committee; as Barzilai explained in the 1959 memorandum, "The lights of the Carmel neighborhoods wink at them from above, while they are caught between the pincers of unemployment and the darkness of the narrow, musty alley."[43] Thus, Hadar HaCarmel was a coveted ideal and an object of rage all at once for the wadi's fictional and actual residents.

Fidelity to reality, even a bitter one, is without a doubt an important value for Hendel. This is evident from the novel itself, but also from interviews that she granted when the book first came out as well as in a conversation I had with Hendel at her home in 2010, a few years before she died.[44] During that late interview she said that her book's characters were based on people she knew, people who lived on the Street of Steps, whose words she heard and integrated into the book.[45] Later, I learned that she was just as detailed and accurate in painting the route that led her down to the Street of Steps as she was in portraying her heroes.

In 2014 Yehudit Hendel died, and I tried to walk in her footsteps from the top of Yehiel Street, touching Herzl Street, through the Street of Steps, all the way down to the movie theater. But this path had been lost: the steps on which I started descending were severed by a shiny, new highway. Luckily for me, as part of a group tour in the lower city, I reached Kibbutz Galuyot Street. Like all the visitors, I looked upward toward Wadi Salib, which was the focus of the tour. On the mountain, above the Arab buildings that remain in the wadi, I saw Gerstel's impressive market, like an aging beauty whose wrinkles are erased by distance. And then I turned my back to the slope, and, behold, there was the Hadar Cinema of which Hendel had told me. In 1947 Maximillian Romanov had planned it in the International Style for Taufiq El-Khalil, who named it Cine El-Naser (Victory).[46] After its abandonment by the Arab owner in 1948, it was converted into the Israeli Hadar Cinema, for which Meirovitch, Hendel's husband, had painted posters. Now, with my back again to the cinema and my face toward the mountain, I searched for the steps and I found them. I knew I was standing in the place where the author walked six decades earlier. This is the lower end of the Street of Steps; this is where she arrived from Hadar HaCarmel to meet her husband the painter. I bought a falafel and started climbing the steps upward, when my path was blocked by the same highly trafficked, wide highway, devoid of pedestrian crossings. I persisted, crossed that street running, and then another highway, but I made it to the top segment of the Street of Steps, and, from there, to Yehiel Street.

Thanks to Hendel's poetics of documentation, the reader of *The Street of Steps* is able to return to the past. In its pages Haifa of the first years after the 1948 war becomes palpable. It is a city that is no more, but still lives and breathes in the novel. *The Street of Steps* is not merely a social-realist novel with prophetic insights but rather an introspective, multilayered work. Hendel's writing internalizes the slope of the mountain on which the city lies and is meticulous about forging the experience of walking within it. She uses the components of reality — here, the city of Haifa, its people, and its landscape — to unearth the depths beneath it. The fabric of Haifa becomes a secret language in which the author is fluent and through which she virtuosically depicts her characters, her plot, and, yes, also her social perception.

Like photographers whose pictures reveal, in their artistry, what is hidden in the landscape, so is Hendel in this novel. Within her pages there is a constant conversation between the various layers of the city, while the angle of the camera changes incessantly. Sometimes the lens turns from the bottom upward to the ridge and sometimes the reverse, from the mountain to the sea. Merely switching from one angle to another is an original Hendelian way of seeing.

The iconic gaze on Haifa until the 1990s — and, to some extent, even later — was the gaze from the Carmel toward the port and the bay. This is the view that is familiar from postcards, the view that the city planners and famous landscape architects tried to preserve.[47] Below an observer standing on the vaunted Panorama Street on the ridgeline, the Carmel spreads like a colorful rug, all the way to the foot of the mountain that touches the shore. But behold, Hendel, with her subversive gaze, insists on also looking from the bottom up. In so doing, she turns the hierarchy upside down, granting importance to those who supposedly look from the wrong direction, the residents of the Street of Steps. They are neighbors of the sea and the train tracks, but she induces them to look up at the green mountain or its shimmering pearls at night: "The canopy of the mountain above, the slope of the houses and rocks . . . and the white roofs" (109; 125). The novel's hero, Avram, climbs up the stairs, again reversing the classic Haifa angle: "every day I come up here from my street" (35; 38). From his low vantage point near the sea, he sometimes looks up at the mountain and sees "the city of the Carmel ridges was swallowed in darkness, and the lights from its windows twinkled nearby like stars." The superior people, so to speak, who live higher on the Carmel are "swallowed in" darkness or, at the very least, seem closer to Avram, as his reversed gaze cancels their differences for a moment (52; 58).

But beyond the equality granted by the multitude of perspectives of the landscape, those perspectives have an added benefit: they allow Haifa itself — the city and the bay, the ships and the trains, the pine trees and the lights — to be reflected with all its facets. The sea, for example, can be seen in the novel, as in the city, from many angles and in different colors, mirroring the changes not only in the landscape but also in the beholders themselves. While Avram, who grew up near the shore and stands on the "downward slope of the steps," sees the "*violet-red* sunset [that] covered *the sea*" (325; 360), Erella, who is on the top of the mountain, observes the "*gray* waves *of the sea*." The narrator's voice adds a third sympathetic viewpoint from the highest house on the Street of Steps: "here, the sea is suddenly exposed, *blue in the sky that is inside the sea*" (166; 190; emphases mine). The narrator's intimacy with the city is evident here, both from the quintessential blue that looks back at her and from her knowledge that, for someone who strolls through Haifa, the sea is always alternately present and hidden, forever revealing itself "suddenly." Avram's uncle Ovadya understands the sea and its language, "I hear 'em [the ships] . . . how they whistle at night, and know whether they're sailing or docking" (186–87; 210). The codes of the sea are clear to the uncle, but not to the girl who grew up on the mountain far away from it.

As with the sea, Hendel applies a kaleidoscopic, poetic principle to her depictions of the Street of Steps. In the first half of the book the street is described as it is perceived by its residents, while in the second part it is seen from the outside, through the eyes of Erella, who visits it as a tourist and whose guides are the residents. The people living on the street are aware of its pathetic state, and while some complain about it, their gaze is full of empathy and their feeling of belonging to the place endows it with splendor: "The street . . . is so narrow. . . . It winds into a series of crooked steps. . . . What of it if parents and children live in one room? . . . Ivy plants on the iron bars of the balconies cast shadows over the basins glistening on the walls . . . and fragments of sea and sky emerge" (73; 81–82).

Despite the crowdedness, flowers bloom in the shiny flowerpots. When Avram returns to the street, defeated, it is seen through his eyes with forgiveness: "As the street lamps went on in an oblique dotted line of light on the slope of the steps . . . the shedding fig tree looked white through the window in the evening light, [and] the shadows of the steps resembled low, thick walls" (325; 361–62). The stairs separate the hero from his dreams, yet he notices that the evening grants the neighborhood grace; the streetlights adorn it with beads and surround the fig tree with a romantic halo.

Erella's experience of the street is one of a visitor, and it is entirely different. She is repulsed by the sight of a little girl who plays with "a headless object that she called 'my doll.'" She notices the peeling paint of a wicket in the yard and armoires that, in her eyes, are "wooden crates filled with rags" (212; 236). When she returns to her fragrant home, hidden between the cypress trees, she reflects back on the Street of Steps: "Once again, she saw the narrow alleys . . . and poverty peering through the open doors" (304–5; 339). Erella remembers how the street seemed to be plotting against her as she walked in it. In her imagination the street becomes an active character, with its own will and passion that threatens the outsider who treads on it: "Suddenly she saw herself . . . opposite that girl . . . and she, Erella, nearly fell into the dirty water" (304; 339). It seems that in a moment of crisis, the street sides with its residents. Erella is trying to steal away a man who belongs to the street or, rather, to one of its daughters. Therefore, the street tries to trip her with its sewage water, while Rivka, the local girl who is in love with Avram, puts the curse of the place on Erella with her stare.

The mother of Rivka, whom Avram abandoned, rails against the blond Erella, saying, "And today this yellow one, damn her, has to come and walk around the street!" (238; 264). It becomes clear that the street itself also hates the intruder and, by association, the hair color of the "yellow one": "the remnants of rotten vegetables lay strewn about, and orange and lemon peels shone golden yellow in the mucky, stinking puddles" (239; 265). To show the street's attitude, Hendel deliberately uses the color yellow to capture decay. She specifically refers to the "lemon peels," elaborates on their "golden yellow" appearance, and places them in the muck. The street speaks through the yellow and orange of the rotten fruits, exposing its hostility toward the blond outsider.

Significantly, Hendel gives the Street of Steps the right to speak throughout her entire novel. Its residents, who had been otherwise silenced during the early fifties, when the book was published, are offered an appearance on the national stage through the book that bears their street's name. Indeed, Hendel uses the city, its streets, colors, and scents, the slope, and the slices of sea as a language through which she creates her artistic world. But through this language her preferences are also revealed. It is clear that, for Hendel, the city has a power and a spiritual existence beyond the individuals who populate it. Haifa is the background but also one of the characters; the scenery but also a mirror that reflects the inner world of the protagonists.

The Street of Steps, the first Israeli urban novel, created a revolution in

Street of Steps *Photograph by Aviv Itzhaki*

the literary arena of its time and presaged the style of the generation that would follow it. It is a groundbreaking work in many ways, an original, masterful, artistic depiction of a city. Indeed, the first city in Israel that had a book dedicated to it was Haifa, the city of steps.

Haifa is filled with streets of steps, and many of its houses have entrance steps that precede the building itself. Many buildings lie downward on the slope from one street to the other, tied together by steps — narrow or wide, private or public, secret or known. The ease with which one can sail from the top of the Carmel to its feet flows in the veins of Haifa and its residents. They know where to find the paths of steps that slide from the top of the mountain to the bottom, from the Carmel Center neighborhood to the top of Hadar and, from there, to lower Hadar and then the bottom of the city. There is no border between these layers, but one easily notices the changing character of the neighborhoods, their styles, their density, and the ratio of gardens to houses. The steps are, to a certain extent, the quintessential expression of the slope that is Haifa's soul, one of the only traits that the gnawing of time and erosion cannot erase. The language of steps is the secret language in which the residents of the city express their love to this slope on which they live. Only those who have skipped from one step to the other, raising their head intermittently to glance at the sea that peeks out between the trees and buildings, know its language. There are steps made from concrete and stone, from marble and wood. There are wide steps and shallow ones, comfortable and steep, narrow and cracked and winding. There are steps on which trees lower their branches on either side, and there are steps bordered only by a tall fence and erect buildings. There are steps where one hears yelling from the houses and those accompanied by the sounds of music. All of them, however, have the same background melody: the horns of the ships in the bay. Like the architect Gerstel, who sang his love song to the city with his buildings and staircases, so Hendel does with her novel. Haifa is Hendel's city of steps, to whom she made love with her feet and whom she serenaded with her pen. The heroes of the streets of steps are all the people of Haifa, those who live along them, and those who climbed them up and down, like me, on the way to the store from Herzl Street and those who ran to and from the market. And for all the sea reveals itself at every turn, and for all the ships sound their horns.

4

THE SCHOOL AND THE SYNAGOGUE

At the End of Herzl Street

Near the end of the wide Herzl Street, between Sokolov Street and Bilu Street, the Central Synagogue and the Alliance School stood directly across from each other, flanked by low residential homes and stores. Both were planned by some of Haifa's greatest architects; both witnessed the British Mandate's rule over Palestine and the historical war that led to the creation of the State of Israel. As a child, I passed by that portion of the street endless times, and I knew each house and store by heart, but while the Alliance School will eternally remain for me the symbol of goodness, nobility, and generosity, the big Central Synagogue is inscribed in my consciousness as a locked fortress whose gatekeepers were evil, bearded men.

The impressive synagogue was the command center of Haifa's religious establishment and over time became the most significant landmark in that area. Even decades after its greatness had declined, people would say, "over there, on Herzl Street, near the big synagogue," and the city's authors and poets repeatedly call it that in their writings. The fate of the synagogue was better than that of the school. Even as the surrounding neighborhood crumbled, the synagogue largely kept its grand façade, while only the ornate iron gate and the entrance steps remain of the original beauty and clean elegance of the Alliance School.

What a contrast to their beginnings! During the sweeping construction of the Hadar HaCarmel district, the Palestine Jewish Colonization Association (PICA), established by Baron Edouard de Rothschild, bought the piece of land that slopes downward from Gilad Street in the south, past Herzl, to Yalag Street in the north. In the mid-1920s the higher southernmost portion of the plot, from Gilad Street to Herzl, was designated for the synagogue, while the school, owned by the Alliance Israelite Française, was later allotted a large lot of five *dunam* (about fifty-four thousand square feet), spreading down from Herzl Street to Yalag. This is how a continuous line of buildings was formed on Hadar's main thoroughfare of Herzl, closing the rocky gap that had separated the houses on the east and west sides of the street. The synagogue went through many transformations, constructed in stages over three decades, as its design was assigned to one architect after another. The Alliance School building, on the other hand, was erected in less than a year.

The Alliance School and the Man Who Designed It

The architect of the Alliance School, Benjamin Orell, was an artist, a painter, and a sculptor who received his architectural education at the beginning of the twentieth century at the Bezalel Art Academy in Jerusalem, but he did not have an architect's diploma. Instead, he completed his training at architecture firms in Berlin and Paris, where he absorbed the spirit of modernism. In 1926 he settled in Haifa and opened his architectural firm in partnership with fellow architect Ezekiel Zohar.[1] In 1935 the architectural office of Orell and Zohar won first prize in the international competition to design the Alliance School building. On October 12 of that same year, the *Ha'aretz* newspaper covered the ceremonial laying of the cornerstone, attended by the principal, Yitzhak Nahon, and honored guests from Paris and Palestine. In 1936 the brand new home of the first Jewish school in Haifa was inaugurated. Fifty-four years after it was first established, the Alliance School moved into this "modern building, large and comfortable, with a garden, a dining hall, and a large sports field paved with tar in Hadar HaCarmel."[2] It contained eighteen classrooms to serve approximately a thousand pupils, ranging from kindergarten to twelfth grade, and its cost was estimated at 12,000 Palestine pounds, paid for by the Alliance Israelite Française in Paris.[3]

The rocky slope of the school's plot of land posed a challenge to the gifted architects, but their solution did not merely overcome the topography — it used the slope to serve the interests of the institution. To counteract the sharp height difference between Herzl Street and Yalag, the architects constructed three levels, with the building in the center of the plot, a large yard in front of it on one level, and two smaller yards behind. The entire area was insulated from the outside world. A chain of stores, built low so as not to block the sunlight from the classrooms, marched outward from either side of the school's magnificent entrance gate on Herzl Street; on Yalag the plot was walled off by a tall fence. Every corner of the strangely shaped plot was utilized. In the asymmetrical tail sticking out of the west side of the lot were vegetable patches used in agriculture classes for grades one to three. In the west wing, on the lowest level of the plot, was the dining hall. From the upper floors of the building, one could gaze out over the "big yard," as we used to call it, next to Herzl Street to the south, or down past Yalag Street to the blue Haifa bay to the north.

The only book written about Benjamin Orell's work, *Binyamin Orell: adrikhal lelo diploma* (Benjamin Orell: An architect without a diploma) was published after the original Alliance building had been changed beyond recognition. Its authors underline the asymmetry of the original school building and provide a succinct description of its plan: "The building consisted of two wings in the shape of an L, on a foundation lower than the level of Herzl Street. A large stairway connected the two wings. The wing facing Herzl Street [to the south] featured an open, columned floor that allowed the entire depth of the yard to be used for the movement of the students. It also served as a source of shade in the summer and

Alliance School
as viewed from
the north
*Permission from
PalPhot; photographer
Yehuda Dorfzaun*

cover from rain in the winter." The book dedicated to Orell comments on the "horizontal balconies that were also outdoor corridors between the classrooms," one of the many details that made it beloved by the students.[4] All these unique qualities imparted their grace to the children and teachers at the school for many years. For me, the school was a refuge, a place protected not only from the winter rains and the hot summer sun but also from the outside world and its attending afflictions.

I did not arrive at the Alliance School until I was in third grade. I had attended first and second grade at the Ge'ula public school, where my second-grade teacher, Sima, did not especially like me. In our class's dramatization of the biblical story of "Rebecca and Eliezer at the Well," I was not cast as Rebecca, not even Eliezer, but rather as one of the maidens with a clay jug on her head. From my second-grade perspective, it was the teacher's marginalization of me that motivated my parents to transfer me to the private Alliance School (I assume, however, that they had other reasons). Unlike the public school, the Alliance School charged tuition and cultivated a formal atmosphere. Even in third grade, when a teacher entered the classroom we had to stand up until she instructed us to sit. Additionally, we were expected to address our teachers in the third person, calling them not by their name but rather, "the teacher" (*hamore*, or *hamora*, depending on whether they were male or female). While I do not remember my first day at Alliance, I know I felt lucky to be at this beautiful new school, which was closer to my home than Ge'ula and was part of my immediate neighborhood. I will never forget my teacher *hamora* Sara. She was as beautiful as an angel, her bright face adorned with brown locks. More than anything, we were enchanted by her soft, manicured hands — her long fingers and her fingernails painted with light pink polish. When she walked toward the classroom before the bell rang, we would run to welcome her, to have the privilege of touching her hands, and we'd hang on to them until she could barely move.

I loved my school: each morning sprinting the short distance from my home on Herzl Street, passing through the large wrought-iron gates, and galloping down the wide entrance steps that led to the big yard where the morning assembly had just begun. On either side of the steps, tall walls stood like groomsmen, their recurring brick design softening their harsh height, almost domesticating them. I took the magnificent gate and its steps and welcoming walls for granted. Five decades would pass before I would understand that the uniqueness of these entrance walls was derived from their intricate brick laying: above every four rows of bricks, there is one row laid diagonally, the corners of the bricks pointing out, creating the illusion of a series of serrated triangles, like a row of pointy teeth. This simple, ornamental device divides the expanse of the wall into shorter, less threatening segments and plays with light and shadow. The artful design stemmed from the genius of Orell, the architect who was so attentive to both the needs of his clients and this "impossible," sloping, rocky plot in Hadar HaCarmel.[5]

When I ran breathless down the steps to the ringing of the eight o'clock bell and tried to slip into the rows of my class in the big yard, I did not pause to think about the capacious width of the steps or the pattern of the bricks. Nevertheless, this impressive entrance announced to me that I had arrived at the place where, daily, the essence of life is taught. At the same time, these steps were an architectural solution to the difficult topography.[6] They matched the downward slope of the plot, connecting the main gate on the high Herzl Street with the lower level of the big yard and the school building.

During recess, the role of the steps changed. No longer were they a passage from one world to the other but rather a comfortable place to sit in their own right, to hide under the roof from the rain, to play jacks with rocks, to whisper secrets, to carve initials into the bricks, or just to watch others playing in the yard. While the central part of the stairway continued to serve as a thoroughfare even during recess, both sides comfortably housed the many pupils. This deft trisection of the entrance space was accomplished with three pairs of columns, each with a niche for a light and a scored horizontal incision at its head. The attention to detail shows the architect's desire not only that the building would be functional but that each part of it, including the entrance, would bestow an emotional experience on its inhabitants.[7]

At the foot of the expansive stairway stretched the big yard. Like the stairs, it too changed faces over the course of the day. In the morning it was home to our daily assembly; during the school day it hosted gym classes; and during recess it became a giant playground. The school building itself rose in the middle of the lot. In front of it was the big yard, the dominion of the high school and older elementary school pupils, and behind it was the "small yard," which was specifically intended for students in grades one to three. The building stood on columns, so it was possible to pass beneath it from one yard to the other. Behind the school there were three levels. On the upper level was the small yard, and on the narrow middle level were a few palm trees and flower beds. On the lowest level the kindergarteners frolicked in the sandbox, which doubled as the landing area for the older students when they practiced the high jump and broad jump in gym.

When I began my studies at Alliance, our third-grade classroom was located on the ground floor next to the small yard, where we could play securely without fearing the older kids and their wild games. *Hamora* Sara taught every subject (as did all third-grade teachers), and I excelled in Torah. I took pride in the fact that I had read from my father's Bible, which contained much more detailed stories than the rewritten, abridged "Torah for children" that we studied in class. I used to sit under the table in the living room and leaf through the thick, mysterious book, its pages divided in two columns: Hebrew on the right and German on the left in ornate gothic print. At the end of the year, *hamora* Sara asked for special permission from the principal to write the following remark in my report card: "a praiseworthy student." This note is how the principal, Mr. Yungerman, heard about me for the first time. Later, however, even when I was not a praiseworthy student, Mr. Yungerman continued to influence my life, lifting me up with kindness even when I fell.

At the end of third grade we performed a kind of morality play, titled

Dirty Ruthie. I was ecstatic to be cast as Ruthie, a dirty girl who does not obey her mother and eats contaminated sweets from the filthy peddler on the street corner. When Ruthie is plagued by terrible stomachaches, two apparitions visit her: the devil, Ziftuni (Tar Man), who tries to seduce her to come to Dirtland; and the beautiful fairy who rules Cleanland. Of course, Ruthie chooses Cleanland. For years the adult spectators of that play would imitate the way I squirmed on the stage, screaming, "My stomach! My stomach! Mommy, my stomach!" Mr. Yungerman himself, my mother, and even our pediatrician, Dr. Emed, were in the audience. My father could not attend because he had to tend to the store. We would perform a play at the end of fourth grade as well. This time it was an adaptation of a Hans Christian Andersen folktale. I played the boy searching for the flower with the golden heart, the only remedy that could save his sick mother.

A mere four months after my search for the healing flower, at the beginning of fifth grade, my father fell ill and ultimately died. This time there was no remedy — no flower, no magic potion — only the sea outside his hospital window.

In the meantime, life at the Alliance School continued as before. In fourth grade we started taking part in the morning assembly, a decades-long tradition for Alliance students.[8] We lined up in the big yard in pairs according to our classes. Our faces were turned toward the microphone, which amplified the voice of Mr. Yungerman, who made the announcements, and of the student who read aloud a Bible chapter. Behind them, the building stood erect, its simple, straight lines bequeathing calmness and a feeling of order and security. On special days more formal assemblies were conducted in the big yard while the lines of "The Silver Platter" or "The Partisan Song" echoed between the grand entrance and the school. After the daily assembly we would enter the school through the generously wide inner staircase between the two wings of the building and climb to the higher floors in ordered lines.

When I returned, almost fifty years later, to the building with Itamar Shoshan, my former classmate, he tried to slide down the railing of the stairs the way some of us used to, but he could not — the railings had been changed. Back when we climbed up or slid down the stairs, neither he nor I understood that this symmetrical, sculptured staircase was deliberately designed.[9] The breadth of the stairs demonstrated Orell's desire that this

A hazy day on Alliance's corridor balcony
Courtesy of photographer Gabriel Laufer

space be elegant as well as functional, enabling droves of students to move about the school comfortably. He separated each flight of steps with a sort of wide island between the railings. This architectural feature of the 1930s and 1940s, often called "the eye of the stairs," created a spacious stairway that allowed those on one flight to see people on other flights and the teachers to oversee the students and maintain order and safety. On each floor's landing a corridor greeted those disembarking with a generous opening that shed sunlight on the entire staircase and opened out onto the sea — this corridor that connected the wings of the building was, in fact, a roofed balcony that also protected the students from raindrops and the heat of the sun. The height of the balcony's railing was made to fit the height of the students — high enough that the younger ones could not fall over the edge and low enough for the older ones to rest their elbows on it and look out at the bay. This was an ideal place for flirting and chatting; here the boys from the higher grades checked out the girls from the lower ones and vice versa. During recess, the older students could look down on the younger ones playing in the small yard or stand, memorizing material for their next exam. The blue of the sea and the horns of the ships accompanied their words and penetrated their souls.

In the fourth grade we received not only the privilege of taking part in the assembly but also of going up the stairs to the upper floors with the "big kids," the high schoolers among them. When we reached the landing on the first day of classes, that corridor balcony welcomed us and led us to the roomy, high-ceilinged classroom on the top floor, bathed with light.

It was the school year of 1957–58, and we were the first ten-year-old pupils in two thousand years in a free Israel. We had almost all been born in 1948, the year of the establishment of the state. We were called the Children of the Decade (*Yaldei He'Asor* in Hebrew), the First Generation for Salvation, and we were celebrated. We were the only grade in school selected to travel by train to plant trees in the Forest of the Decade near the village of Kfar Galim. In truth, we did not understand why the adults were so moved by us, the Children of the Decade. We were born into a land where the dominant spoken language is Hebrew, where the policemen and soldiers are Israeli, where the capital is Jerusalem, and where most leaders, officers, and advisers are Jewish. While we studied the 1948 "War of Liberation," the draining of the swampland, the pioneers, the British Mandate, and the battles, the reality in which we lived was both Israeli and Hebrew, and we took it for granted. To us, it seemed that Israel's Independence Day had been marked in the calendar since the beginning of time. Nevertheless, when we were given special favors as the Children of 1948, we did not object.

Independence Day in Haifa was celebrated that year with a colorful parade of dancers filling Herzl Street, the main thoroughfare of Hadar HaCarmel. This period of the late 1950s was relatively stable in terms of security and economics, and the surrounding euphoria stuck to us too. In the large classroom that also served as a synagogue on Saturdays, an exhibition dedicated to the city of Haifa was presented by the entire student body in honor of the tenth year of Israel's existence. Bella Pevzner and I were tasked with creating an album, our class's contribution to the exhibition, and we filled it with Bella's perfect handwriting, photographs cut out from city publications, and my own childish historical research. Into the album we glued pictures of ships, as well as the hypnotizing landscape of the bay, port, and mountain. We did not know about the Arabs who had once made up half the city's population or that a mile away there was an ancient Arab neighborhood that had been destroyed in 1948.

Grades Five through Eight and Their Travails

Entering the fifth grade marked the beginning of a more advanced stage in our education. We no longer had a homeroom teacher who taught every subject, but rather specialized teachers, each experts in their subjects: a stern science teacher, an old and distant geography teacher — a new world. That year we also started to learn French: a different alphabet, the Latin one, with unfamiliar syllables. But before I could absorb the French letters and learn how to form my lips to pronounce the French vowels U ($[y]$) or E ($[ø]$), which do not have Hebrew parallels, I had to confront the event that would tear my life in two. That summer my father suffered a heart attack and on the ninth of the Hebrew month of Heshvan, the twenty-third of October, he died. My brother and I were not taken to the funeral, but in the evening we were brought home for the shiva. I got sick. My pediatrician, Dr. Emed, made a house call. Seeing that the family was sitting shiva, he asked who died. When he realized that it was not my mother's father, but mine, he became embarrassed. But what could he have done?

The school year of 1958–59 was the most terrible of my life. I was entrenched in misery and stopped studying, but the teachers ignored the decline in my achievements. I found some comfort in the structured, rigid nature of science classes. The stern *hamore* Shoshan, who was also our vice principal, would approach our fifth-grade classroom on the top floor, and, as a magician carries his mystery box, so did he carry connected glass "communicating vessels" and an alcohol lamp. As soon as the class was quiet, he would stand on the little stage that resembled the French Jesuit podium and show us with his magic wand how the purple-tinted water balanced out in the interconnected vessels, even when they were oddly shaped, and how the ethanol squeezed out of an orange peel makes the blue flame of the alcohol lamp dance.[10] After performing each experiment, he would instruct us to open our notebooks and copy the diagram on the board, and then he would dictate the experiment to us stage by stage. Our hard-covered science notebooks would fill with notes, whose contents accompany us to this day and continue to explain the wonders of the world around us — the rule of gravity, the three states of matter, and the composition of rocks. I loved science classes — the exactitude, the formality, the dignified *hamore* Shoshan, and the respect that he felt toward his work.

Author's graduating class (eighth grade),
principal and vice principal (*top center*)
*Courtesy of Studio Gavra Tel Aviv; photographers
Moshe and Ella Mandil, Photo Studio Talpiot*

Only my French teacher would tell my mother about my failures. She
called on me when she knew I did not know the answers to her questions, and on the dictations, for which I never studied, she would give
me a zero or a two and a half out of ten! In one of her classes I started
humming loudly to disrupt the lesson. To figure out which student was
humming, the teacher ordered five boys, the known troublemakers
of the class, to stand in front of the board and demanded a confession.
Only then did I get up and admit to the crime. The response was swift,
the kind of humiliating punishment that the school inherited from the
French tradition and that this particular fifth-grade French teacher liked.
She "lowered" me two grades, sending me to sit with the third grade for
the remainder of class. I arrived, reprimanded, but fortunately my beloved *hamora* Sara was still teaching third grade. As soon as the French
teacher left the room, Sara smiled her kind smile at me and appointed me
her production assistant. Her third-grade class was once again putting

on a production of *Dirty Ruthie.* I, who had been chased out of French class, became the acting coach for the golden-haired Liki, who was now playing Ruthie. My punishment had been turned upside down. I felt so important.

Thankfully, fifth grade did not last forever. In sixth grade the good-hearted *hamore* Shadmi taught us Hebrew classics and, like most of my teachers in fifth grade, ignored the fact that I did not do the homework. One day in class we read an excerpt from *Motl, the Son of Pessi the Cantor* by Sholem Aleichem in our reader, titled "Lucky me, I'm an Orphan." In the story the child Motl takes advantage of his status as an orphan. At that moment I decided that I would not talk about my father's death anymore. I would try to be like everyone else. Still, at home I continued to make life difficult for my mother, so in seventh grade I was sent to a boarding school in Alonei Yitzhak. I survived there for three months, until Hanukkah. My mother understood that there was no sense in forcing me to stay. But who would accept me in the middle of the school year?

The principal's office at the Alliance School was located at the heart of the building, on the middle floor, near the staircase between the two wings. Thus, from his window the principal could observe the big yard and from his door, which opened onto the entire building, he could easily supervise everything that was taking place in the school. He received my mother and me in his roomy office, where the large book cabinet looked at me with its glass doors and the wide desk stood quietly. Mr. Yungerman did not sit in his chair but rather got up, came to me, and said, "Yes, of course, the Alliance School will take you back. A student like you? Of course! I remember you and I know." Later I found out that Mr. Yungerman had also promised my mother that, although it was a private school, Alliance School would waive my tuition and provide me with books. He took me straight to my class, and so, in the middle of the seventh grade, I returned to Alliance. Mr. Yungerman watched over me then, and even throughout high school. In Israel of the 1960s, high school attendance was not mandatory, and tuition in every high school, including Alliance, was scaled according to the family's income. My mother could not even afford the low sum she was required to pay. If not for the school's support, I would have been forced to stop my studies, and if not for Mr. Yungerman, I may never have reached the university.

Fifty years later Itamar revealed to me that, as a child, he used to visit Mr. Yungerman's house with his parents because his father, Mr. Shashon, was our school's vice principal. Itamar and I made the pilgrimage up the steep slope of Balfour Street, all the way to its highest point, where it crosses Arlozorov Street. At this crossing stands a house also designed by Orell, where dear Mr. Yungerman lived. In the building file of 31 Balfour Street, in the archive of the Haifa History Society, there were a few details about the owner, Asher Yungerman. Born in Poland in 1900, he immigrated to Israel after finishing his studies in 1921 and died in Haifa in 1972. He was married to Flore, the daughter of Yitzhak Nahon, who himself had been the principal of the Alliance School for many years.[11] From the mostly negative school memories of one graduate, Moshe Barak, who studied at the school in the 1930s and 1940s, the image of Mr. Yungerman emerges as a ray of light. Mr. Yungerman did not initially know French, and he was the first Hebrew teacher to become the principal of the Alliance School, according to Barak.[12] Until then, all the principals and most of the teachers had been graduates of the Alliance School system. Yungerman, however, slowly became a central fixture in the school's faculty; he emphasized the study of Hebrew at the very time that the State of Israel was being established and the Hebrew language became dominant.

Although we remained in the same building, the passage from elementary to high school was extremely significant. On the face of it, we only changed floors, from the top floor to the middle, but in fact our lives changed completely. First, more than half of us left the school. My friend Esther, who was the oldest among us and lived with her large family on the Street of Steps, married a rabbi in his thirties. Others spread to professional schools, military academies, or other high schools. Those of us who remained formed a solid kernel of brave Alliance students, united in one class, loyal to the studies of French that made us unique (all the other Israeli schools taught English as the first foreign language). We were also loyal to the strict discipline in academic studies. As I look back, it becomes evident that we were one of the last grades who had the privilege of studying under the wings of the French culture in good old Alliance. Less than a decade after we had graduated, the school was dismantled, the elementary school closed, grades seven to twelve moved to a different place, and the tie to everything that was French was severed.[13]

Pouring the Foundations of Culture

Almost five decades would pass before I would read touching correspondences between the principals of the school and the local and national
authorities, found in deeply buried archival documents. Written under the
duress of war and during times of peace, these letters serve as distant testimonies to the sense of mission felt by the Alliance faculty. On January 21,
1948, principal David Sasson wrote to the Committee for the Community
of Hadar HaCarmel, with a copy to the National Committee for the Community of Israel at Large: "This is the second month that our school building has been occupied by refugees who overran it on the 24th of Kislev. . . .
Following this invasion, our ability to continue our orderly educational
work has been taken from us and much damage has been caused to our
institution and to the hundreds of students who have been evicted from
their classrooms."[14]

At the time Mr. Sasson wrote this letter, the war of 1948 had already
begun and would directly impact not only the school but every aspect of
life in Haifa. The city had already become a battleground. The Jewish minority of the lower city was in danger of death and had fled to the higher
Hadar neighborhood, which was only relatively more secure. The Alliance
School was now a giant shelter, but its principal still complained about
the disturbances to the curriculum. Although his priorities read as strange
today, it is difficult not to admire his attitude toward education as holy
work that must not be interrupted, even when cannons are thundering.
In his letter Mr. Sasson mentions that some of the Alliance students had
gone to study in the Ge'ula School temporarily.

An unexpected source provides a description of the situation from the
point of view of those at Ge'ula who hosted the "evicted" Alliance students. During that period the as-yet-unknown poet Yehuda Amichai was
a teacher in the Ge'ula Elementary School, while his beloved, Ruth, was
living in New York. The poet used to write her three letters a week, and
in them he gave many details about his life and his work as a teacher. In
an aerogram that he sent to Ruth on December 19, 1947, approximately
a month before Mr. Sasson sent his formal letter, Amichai describes the
same situation. Despite his generally tolerant and obedient nature, one
can read between the lines his resentment toward the uninvited guests:

"Half of the Alliance School is at our place." And also "We study in two shifts and the noise and the commotion are great . . . and it's a little difficult to teach." Unlike Mr. Sasson, Amichai did not demand that someone change the situation, accepting reality for what it was.[15]

The situation continued to deteriorate and would have become almost unbearable in the month that passed between Amichai's personal letter and Mr. Sasson's official complaint to the establishment. In fact, by the time Mr. Sasson sent his letter, Amichai himself was no longer at Ge'ula. He had been reassigned to a school in the lower city, where the fighting was thickest.

Twenty years later, against the backdrop of a relatively peaceful Haifa, disagreements of a different nature arose between the principals of Alliance and the "authorities," as reflected in archival documents. The supervisors from the Ministry of Education reprimanded the principals because they believed the Alliance high school curriculum was overloaded. "The number of hours in all the classes . . . is much above the required," writes the supervisor Mordechai Cohen in a letter from October 23, 1968.[16] He suggests to the principal at that time, Bezalel Yofe, "the following reductions": cut one hour per week in "Bible, Hebrew, English, French, and also math for the humanities track." As far as I know, however, the "superfluous" classes continued as before at the Alliance School. The common trait between the correspondences from the 1940s and the 1960s is the devotion of the Alliance leaders to their goal of imparting first-rate education to the students, no matter the conditions and external circumstances.

One of the issues on which the principals insisted was guarding the favored status of French in the Alliance School. In a February 22, 1965, letter to the supervisor from the Ministry of Education about the baccalaureate examination, Mr. Yungerman, now approaching retirement, clarified in his dignified style: "I would like to note that according to my suggestion . . . our students in both the humanities and the math/physics track will be tested in the intensive curriculum in French. I'm speaking of students in both tracks who have studied French for eight years, four of which were in elementary school."[17] The supervisors opposed this demanding requirement and ultimately won the battle, but as long as I studied at this school, and for a few years afterward, Alliance had the upper hand. Thus, even when we were divided into two tracks in the eleventh grade, our class was reunited for one or two sweet hours a day for French classes. My French class was made up of the original Alliance students and even if we did not excel in that language, we belonged there thanks to our studies at the Alliance Elementary School. In fact, when we went on school trips and other activities, we asked to be grouped according to our French classes.

Those integrated French classes were special for another reason. Our French teacher from tenth to twelfth grade was the legendary Charlotte Wardi (pronounced *Vardi*), a woman who seemed old to us then, like all the teachers, but was probably only in her thirties. Her skin was as white as alabaster, her hair as black as a raven. She spoke Hebrew with a strong French accent and confused the "resh" and "het." On her arm a blue number was tattooed. The clacking of her heels sounded from afar as she marched toward the classroom along the corridor, a heavy bookbag under her arm. Madame Wardi hypnotized us and kept us spellbound. When she taught us the sad poem about the toad, "Le Crapaud" by Victor Hugo, she stood in front of her desk and looked out the window. Did Orell, the wise-hearted planner of our school, think of teachers like her when he placed large windows in the classroom, so high up that only the sky would be visible through them? In the colors of her native language, Wardi painted the long European twilight hour, and when we looked, like her, toward the window, we did not see Haifa skies but rather the pinkening horizon against which the children in the poem tortured the poor toad. To ensure our future as erudite, intellectual human beings, educated in the bosom of Western culture, she demanded that we buy two three-ring binders in different colors: one for French grammar, the other for the history of French literature. Like an inexhaustible fountain, she poured the foundations of our education into those three-holed pages: the hierarchy of values in El Cid, the Aristotelian unities, Proust's madeleine. Wardi did not woo us, did not entertain, and did not make us laugh. She taught with unfathomable seriousness, as if her life depended on it, as if our lives depended on it.

When we arrived in twelfth grade, we were privileged to be invited to her home for extra classes — the seven weekly hours in school were not enough to bestow on us the treasures of French literature. And when we traveled, almost each one of us in his time, to the enchanting city of Paris, we followed her footsteps to the Jardin du Luxembourg and Gare du Nord, to the Sorbonne and to the *bouquinistes* (booksellers) on the banks of the Seine. She never spoke about the blue number on her arm, but later we found out that while she was teaching us, she was immersed in writing her doctorate, *Le Juif dans le roman francais: 1933–1948*, about the image of the Jew in the French novel.[18]

We had other unforgettable teachers who wanted to confer on us all the knowledge they had to give. The biology teacher, Mrs. Malka Kolodny, who taught us about the human body and did not rest until we all knew the heart, literally and figuratively. A yellowing supervisor's report on Kolodny from the middle of February 1966 explains, "the methodology of the veteran teacher rouses the students to vigorous participation in the discussion and allows her to bestow a lot of knowledge."[19] Under the heading "Teaching Aids," the report indicates simply "blackboard and map." Yet the supervisor was right; we truly learned a lot. Mr. Yitzhak Ring, who taught the Bible in a whisper, revealed the secrets of the biblical language to those of us who wanted to listen. And there was the math teacher, Dr. Yofe, who we all thought had advanced degrees, although I recently discovered in an archival document that he had only a bachelor's degree. That, however, was entirely unimportant because he solved geometry proofs like a ballet dancer, and when he explained algebra problems, everybody could understand. We were in love with him and afraid of him. Those who came late to class he would put in front of the chalkboard to solve math problems, and when Itamar solved one too easily, he promised him a more difficult one in the next round.

At our graduation party in June 1966, we each recited an excerpt that we studied in French from "The Little Prince" by Antoine Saint-Exupery: Love makes parting painful, and the fox is sad because he has become so attached to the prince. We did not know then that the glory days of the Alliance School in Haifa and the wonder-filled building that both contained and contributed to its undertaking were gradually waning. The striking building, whose steps, balconies, and yards gave us so many hours of joy, was sold to Maccabi Healthcare Services. It became a different place. The corridor balconies that overlooked the sea were walled in, the generous yards became parking lots, and the vegetable patches were paved over. The architect Benjamin Orell was also seemingly forgotten.

Yet there is a man who remembers. Waleed Karkabi, the architect with the soul of an artist who heads the Department of Conservation in the

Haifa Municipality, has much love for the city's architectural legacy. On a walking tour he conducted in Hadar in November 2010, Waleed told the following story: "One day a man about eighty years old comes to my office and says, 'I am Aluf Orell, a professor in the faculty of chemistry in the Technion; I'm the son of Benjamin Orell. My dad was an architect, and he was very active in Haifa. As a child, I remember that my father used to take me to all his projects, and I latched onto him. And my dad did not leave anything, not an archive, no nothing.' And then we started working together to locate all the buildings Benjamin Orell had designed and very quickly found about thirty such structures all over Haifa. It was a moving project. At the end we published a booklet, and we designated almost all Benjamin Orell and Ezekiel Zohar's structures as structures for preservation."[20] Sadly, the declaration of preservation came too late for the building that I loved so much. Only the gate and the entrance steps remain as they were. The building of the Alliance School is preserved mostly in the memory of its students and within these pages.

The Central Synagogue and the Struggle of Its Construction

Unlike the school building that stood across from it, the synagogue still serves the purposes for which it was built: prayer, religious study, and worship. For decades its presence dominated the end of Herzl Street, between Sokolov and Bilu, without competition, the long stone wall at its front dwarfing the buildings on either side. This solid wall has been altered little since it was built, and its top still boasts a symbol-filled engraving, one of the public art projects that flourished in Haifa in the 1950s. The massive, sturdy building demonstrated the power of religion in Haifa and the special status it occupied in the lives of its inhabitants, even throughout the decades during which Haifa was known as a "red" workers' city. The Central Synagogue is imprinted in the Haifaian collective consciousness —its exact location is known to all. Often called "the big synagogue," or "the great synagogue," it floats to the surface in works by those who grew up or lived in Haifa, and the memories of those who worshipped there as children caress it fondly.[21] But when Yoel Hoffmann, Natan Zach, and Yehudit Katzir write about this segment of Herzl Street, they do not glorify it; in fact, the opposite is true. The casual reference to the synagogue in Zach's autobiographical poem hints at the poet's hostile feelings toward the religion that complicated his youth.[22] Yoel Hoffmann relates to the synagogue mainly through the public toilet attached to it, and in the story "Disneyel" Yehudit Katzir's young protagonist does not arrive in that neighborhood until the day her world collapses.[23]

The synagogue was erected on the side of the mountain, on the slope that descends from Gilad Street to Herzl Street, from the south to the north, respectively. Rising tall, the introverted building presents an expansive wall to Herzl Street, although openings and engravings lessen, somewhat, its forbidding massiveness for passersby.[24] Its front is made of stone — a gesture toward its traditional, religious role — but the multitude of square and rectangular windows creates a grid and testifies to the modernist tendencies of its planners. Its lower, more modest, level, whose entrance is on Herzl Street, was named Bet HaMidrash (House of Study) and also functioned as a synagogue, while its upper level, whose entrance is on Gilad Street, is considered the fancy Central Synagogue.

On my daily route to school, I passed the Herzl Street side of the synagogue. My father preferred to pray in the humble Bet HaMidrash on the lower level, so the upper part of the building remained terra incognita for me. I only seldom glimpsed the spacious Gilad Street entrance terrace, the doorway that boasts two stone lions and, between them, the tablets and the giant arches held aloft by columns, full of self-importance. Ya'akov Weiss, who as a teenager frequented the central hall, describes in his memoir the main sanctuary in all its glory:

> [The synagogue was housed in] a large building with two levels that were each administered separately. The top level, accessed from Gilad Street . . . was the fancier of the two. The Holy Ark stood by the eastern wall, eternal candles on either side. . . . On both sides

of the hall, at half height, were two balconies attached to the walls of the synagogue, facing from west to east. This was the women's gallery. The synagogue held about 2,000 male and female worshippers. On Saturdays and holidays, it was full from end to end, and anyone who wanted to find a worthy sitting place was forced to buy it at full price or wake up early for prayer to get an available seat. . . . A *bima* [stage] stood at the heart of the synagogue, and the pits of benches surrounded it in perfect order. In the center of the *bima* was the prayer lectern and behind it, the cantor. . . . In the synagogue a multiparticipant choir was founded. . . . From time to time the synagogue hosted renowned cantors. . . . The lower level was used as both a house of study and a synagogue. Here, too, famous cantors visited. Toward the beginning of the Sabbath or holiday, the street segments on both sides of the synagogue were blocked to traffic.[25]

With the decline of Hadar HaCarmel, the days of the synagogue's greatness passed, and its prayer halls are no longer humming with people. Nevertheless, it is still an impressive structure, at least from the outside. On Herzl Street, to the right of the entrance to the Bet Hamidrash, the city placed a blue information sign in Hebrew and English that attempts to summarize the synagogue's history:

CENTRAL SYNAGOGUE

The construction of the Central Synagogue commenced in 1926 according to plans by Architect Alexander Baerwald on a plot of land donated by the PICA Company. Its first section was dedicated in 1927. The construction of the synagogue progressed in stages due to lack of resources and leaned on collection of levies from the residents. By 1938, only the skeleton of the main hall was completed. The building's finishing work and exterior design were completed only in 1955 with the support of the Ministry of Religion according to architectural plans prepared by Architects Al Mansfeld and Munio Weinraub (Gitai). The building served for many years as the main synagogue of Hadar Hacarmel and Haifa.[26]

This short sign merely hints at the travails that plagued the synagogue's construction, which unfolded over thirty years. The first architect who designed it died prematurely in 1930. The second won the 1936 competition for its design, but his plan was never implemented. Finally, the partnership between the pair of architects, into whose hands it was entrusted in the 1940s, fell apart before the building was completely finished. The sign makes no mention of the political struggles that hindered the progress of the construction.

According to the appointed documentarian of the Committee for Hadar HaCarmel, Hayim Aharonovitch, on April 21, 1927, a parade of men carrying Torah scrolls marched from the Technion to the consecration of the Central Synagogue; this was after three years of preparation and one year of construction. Aharonovitch also notes that the intention was to build a spacious house of prayer that would contain about a thousand worshippers. For the purpose of its construction, a special tax was collected from all the inhabitants of Hadar HaCarmel.[27] The photograph of the first floor of the building (built in the 1920s) that appears in Aharonovitch's book does not name the architect, but there are sources that support the blue municipal sign's assertion that Baerwald was its initial planner. Yet the existing lists of buildings by Baerwald do not include the synagogue.[28] In any event, the desire to attribute the building to Baerwald is understandable. He was admired, the first Zionist architect who imprinted his signature style on the city and designed the historical Technion building on the then bare northern slope of the Carmel in 1912. The fact is that in 1930, the last year of his life, Baerwald did indeed create an original, elaborate design for the synagogue, but though his plan survived, it never came to be.

As soon as its first section was completed in 1927, the synagogue was continuously in use as a house of prayer; nevertheless, for the next decade additional construction was halted due to lack of funds. In 1936, the same year that the Alliance School was inaugurated ten months after its construction began, a design competition was announced for the completion and expansion of the synagogue.[29] The architect Max Loeb won first place with an ambitious and expensive plan that combined grandeur with simplicity, but this design, too, was never implemented.[30] In the spring of 1938 Solel Boneh erected the skeleton of the central hall on exposed columns over the existing bottom floor of the synagogue.[31] For the holiday season of that year, the directorship of the synagogue announced in the religious newspaper *HaTzofe* that there were 1,100 seats for sale in the synagogue.[32] Nevertheless, the work stalled again and the building stood in its unfinished state.[33] Because of the constant stoppages, in 1940 the municipality threatened to cancel the synagogue's building permit if the front was not fixed and other vital improvements to the structure made.[34] Consequently, in the midst of World War II, a new committee was created: the Committee for Clarification of the Matter of the Central Synagogue. This committee met at the beginning of 1943 and decided to shelve Loeb's design and instead adjust the existing structure to fit Baerwald's original plans, which had been transferred to the Committee for Hadar HaCarmel by the executors of his estate.[35]

The committee agreed that the architect Yohanan Ratner, a member of the Technical Building Committee, would be responsible for ensuring that the work would be "executed in the spirit of Baerwald."[36] Indeed, Ratner was Baerwald's heir at the Technion and worked in the latter's office before he died, but in the end that did not matter. The sad fact is that Baerwald's 1930 design for the synagogue, for all its beauty and splendor, remained a sketch in the Technion library.[37] Yet some comfort can be derived from the remnants of his spirit in the current synagogue building. Like the Technion, its façade is covered with smooth-hewn stones, even though at the time of its construction, the cheaper concrete and cement were the favored materials. Additionally, the Byzantine-style main entrance, with its three arches and a few small, arched windows, echo Baerwald's sensibility. Baerwald's signature pointy stone arches, however, did not survive. Ratner and the Technical Building Committee ultimately entrusted Mansfeld and the Bauhaus graduate Weinraub with the building in 1946, and they clearly pursued their modernist agenda, albeit while nodding to their revered predecessor.[38]

The financial difficulties continued in the late 1940s, in part because the representatives of the workers in the Committee for the Community opposed aiding the completion of the synagogue.[39] An elaborate correspondence found in the Haifa City Archives documents the treacherous road that the building of the synagogue traveled before it was completed. In February 1948, during the war, when there was shooting on the streets and snipers would target pedestrians, there was not yet a sidewalk on the side of the synagogue facing Herzl Street. The representative of the synagogue demanded that the municipality pave a sidewalk for people to walk

The Central
Synagogue on
Herzl Street
*Courtesy of Haifa
City Archives*

on the side of the road — not the middle of the street — so they could "avoid being hit by bullets." But even after the war ended and six years of relative calm ensued, the building had still not been completed. Contrary to the record on the aforementioned sign, work on the synagogue extended well beyond 1955. In the spring of 1955 the leadership of the synagogue asked the mayor for funds to finish plastering and flooring the Bet Midrash. Furthermore, we can conclude that the building was still unfinished in the summer of that year, because that was when the architecture firm demanded additional payment from the city engineer for finishing work. In 1956–57 the façade was prepared and a mural was engraved on it. Concurrently, the city approved the artist Perli Peltzig to decorate the inner wall of the Holy Ark. At the end of 1958 an agreement was signed with an acoustic engineer. In 1959 the architects Weinraub and Mansfeld split bitterly, and this caused more delays. To the great frustration of the synagogue leadership, even in 1964 some issues remained unresolved as the synagogue continued to serve its congregation.[40]

In their dismay, the community leaders wrote, "It is more than six years since the city of Haifa stopped the work of completing the building, and it stands today in an unfinished state in many vital aspects." As they continued, they invoked the dead: "It is clear that the intention of Baron Rothschild, the renowned benefactor, may he rest in peace, when he contributed the lot for the synagogue, was not for the secular use of

warehouses and workshops on the premises."[41] In other words, PICA donated the lot to the synagogue in the 1920s, and at the time of the writing
of this complaint in October 1964, not only was the building incomplete,
but parts of it were being appropriated by the secular city hall. The writers
were also aware of the changes that had taken place in the composition of
the neighborhood's population: the well-to-do had moved to the Carmel,
and the present community of worshippers was composed of workers and
small businessmen. It seems, then, that before the building had fully realized the vision of its founders, its leaders understood that it was already
serving a less affluent population than the one for which it was built, a
population that would not be able to support its maintenance. But the extent of the decline of the synagogue building and of the entire neighborhood was not clearly noticeable until two or three decades later.

Shattered Dreams and Prayers

Indeed, one could already see signs of deterioration when Yehudit Katzir
published her first story, "Disneyel," in 1988. She even uses the familiar
marker "Herzl Street . . . a little bit after the big synagogue" to foreshadow
the end of the age of innocence and bliss in her heroine's life.[42] This heroine, the fictional double of the writer, is a girl around the age of ten. In
her twenties, she relives the story of her coming-of-age and her family's
demise, retelling it to her dying mother. The story, which alternates between past and present, the early 1970s and the mid-80s, interweaves the
mother's doomed love affair with the girl's maturation. The city's history
and landscape suffuse the narrative: on the one hand, the green Carmel
and the blue seashore radiate the glow of the mother's infatuation with
her lover, Michael, and the daughter's enamoredness of him and of her
mother. On the other hand, her arrival with her mother in the synagogue's
vicinity, described in the middle of the story, marks the last station of a
journey that culminates in catastrophe.

Ever since the narrator was four years old, she and her mother had glee-
fully performed a ritual, of sorts, preparing for the visits of the attractive
but unreliable man who burst into their lives every April and August. As
described in chapter 2, they would set off on a route from the center of
the Carmel to the intersection of Herzl and Balfour Streets in Hadar, to

acquire the necessary treasures for welcoming their guest. Michael's final visit, however, deviates from his regular schedule, and occurs in the midst of a rainy, stormy winter. The joyous, sunny romp of mother and daughter through the streets of Hadar becomes a nightmarish obstacle course that leads to the ruin of those who run it. In this violated preparation ritual, both of the girl's favorite stops — the children's clothing store and the ice cream at Café Atara — are omitted from the route. The mother and daughter run hand in hand along the rainy Herzl Street while the red, yellow, and green traffic lights reflect off the pavement. It takes the pair a quarter of an hour to run from the Herzl/Balfour intersection all the way past the Central Synagogue at the opposite end of Herzl Street, where there is the "dark little" linen store belonging to a family friend.[43] The fact that the girl knows the store owner is meaningless because a curse already lies over this end of Herzl Street, and even this friendly acquaintance now looks like a different person. This last station of the journey, the one that had never before been part of the mother-daughter-preparing-for-Michael ritual, presages the catastrophe, and it is none other than the area of the Central Synagogue. Only when the dreams are about to be shattered is the synagogue's vicinity at the end of Herzl Street introduced into the story.

Is it that, subconsciously, Yehudit Katzir, the daughter of Haifa, sensed the looming disintegration of Hadar? Even if not, choosing the area of the synagogue as the final stop in the tragic journey of "Disneyel" augurs the decline of the city or, at least, of the neighborhood.

In the late 1950s and 1960s, the years that I lived in that neighborhood and studied at the Alliance School, it was hard to foresee Hadar's sad fate. Then, it seemed as though Herzl Street and its businesses would always flourish and that the synagogue would stand firm as the center of Jewish religious life in Haifa for eternity. But in that period of apparent local stability, cracks formed in my personal connection with the synagogue or, rather, with the Bet HaMidrash section of it. My father, who frequented the synagogue on Shabbat and major holidays, would often take me there. The prayer hall that I remember was much more modest than the upper hall described by Ya'akov Weiss. Behind a lace curtain, along the wall, sat one or two rows of women. My mother rarely came to the synagogue, so ever since I was a little girl, I sat with my father in the men's prayer hall. Long, wooden benches stood on both sides of a raised *bima* that faced the Holy Ark, on which the rabbi and other community leaders would stand. My father's regular seat was on the left side, facing the ark, approximately in the middle of the tenth row. We sat with my father's friends; they were all very amiable to the little daughter, and their pockets were always filled with candy. I did not listen to the prayers, but I felt that I belonged to that place, where my father and the other worshippers, wrapped in prayer shawls, got up and sat down, swaying back and forth while they quickly mumbled endless sentences in which I sometimes caught a familiar word. Periodically, the Torah scrolls, in red velvet dresses, were taken out of the Holy Ark.

On Yom Kippur I sat with him and was entertained when he and his friends passed a small snuffbox from hand to hand, asking one another, "*ah shmek tabek?*" and sniffing tobacco. A couple of times a day I would sprint home to my mother to say that my father, who was fasting, was holding up okay, and then back again to the warm bosom of the synagogue.

After Yom Kippur, on the sidewalk in front of the big synagogue, long tables, with many etrogim *(citrons) and* lulavim *(palm fronds). And I'm with him, smelling the* etrogim *and examining them until we find the one perfect* etrog. *Many men stand all around, and there is the buzz of the excitement before the holiday. Then every morning of the Sukkot holiday, at home in the living room, picking up the* lulav. *With small hands, I hug the dried, woven palm leaf that wraps the* lulav, *the willow, and the myrtle. The other hand, carefully and with awe, cradles the* etrog, *its scent increasing from day to day. One after the other, my father, my mother, myself, and my little brother repeat the words of the blessing. The dining table is behind us, the bookcases in front of us. Facing east. Afterward he goes to the store. But the* lulav *is at home, the feeling of holiday, and the dry palm leaf hugging our small family, all of us unaware that we'll be together only a short while longer.*

As a Levi, my father frequently had the privilege of carrying the Torah scrolls, and on the holiday of Simhat Torah he received a scroll early, in the second of the seven rounds at the Bet HaMidrash. *I am sitting on his shoulders, proudly, circling this entire space full of men, holding the illustrated paper flag with the Holy Ark and paper doors that opened out from its middle.*

And my father goes up to the bima *and kisses the Torah with the corner of his prayer shawl.* Only the washing of the hands disturbed my joy. According to custom, the Levis pour water on the hands of the priests before the priests bless the community. My father would fill up the big copper mug that hung over the sink at the entrance to the synagogue and pour water on the hands of others. *Why do you have to wash their hands?* I got angry. As an adult, I found comfort when I read that "a priest who wants to raise his hands in blessing needs to add holiness to his holiness from the hand of one who is holy. And that is the Levi." My father the Levi gave of his holiness to the priest on whose hands he poured water. *My father is a Levi, and there is nobody more important than him in the world. Dressed in a Shabbat suit and wearing a hat, he goes to the synagogue and then wraps himself with a prayer shawl like a cloak; the embroidered forehead piece on it sparkles, and I'm next to him, dancing, laughing, happy.*

But the synagogue changed its skin overnight when my father died. In Israel of the 1950s, only a male could say the prayer of the Mourner's Kaddish. My mother, who was well versed in religious law, and likely assumed that my father would have wanted it, required my seven-year-old brother to say the Mourner's Kaddish.[44] Since she now had to work at the store, the chore of bringing my brother to the synagogue fell on me. My brother cried, refused, and squirmed while I exhausted all the methods of inducement that I knew, including doing his second-grade homework. Every day in the afternoon I dragged my brother by his arm to the synagogue for the afternoon prayer. To sooth his fears, I wanted to accompany him into the warm hall where I had spent so many Sabbath mornings. But then the "worshippers" revealed their true faces. "You're not allowed to enter," they scolded. "You're a woman." I was ten. They instructed me to wait at the entrance to the Bet HaMidrash. The copper mug was hanging over the sink, and there were no priests wrapped in prayer shawls and no Levis to protect us. After a short time, perhaps also due to the protestations of the second-grade teacher who had identified my handwriting in his notebooks, my brother stopped saying the Kaddish, and I was no longer forced to bring him to the synagogue.

I did not enter that prayer hall for decades. But when I saw a photograph of that place in its deterioration, its walls crumbling, its benches empty, its floor filthy, and its Holy Ark pathetic, I was not sorry. In my last visit to the city, the construction workers allowed me to enter. A few men were praying or studying, but the construction workers did not care that I was a woman. They were busy with the renovation and redivision of the great space that had once purred and sang.

To this day, I avoid going to synagogues that segregate women and men, and I do not utter the words of the Kaddish. These words dwell forever next to the long sink at the entrance room to the synagogue that rejected me in the autumn of 1958.

And, behold, the words of the Kaddish spring up at the margins of the Central Synagogue for Yoel Hoffmann as well. The protagonist of his Haifaian novel, *Ephraim*, abandoned his wife and moved from Tel Aviv to Haifa in December 1999, staying in the house of his friend in the center of the Carmel. The narrator reports on the wanderings of his protagonist with maximum realism and describes how on one winter day in the beginning of the year 2000 Ephraim descends to Hadar HaCarmel. There, his feet take him to the end of Herzl Street and to the synagogue building, but not for prayer: "When he arrives at the big synagogue / at the end of Herzl Street, he enters the public / toilet there."[45] Given this detail, there is no doubt that Hoffmann is familiar with Hadar HaCarmel, not solely the upper Carmel neighborhoods. Indeed, in the middle of the narrow staircase that connects the lower level of the synagogue to the upper, a side door opens on the left to a public toilet. The protagonist, who, like his creator, knows the remote corners of the neighborhood, arrives at the end of Herzl Street and uses the building that was designated for holiness for the most corporeal of business. For Hoffmann, in the year 2000, then, the Central Synagogue building is reduced to fulfilling bodily, not spiritual, needs.

After he goes to the bathroom, Ephraim "remembers a café that he once saw / on Nordau Street," not far from the synagogue.[46] But when he arrives there, he discovers that "the café had become an Italian restaurant, and, in the meantime, the sun stands at its zenith *yitgadal veyitkadash shme raba* [may His great name grow exalted and sanctified]."[47] Quoting the first words of the Kaddish prayer for the dead in this context demands an explanation. Is it because, following the visit to the synagogue building, Ephraim thought of a deceased relative for whom he had once said Kaddish? Or perhaps the "dead" he mourns is his marriage, which has ended? Or does he say Kaddish for the deteriorating Hadar HaCarmel? For the neglected synagogue? For the Viennese café that has disappeared? And who is the narrator? Is there a shade of sarcasm in his invocation of the Kaddish opening words that glorify the creator? Or do those exaltations sincerely express Ephraim's awe of nature and the sun that stands at its zenith? Or perhaps the entire paragraph is propelled not by the meaning of words but by the music of the language, the sounds that drive all of Hoffmann's work. It may be that the consonants *sh* and *m*, that repeat in *bet shimush, shemesh, shme* (toilet, sun, name), motivate the text.

The riddles that Hoffmann's work presents are many. In *Ephraim*, however, the details of concrete Haifaian reality are intertwined with lyrical writing that ties the text to a specific time and place, while sensitively following the fluctuations of the consciousness. The Central Synagogue and the public toilet, the end of Herzl Street and the lost café, touch the chords of the conflicted soul of the protagonist, and the sad urban landscape is another mirror of that soul.

The Chariot of Israel and Its Horsemen

In the good old days, when the Central Synagogue was still humming with worshippers, and its shapely neighbor, the Alliance School, still stood across from it, one could draw an imaginary line from the synagogue over Herzl Street directly into the high windows of Alliance's classrooms. When the front wall of the synagogue was cleaned, a tremendous roar of splashing water would interrupt our lessons and cause a "holiday" on the top floor of the school. Despite the strict discipline of our homeroom teacher at the time, we, the students of the seventh and eighth grades, dared stand up for a minute and observe the performance that was seemingly meant just for us: secured by ropes at the head of cranes or tall ladders, city workers would clean the synagogue's façade as it looked at us from across the street. A mighty stream of water meticulously rinsed the picture engraved on it: a procession, full of vitality. At its head is Elijah, blowing the shofar, draped in a royal cloak, riding a chariot whose horses soar upward toward

Model for the wall relief of the Central Synagogue, by Israel Rubinstein
Courtesy of Haifa City Archives

heaven. The symbols of the tribes of Israel are at their feet and following them is an impressive procession of many people on foot carrying the
seven-pronged menorah, the symbol of the State of Israel. I was fond of
the picture: reliable, fixed in its place, kissing the sky. All I had to do was
glance at it to know that it would always be there. Works of art were rare
in my immediate surroundings, and the engraving that I saw every day on
the way to school won a special place in my heart. I did not know then who
created the engraving, and I also did not realize its meaning, but it always
infused me with a sort of celebratory optimism.

Almost fifty years passed before I wondered about the work of the forgotten artist, Israel Rubinstein, who carved it after he won the job that was
posted jointly by the Haifa municipality and the Ministry of Religion. In
the fancy photo album that the city of Haifa produced in 2012, *Public Art
in Haifa*, the image appears among dozens of works that were captured
by the eye of Zvi Roger, the photographer of the city. In the table of contents and at the head of the short text dedicated to this piece, the book
states, "Unknown Artist" and "Unknown Date." The name of Rubinstein
is brought up as a "supposition . . . because the letter 'R' appears on the left,
bottom corner."[48] A thorough search in the Haifa City Archives brought
up the file and, in it, the adventures of the engraving's creation and the
conflicts that surrounded it. The work's history is chronicled in the newspapers' announcement of the posting, in the summaries of the Judgment
Committee's meetings, and in various correspondences. It turns out that I

was not wrong in my understanding of the message encoded in this work. The euphoria it radiated was deliberate, almost dictated.

In fact, according to the art critic Gideon Ofrat, the collective optimism and the sense of "we" that dominated the early years after the establishment of the State of Israel in 1948 were expressed in contemporaneous Israeli art.[49] Public art, which often combines populism, figurativism, and didactic elements, fits these communal sensibilities. Before 1948 public art had mainly been the domain of kibbutzim dining halls, but afterward it became the ideal in cities as well. In the 1950s and 1960s, public art blossomed in Israel generally, and it is not a coincidence that "red" Haifa, so-called for its high number of workers and the dominance of the leftist Labor Party there, was at the center of this enterprise. Mosaic walls, engravings, and ceramics appeared in its public buildings, underpasses, the Carmelit underground stations, and the new Technion, which was slowly being built outside of Hadar.[50] The interest in displaying an artistic work on the façade of the Central Synagogue was thus consistent with the prevailing atmosphere. Yet combining highly figurative mural art with the Jewish religion and its commandment, "You shall not make for yourself a sculptured image," presented a challenge. According to this commandment in Jewish law, it is traditionally forbidden to sculpt the form of a person in any material, as sculpting a person was reminiscent of idol worship.

From the wording of the city announcement in the newspapers on January 18, 1955, it is clear that any work deemed worthy of being engraved on the Central Synagogue would have to reflect both the national feeling and Jewish tradition: "It is recommended that the engraving should express — according to the ideas of the artist and with consideration of the demands of Jewish law — the changes in the life of the nation in our generation, the generation of the War of Liberation, the rebirth of the State, and the gathering of the exiles."[51] Rubinstein won the competition.[52] Yet there was pressure on him to change or rather, "Judaize" his design. He was asked to attend a meeting of the Judgment Committee on December 14 of that year. There the representative of the rabbinate, Mr. Bialer, demanded that he create a "quintessential Jewish expression" of Elijah, one that is not "of the gentiles." He specified that the artist had to grant Elijah a shofar, add a cover to his head, and shape his beard so that it did not look like an ancient Egyptian beard. Bialer also demanded that Rubinstein make the depiction

of the snake more abstract ("the usage of scales is absolutely forbidden").
Even though it is the symbol of the tribe of Dan, the snake is also associated with evil.

Surprisingly, Bialer did agree to include the "human figures" that the
artist suggested, even though they are "distant from Judaism." His rationale was based on a specific monument dedicated to the ghettos' fighters,
in which human figures were an "expression of the 'New Jew.'" Even so,
he emphasized that "the artist must find a way to blur the body parts."[53]
Despite his protests, Rubinstein ultimately surrendered to most of these
conditions, submitted a compromise sketch (without extra payment), and
was allowed to undertake the engraving. And, indeed, the final product is
quite different from many works of the same genre that sprung up during
that period, many of which were in bas-relief, reminiscent of sculptures.
The lines of the synagogue's engravings contain more abstract elements,
and its content is unique in the extent to which it relates to the Jewish
tradition.

From the heights of the Central Synagogue, the redemption procession still looks out today, after finding favor in the eyes of both religious
representatives and artists alike. It is led by a Jewish Elijah, head covered, wrapped in a cloak, and blowing the shofar, his chariot harnessed
to horses galloping toward the heavens. Behind him marches a crowded
group of figures with blurred body parts, carrying the seven-pronged menorah on their shoulders. When one examines a close-up photograph of
the engraving, one discovers the gender of the figures: those marching at
the head of the procession are women, one of whom is pregnant, while
the men are behind. The idea of equality between the sexes implied by the
image fits the vision of socialist Haifa more than Jewish tradition, but for
now, in the 1950s, that ideological tension was suppressed. In the symbols
of the tribes at the feet of the chariot and the shofar-blower, the snake is
combined with the final *nun* (נ) letter of the tribe of Dan. The prominence
of the symbol of the tribe of Zebulun hints at the Haifaism of the building
— its sailboat on the waves is very similar to the symbol of the city (which
Rubinstein had carved into city hall a decade earlier). Rubinstein, who
specialized in wall engravings and was one of a group of artists from whom
the mayor ordered works, succeeded in pleasing both his masters (the socialist city hall and the Orthodox rabbinate) and satisfying the contradic-

tory demands of the assignment. In Israel of the twenty-first century, such a figurative and egalitarian engraving might not have won first place for decorating the Central Synagogue in the city.

My memory separates the engraving from the synagogue that turned its back on me. Its tidings of deliverance are associated in my mind mainly with the view from the classroom window of my beloved school. Something of the contrast that I felt between the meaning of the synagogue and that of the school is echoed in an epic poem by Natan Zach, whose story begins at the same urban site. The Central Synagogue evokes, for Zach, powerful memories that gradually branch out into other locations in Haifa and into the poet's tortured childhood and youth there.

A Flicker of Hope "In the Fields of Then Perhaps"

Zach's poem "Bisdot az ulay" ("in the fields of then perhaps" or "then maybe") is a long, confessional, autobiographical poem that was written in Haifa in 1988 but was not published in a book until 1996. In this poem the area of the Central Synagogue is dubbed "the beginning" of Herzl Street, although the synagogue is closer to its end. Everyone in Haifa knows that Herzl begins in the west of Hadar and ends in the east. This misnomer, therefore, is not coincidental. It may be that the formative life events that unfurl in the poem endow the arena where they occurred with the status of "beginning," but it may also suggest that the speaker should not be considered reliable. Regardless, according to the awkward word combination "then perhaps" that appears in the title and as a refrain throughout the poem, the events told took place in a twilight zone, of sorts. These are the fields of slippery memory, where there is no absolute truth and no attempt to be precise regarding time or plot. The realm of the poem belongs to the "then," to "long-gone days," and to the iffy domain of "perhaps." And so, before the speaker turns to his ninety-three-line long confession, he prefaces it with a short apology or caveat:

> These are long-gone days so don't ask me
> For an exact account in the fields of then maybe
> I remember that it was by the Great Synagogue
> At the beginning of Herzl Street on a parallel street[54]

But even this opening contains an inner contradiction, for its lines
describe exactly where the events happened. Moreover, despite the dis-
claimers he makes throughout the poem, the speaker shows that he
is well versed in exact details from "then"—his studies in the Hugim
School, the defense balloons that the British flew in the skies of Haifa
during World War II—as well as those from a later period. The urban
topography is seared into his consciousness: on Herzl Street, next to the
"Great Synagogue," and on its "parallel street," young Zach had to come
of age, rejected from all sides. There he walked around, a thirteen-year-
old lovesick boy, memorizing the home address of his first, unrequited
love, Elisheva, the brown-haired daughter of the *yekke* dentist who used
to live next to the synagogue.[55] After a long absence, he returns to the
urban corner that derives its present-day meaning from the significance
it had decades earlier: the synagogue, Herzl Street, and "a parallel street /
[where] a young love lived." The "parallel street" is Gilad Street, the upper
southern border of the synagogue. It is evident that the speaker knows
the area, not only as it was in his youth but also a quarter of a century
later. Like a patient who tries to lead his doctor to the exact spot where he
feels pain, the poem's speaker strives to reveal to the reader the exact location of his desperate love: "a bit lower on Herzl / where furniture stores
opened twenty years later."[56] For readers to be able to identify the spot of
the pain with certainty, they must be able to orient themselves in Haifa,
and for that purpose the speaker draws a street map of the city in words.
But the synagogue building is not mentioned here as a mere geographic
landmark.

As he continues, Zach recounts how the pretty girl visited his house
when he pretended to be sick. He poured out his heart to her, but she
rejected his love. "This is how I learned / to lie the hard way" he confesses.
And, behold, through the screen of the "then maybe" that blurs the borders between lie and truth, one big lie young Zach told is exposed: "and
I raged and I even told some lie regarding religion then perhaps."[57] Zach,
the son of an Italian Christian woman and a Jewish man, immigrated to
Palestine with his parents to escape the Nazis when he was six years old.
Early in his life, he knew that he was different from others because of his
religion, his roots, and the languages in his mouth. And regarding religion,
he probably lied not only to the chestnut-haired girl but also to others.

The area of the Central Synagogue, then, is a dangerous and threatening place for him. It is the juncture of the house of the beloved who rejected him and the building that represents the religion that does not recognize him. This personal intersection may be behind the fact that, in the first lines of the poem, the speaker "errs" and calls the area "the beginning" of the street and not its end. The synagogue's vicinity holds within it the trauma of being different, rejected, someone who will never be loved. It symbolizes the continuous pain to which the adult poet Zach returns almost obsessively: alienation and isolation.

The "fields of then perhaps" are indeed portrayed in the poem as dark fields in which the speaker loses his way, while the Central Synagogue and the beloved girl, two of the dominant forces in those fields, withhold their light from him. But even in those somber fields, "a kindly ray of gold," as the poet Hayim Nahman Bialik says, emerges.[58] In the sixth line of the poem, after the synagogue and the desperate love, the following details appear: "I was studying at Hugim then / with Kurzweil and Eliahu and Naomi the biology teacher." Zach relates, in short, the names of his school and his teachers. He then turns for the next twenty-seven lines to his disappointments, the difficulties of the time, and the horrors of his family life. But then one school figure reappears:

> And Kurzweil was a German-speaking Moravian so maybe I
>   didn't exactly
> Understand the difference and he painted me an aquarelle and
>   showed me, foreigner that I was, and this
> Helped me some, not much, years before he became religious
>   and later
> Committed suicide and actually he couldn't even
> Help himself, my teacher, my teacher![59]

For Zach, the antidote to the synagogue is the school, and especially Baruch Kurzweil, one of its legendary teachers, who tried to give him a helping hand. In contrast to the dark area of the synagogue and other places where the speaker felt foreign and unwanted stands the bright Hugim School, with Kurzweil, who taught literature there, at its center. The school and two other teachers are mentioned briefly, but six lines are dedicated to the towering figure of Kurzweil, among them a twelve-word line, the longest in the entire poem. Translated, it reads: "Understand the difference and he painted me an aquarelle and showed me, foreigner that I was, and this." Kurzweil is a ray of light that penetrated the darkness of "the fields of then perhaps." The teacher could not fix all his student's problems, and yet the aquarelle (water color) that he painted for the rejected boy lessened his suffering and loneliness, perhaps to a greater extent than the pupil was aware of at the time. In an article Zach wrote twenty years before he composed this poem, he described this episode: "I remember that he showed me one evening, in his house, the aquarelles of Haifa's landscape, which he had painted with so much love, and I congratulated myself in my heart that I had received a great honor. I ran the whole way home that evening."[60] Kurzweil, then, noticed the qualities of his unusual pupil, and with his gift caused him to feel chosen and favored. Moreover, Zach's "foreignness," the cross he bore on his shoulders, so to speak, was irrelevant for the teacher and, apparently, also for the school as a whole.

The poem also recounts the death of the generous teacher, who committed suicide because "he couldn't even / Help himself." The segment that is dedicated to Kurzweil in the poem ends with a dramatic outburst that echoes the rise of Elijah to the heavens: "and later / [he] Committed suicide ... / my teacher, my teacher!" Like Elisha, the disciple who saw the disappearance of Elijah, his beloved teacher, and cried out, "my father, my father! The chariot of Israel and its horsemen!" so too did Zach call out to Kurzweil in a poem published about fifty years after he was his pupil: "my teacher, my teacher!" It is important to note here that the poem in its entirety is written in a stream-of-consciousness technique, seemingly free associations from the writer's past. The structure of the poem and its style are also "free": the division of stanzas and lines is not uniform and seems random, and a few scattered punctuation marks—periods and commas alone—emerge sporadically. The exception to this minimalist punctuation is the sole exclamation point that accompanies the cry "my teacher, my teacher!" There is no doubt that this punctuation mark is deliberate, especially when speaking of a superior poet like Zach. Although the poet's gesture to his teacher is understated, one ought not mistake its forcefulness.

In the 1967 article that Zach wrote when Kurzweil turned sixty, the former pupil thanked his teacher for his kindness of heart. In it, Zach revives

British Mandatory Haifa of "then" as well as the Hugim School, with its advantages and disadvantages. In addition to Kurzweil, there were others at Hugim who were kind to the young Zach, like the teacher Meir, whose last name Zach admits to forgetting but whose "gentleness of soul and hidden affection" he remembers. These teachers, who granted the boy the love and respect that he so sorely missed because of his lonely, violent family life, served as a balance to the traumas, whether they were experienced in connection with the Central Synagogue or not. The article ends with the last time Zach met Kurzweil in Haifa. They coincidentally ran into each other on the corner of Arlozorov and Balfour Streets, not far from where the Hugim School was located in those days. The boy could not reveal to his teacher that his family was moving to Tel Aviv, but Kurzweil, in his sensitivity, noticed his pupil's despair and, as quoted in the article, tried for the last time to lift his spirit: "you can come to me any time you want."[61]

As it was for Zach, school was a shelter for me, and some of its representatives and teachers were heralds from a higher, benevolent authority. On the corner of Arlozorov and Balfour, the place of Kurzweil and Zach's last conversation, 31 Balfour Street still stands. This was where Mr. Yungerman, the principal of the Alliance School, used to live — the man who shone his light over me about twenty years after the events related by Zach took place. It was Zach's good fortune that, in the article he wrote in his honor, he managed to thank his teacher while he was still alive. I never got to thank Mr. Yungerman. Let this chapter be a belated attempt to praise him.

The corner of Arlozorov and Balfour is found on the ascent of the mountain, where steep Balfour Street reaches its climax and its end and kisses Arlozorov, which continues winding on its way to the ridge. One can stand there and look out at the blue of the bay. One can also quote the last lines from Zach's Haifaian poem, lighting a candle, of sorts, for the souls of the good-hearted teachers who tried to sweeten the lives of their students and sometimes even succeeded in changing their fates:

maybe there will come a time when
Some little flicker of hope from the fields of then maybe arrives
    and ignites some little light
To illuminate the dark I don't know when.[62]

5

CONQUERING THE SLOPE
Building and Writing the Mountain

On September 1, 1954, the first day of the school year, which was also my first day in first grade, we moved to the other end of Hadar HaCarmel. We were now farther from the colonial city hall and Memorial Park, as well as from the historical Technion and its garden. But we were closer to the central landmark of our family life — my father's store. It was located on the ground floor of the rounded Bet Talpiot building, which observed the point where the horizontal Herzl Street bids farewell to Arlozorov, as it branches off and climbs diagonally toward the top of the mountain. Our new home, 85 Herzl Street, stood higher on the slope than our old house and was only a little over a mile southeast of it. Nevertheless, it felt as if we had come to an entirely different neighborhood.

Looking back, I think my parents must have had a special affection for intersections. Attached to Bet Talpiot, where they bought the store in 1952, was the stylized passage that crossed the two main horizontal streets of Hadar HaCarmel: the parallel Herzl and HeHalutz Streets. Similarly, the apartment building to which they decided to move in 1954 stood at the crux of a T-shaped intersection that served me faithfully for my entire childhood and youth. The short arms of that 'T' spread in either direction along Herzl Street. Usually, I would turn right (westward) upon leaving the house: every morning from third grade until I graduated high school, I would walk scarcely three minutes to the Alliance School and sometimes continue on to the store. Occasionally, I would turn left, eastward, to the pharmacy, where we bought chamomile tea, whose smell I cannot bear to this day. Farther east lay the Lysol-drenched Barzilai Clinic, which we visited when we were sick. Continuing in the same direction, we would arrive at the Rushmia Bridge on the way to Neve Sha'anan, whose green slopes we could see from our terrace. But we hardly ever wandered that far.

The central arm of our "T" was Bar Kokhba Street. From the day we arrived in our new house until the day I left Haifa, again and again I would conquer the mountain with my feet, beginning with that street. Bar Kokhba emerged directly across from the house on 85 Herzl, climbed up the mountain, and formed my constant link to the heights of the Carmel. I used to cross Herzl Street, leaving behind the trees planted on its sides, the store windows, and buses and walk straight ahead up the hill.

On my way to first and second grade at the Ge'ula School or, later, to the Scouts, which met there, I would walk past Yavne, the religious school for boys; peek into the store of the kind shoemaker; breathe in the scents that wafted from the neighboring pastry shop; then cross a small side street and continue to the end of Bar Kokhba, where it is cut off by Hermon Street. At that corner sat a nursery school, its small yard filled with swings and slides. About seven years before I arrived in that neighborhood, Ye-huda Amichai rented a room on the nearby Gilad Street.[1] This was long before he was known to the country and the world as a great poet. In the morning, on his way to teach at the Ge'ula School, he would pass this toy-filled yard, and in the evenings he would describe it in the letters that he wrote to his beloved Ruth in New York. From that corner Amichai would continue his ascent up the steep Betar Street, which leads directly to the Ge'ula School, just as I did. After glancing at the nursery, I would walk along the western sidewalk of Betar, almost touching the thick hedgerow, the living fence that accompanied the upper part of the street. I would try to peek through and see the mysterious house hidden behind it, until I arrived at the horizontal HaShiloah Street.

At the corner of Betar and HaShiloah stood two modern buildings, which hugged the slope, and a lush public garden that cuddled it. The two buildings were erected in the late 1930s and were the first public buildings in the Ge'ula neighborhood, albeit very different from each other. The former Magen David Adom Trauma Center curved humbly along the turn of the street, while the Ge'ula School rose sharply across from it on the rocky ground between the parallel HaShiloah and Bezalel Streets.[2] Surrounded by a large yard, the Ge'ula School dominated the intersection from its height. Amichai, the perceptive junior teacher-poet, reported how this lookout from the school windows toward the lower HaShiloh Street changed from an advantage to a liability during the 1948 war. From their classrooms, his pupils saw shot-up city buses unloading wounded passengers at the Magen David Adom.

The public garden adjacent to the Magen David Adom building has two entrances. The steps at its heart connect HaShiloah to the sharp turn of Arlozorov Street above. On Arlozorov stand the venerable Struck House and the Itzkovitz House, both designed by Alexander Baerwald, the architect of the Technion. In 1940 the Itzkovitz House became the home of Haifa's rabbinate. The apartment building where my mother lived before she got married was also on that street. The public garden that connects Arlozorov and HaShiloah is called Struck Park, after Hermann Struck, the artist whose home hid behind the hedges that surrounded it like an abandoned castle.

Near the lower entrance to Struck Park, the vertical Betar Street crosses HaShiloah, ceases to accommodate cars, and continues upward as a narrow alley designated for pedestrians. The Betar Alley leads to the gate of the Ge'ula School and continues a little bit farther on its way, until it meets the horizontal Bezalel Street. At that corner rises the Dunie Weizmann Music Conservatory, a building that resembles the rounded hull of a ship, or an iron with its tip pointed downward. Next to it, Betar again changes its skin — no longer an alley, but a bank of steps. The Betar Steps: One of the step paths that cuts through the horizontal streets of Hadar HaCarmel

Corner of Betar Steps and Bezalel Street, near the Ge'ula School
Courtesy of Haifa City Archives; photographer Zoltan Kluger

on the side of the mountain, creating the wonderful grid of the quarter. The Betar Steps are a relative, of sorts, to the classic Donkey Steps, the ancient Haifaian transportation route and a feature of many mountainous Mediterranean settlements. We would be drawn from everywhere in the city, as if by magic strings, to the webs of these stony stairs that stretch up the side of Mount Carmel. Indeed, when I asked the author Avraham B. Yehoshua, who lived in the city for decades, which of his books was the most Haifaian, he answered without hesitation: *"The Lover!"* In it, even before love blossoms between an Arab boy and a Jewish girl, their creator brings them together to those very steps. Yehoshua seems to imply in this book that these steps are the expression of pure, romantic Haifa, the city where a love that crosses boundaries is possible.

I remember seeing the bottom tip of the Betar Steps from the entrance of the Ge'ula School both as a pupil there and later, once I joined the Scouts. As Scouts, we often went out to the as-yet unbuilt areas of the Carmel slope, which were an easy walking distance away. From the schoolyard, we would march in strict rhythm out of the gate, turn left on the alley, and then left again on Bezalel, and take it eastward all the way to its end, where it meets the straight Ge'ula Street above it. On the north side of the street stands 21 Ge'ula, the house where the doctor and author Yitzhak Kronzon spent his childhood and youth. I did not know Kronzon then; when I marched by his house for the first time with my Scout group, he was already in medical school. In his stories he resurrects the Ge'ula School and the sounds of pianos that rose from his neighbors' apartments. With a bittersweet smile, he incessantly lists the names of the small streets he would climb up and down, the streets that led to the still-untamed portion of the Carmel, which we affectionately called "The Mountain" (*HaHar*), as if there were no other mountain in the world.

About a hundred footsteps from the meeting point of Bezalel and Ge'ula, the houses ended. We continued marching in threes, an excited group of girls with our beloved Scout leader. The unforgettable landscape of Haifa spread in front of us, as if laid out on the palm of our hand.[3] On our left the slope rolled all the way down to a deep valley, the Rushmia Wadi, a green mountainside with scattered stone houses and natural caves that gaped into it. The bay glistened at the bottom and the two refineries stood upright in the east.

To our right were the quarries, a white gash in the landscape. As we marched, we would sometimes hear the screams of *barda*! and know that in a minute, the rocks would explode.[4] We would continue along the busy sidewalkless road that connected Hadar HaCarmel to the upper neigh-

Author's friends at the end of Ge'ula Street, with the Rushmia Wadi and the bay behind them
Courtesy of photographer Zvi Roger

borhoods on the mountain. A few minutes later we would leave the paved road and walk up a wide dust path to the aptly dubbed Eucalyptus Grove nearby. On long summer Saturdays we would venture farther, to other enchanted spots on the mountain, whose paths and rocks, bushes and trees, pine needles and fallen pinecones, were imprinted in our hearts forever, along with the sea, sparkling in the distance.

Far in the future, lines from a poem by Dahlia Ravikovitch, who spent her sad youth in Haifa, would send us back there:

> The woods of green sheep flowed down the slopes
> and the sea below splashed and turned blue in the sun.
> . . . .
> and we were still girls.[5]

The Ge'ula School

At first, my father would take me to the Ge'ula School in the morning, before he went to the store. We would cross Herzl Street, starting our climb on the middle arm of "our" T, that is, Bar Kokhba Street, and continuing on the street above it. Afterward, we would cross HaShiloah Street and then ascend through the alley. The conservatory faced us, and to our left was the low iron gate of the school.

Even before I crossed through the gate and entered the school premises for the first time, my heart was drawn to the thick-trunked eucalyptus tree, which I could see from the alley. The tree stood at the edge of the giant schoolyard and rose up to the sky, while its long-leaved branches bent down toward us. Next to it were steps that led to a smaller yard, partially roofed, that spread between two buildings. By these steps I bid my father farewell and joined the pupils of the first grade, who stood there in front of a thin man whose round glasses especially impressed me. The teachers arranged us in pairs, and then we turned right to the smaller western building that — as I found out later — housed the lower grades. We went up to the first floor. *Our first-grade classroom is left of the steps. We enter a large, light-bathed room, with our teacher,* hamora *Rina. Her light, curly hair combed backward, her eyes small and blue, her smile warm and pleasant, and she is a little chubby.* I immediately knew that I would love

The Ge'ula School,
the eucalyptus
branches hovering
over the steps
*Courtesy of Haifa City
Archives; photographer
Zoltan Kluger*

going to a real school with rows of desks and a teacher standing in front of
the class.

Kronzon, who attended Ge'ula before I did, remembered that first day
in darker tones:

> A scary man in a gray, wool suit and thick-lensed glasses wandered
> around the yard and screamed in a voice hoarse from smoking, "First
> grade here, first grade here!" . . .
>
> The scary man said, "I am the vice principal Haklay." . . . Mr. Hak-
> lay screamed at the parents . . . to go home. . . . One boy started crying.
> . . . Mr. Haklay approached him and yelled next to his ear, "Stupid! If
> you don't stop immediately, we'll send you back to kindergarten."[6]

From that moment on, Kronzon the boy was afraid to cry at school, but
that did not prevent him from loving his first-grade teacher, Ziva, "the
first and the admired one," for eternity, exactly the way that I loved my
teacher, Rina.[7]

For the first few days of school, my father walked me all the way to the
schoolyard; later he just took me to the rounded building at the intersec-

tion with HaShiloah; and, finally, he walked me only up to Hermon Street. In this way, he gradually weaned me off of my dependence on him. In 1954 Herzl Street was a major two-way thoroughfare, and there was no light at the intersection I had to cross. My father taught me to look both ways and to observe and follow the behavior of the adults crossing that street, but he continued to help me cross Herzl Street for many months.

The autumn days of first grade were as bright as the face of *hamora* Rina.

I had a small rectangular notebook, a kind of half notebook, a pencil, and an eraser. On Hanukkah, after we already knew how to read, we received our very first reader in a party for all first graders. One of the children played the wise dwarf, a pointed cap on his head: "There was a dwarf in the past / All night he studied so fast / One day he got up / And behold he was smart!"

But in the middle of the school year, we found out that *hamora* Rina was pregnant and a short time later she said good-bye to us. My mother and I went to visit her to give her a present after she gave birth. Rina served us chocolate candy, flat and round, on top of which were scattered sweet, small dots in a variety of colors — nonpareils. Since then, every time I see nonpareils, I think about that visit at *hamora* Rina's. Her replacement was the tall, chopped-haired Sima, whom I did not like. She was my teacher in second grade as well, at the end of which my parents transferred me to the Alliance school.

The Ge'ula Elementary School or, as it was initially called, Amami Bet (P.S. 2) was built due to the boom in the Jewish population during the rise of the Nazis in the 1930s. Initially independent, the Ge'ula vicinity was absorbed into the district of Hadar HaCarmel, which spurred the construction of a public school in the neighborhood. The Committee for Hadar HaCarmel, aware of the grave need for appropriate facilities for educational institutions, allotted grounds for the school and pursued its quick construction.[8] Ge'ula was the second public, or "folk," school in Haifa. P.S. 1, established in the 1920s with the support of the private Reali School, preceded it. P.S. 1 provided the new school with veteran teachers like Mr. Ya'akov Haklay, who would eventually become its principal. Following the model of the Reali School, Public School 1 contributed to the

Magen David Adom Trauma Center, with Struck Park on the left
Courtesy of Haifa City Archives; photographer Zoltan Kluger

emphasis on physical education in the Ge'ula School as well, incorporating the Scouts movement into the curriculum.[9]

During the development of the Ge'ula neighborhood, another public building, Magen David Adom, the first free-standing trauma center in Haifa, was constructed across the street from the school. A sign in bronze letters on the façade of the building testifies to its glorious past: "Magen David Adom, 1938" and, above the letters, the six-pointed Jewish star. The building was designed by the engineer Gedalya Wilboshevitz, one of the builders of the Technion and one of the founders of Hadar HaCarmel. A metal plaque still affixed to the building commemorates the builder's son, Alexander, who died suddenly in 1932.[10] Wilboshevitz's Magen David Adom building boasted a smooth, clean façade and a special awning above its entrance. Its rounded form nicely solved the problematic meeting of HaShiloah Street and the steep Betar.

At that intersection, a bit higher on the Carmel slope, lay the plot of land designated for the Ge'ula School, sandwiched between HaShiloah and Bezalel.[11] It was a narrow lot, akin to an asymmetrical trapezoid. The original plan of the school included one long, multistoried building on the eastern edge of the lot, following the incline of the ground. Its wide windows all faced westward toward a large yard. The basement floor contained workshops for crafts as well as a cafeteria and kitchen, while offices and classrooms were on the upper floors. In the middle of the long structure was a staircase that split into three branches. The entry was beneath the roof that attached it to a smaller building, which held only the bathrooms (over the years that smaller structure was expanded into a building for the lower grades).[12]

The Ge'ula School was designed by the architect Max Loeb, considered "one of the pre-eminent exponents of Modern architectural style in Palestine." He was born in Kassel, Germany, in 1901 and studied architecture in Dresden and Munich, but ultimately earned his diploma in 1925 at the Technische Hochschule Darmstadt. Loeb grew up in a Zionist home and visited Palestine when he finished his studies. In 1929 he immigrated there and joined a Jerusalem firm, where he planned and built the main branch of the Anglo-Palestine Bank as well as some private residences that were clad in stone but were modern in form.[13] Yet Loeb's place in the annals of the country's architecture is preserved in no small part due to his innovative plan for the New Business Center in the lower city of Haifa near the port. His design was "extreme in its simplicity" and remarkable in its "unity and diversity" as well as its "disciplined flexibility."[14] To supervise a project of such massive dimensions, Loeb moved from Jerusalem with his business partner in 1934, settled in Haifa, and, before the center was even completed, became a sought-after architect.[15] He planned the first printing house in the city in addition to a variety of businesses and residences. In 1936 photographs of his New Business Center in the lower city were published in the journal *Architecture d'Aujourd'hui* as a prime example of urban architecture worthy of international attention. That very year he also won first prize in a competition to build the Central Synagogue of Haifa for a design rich in contrast, which was simple yet full of grandeur. This ambitious plan, however, was never executed, despite protests from Haifa's Association of Architects and Engineers.[16]

Loeb, who believed that architecture in Palestine should be a harmony between "material, form and landscape," was also renowned for the schools he planned.[17] Julius Posner, another German Jewish architect, praised Loeb's village schools in a 1938 article published in the Palestinian architectural journal *HaBinyan baMizrah haKarov* (The building in the Near East). Posner evaluated the schools based on educational, health-related, and structural categories.[18] He commended Loeb for considering the local climate while planning the multistory Ge'ula School by placing the windows on the western side to avoid exposure to the heat and light from the east.

Posner, however, criticized city planners in Palestine for failing to allot appropriately spacious grounds for schools and settling instead for lots devoid of open space and greenery, squashed between buildings and streets. With Ge'ula, Posner complained, "the constriction of the lot causes an arrangement of elements that does not seem ideal to us."[19] However, he emphasized that Loeb's hands were tied, as placing the building on the opposite side of the lot would have resulted in even greater deficiencies.

Despite its limitations — topographical and otherwise — the Ge'ula School faithfully served generations of students, and its original plan proved flexible enough to enable expansion both upward and laterally. When I attended this school in the mid-1950s, it had already been expanded.[20] Grades one, two, and three studied in the small building on the west side of the lot, while grades four through eight were held in the original building. The younger children played in the small, partially roofed yard between the two buildings, but when it rained, many pupils, big and small, gathered there. Another rainy-day option was at the northern tip of the large yard, where a newer building on stilts provided an open yet sheltered area perfect for games. The school cafeteria on the basement floor transformed into a synagogue on Saturdays, and on the other side of that floor was the gym, with floor-to-ceiling wooden ladders covering the entire eastern wall.[21] This was also where students gathered and school plays were performed. Every morning, in the giant yard that belonged to the "big kids" during recess, the daily assembly was held. After the assembly the pupils walked in unison to their classrooms to the sound of popular marches played over the loudspeaker.[22] This daily ritual was conducted by Mr. Haklay who, by my time, had already become the principal.

I ran into Haklay's name many, many years later, during my research on Amichai, the poet. I found out that when Haklay offered Amichai — then Yehuda Pfeuffer — a position at the Ge'ula School, he demanded that the young man Hebraize his German last name. Thus the name "Yehuda

Amichai" was born. Haklay's daughter, Ora, was the poet's cherished friend and colleague during his time teaching at Ge'ula.[23]

Literary Accounts of the Ge'ula School

It so happens that the Ge'ula School was exceptionally lucky in the documentation of its early days. One of the most important periods in its life was recorded by two gifted, yet very different, authors, whose lives intersected with its own. While the time they spent under its roof overlapped, their paths did not. One was a rookie teacher, the other a student. One came from Jerusalem and stayed in Haifa for eight months (August 1947–April 1948); the other was born in Haifa and spent his formative years at that school (1945–53). One was a German Jew, who—though he'd been mischievous during his childhood—believed with all his heart in instilling "regular itineraries," order, and discipline; the other focused mostly on subverting the rules that Ge'ula's teachers and principals tried to impose.[24] What's more, their written records themselves are dramatically different: the first wrote letters to a single addressee in real time as the events were unfolding; the second waited over three decades before retrieving his autobiographical stories from memory.

The first of the two "documentarians" of the school was the poet-to-be Yehuda Amichai, who taught at Ge'ula for less than five months, over the course of which he wrote sixty-seven of the ninety-eight letters he would send to Ruth. Haifa was a new city for him and teaching a new profession; also new was his status as a man who saw himself as engaged to a woman on the other side of the ocean. In his romantic letters to her, Amichai's pen captured the school's everyday life and even Loeb's design, like a camera that captures every object in front of it, regardless of whether it was only coincidentally in the frame.

The second is Yitzhak Kronzon, a renowned Israeli cardiologist who lives and works in New York City. His bar mitzvah ceremony took place in 1952 in the cafeteria-turned-synagogue in the Ge'ula School's basement. This school was at the center of the boy's universe and later would play a key role in his stories, together with the small slice of Haifa around it.

That very institution was also a central fixture of Amichai's life in Haifa. Indeed, caught within the frame of his epistolary camera is the everyday life of Ge'ula. He, the fourth-grade homeroom teacher and English teacher for the fifth and sixth grades, meticulously depicts how the large yard changes its face over the course of the day. In the mornings the daily assembly is held there, and each homeroom teacher stands at the head of his pupils. Amichai feels that "forty pairs of eyes of all colors" follow him.[25] During gym class the yard becomes a training ground — forty-two children, all in white uniforms, crouching under the shadow of the building, while "the teacher Amichai stands in front of them."[26]

And finally, at 4:30 p.m., during recess, when he is the teacher on duty, "the sun goes west over me and my shadow is cast long over the yard."[27] Due to the shortage of classrooms in 1947, school hours were lengthened to accommodate two shifts, so both the yard and the teachers had to work overtime.[28] When winter approached, joyful songs about rain wafted from the classrooms, and during recess the yard became a gauge of the "changing seasons." As the "cool days" neared, the children's games became "increasingly energetic."[29]

Through his letters Amichai also captures the broad stairs separating the small yard from the large one as well as the wide entrance gate. "Streams of children" flow through with ease, and at the end of the day Amichai the "photographer" zooms in on the girls' skirts, wrinkled like an "accordion," from extended sitting.[30] The large hall in the basement also peeks out through the letters, albeit not during gym: "I was with sixth grade in the hall. A broadcast [began] about . . . the river of Mark Twain and the boats." In this letter Amichai draws an almost surrealist picture — eleven-year-old pupils in 1947 Palestine listening attentively in the school gym to the sounds of the Mississippi River, the bass voice of Paul Robeson, and the "songs of the black people . . . in the cotton fields." As his pupils listen to the broadcast, Amichai writes that "curious trees stretched their branches through the window."[31] The teacher-artist who, within a few years would write the famous lines, "Of three or four in a room / There is always one who stands beside the window," is keenly aware of the value of the giant windows Loeb set in the western wall: "the windows in our classrooms are very large, a kind of a wall that is all glass."[32] While the pupils are busy with their work, he gazes out at the world and dreams up visions. One time he imagines that his beloved has returned from America and is crossing "through the yard."[33] Another time he looks beyond the yard and the nearby buildings and sees the ridge of the Carmel, and, for him, it is reminiscent of Mount Moriah.

The thoughts about Mount Moriah, and the altar that Abraham built on it, pop into Amichai's head after one particular Friday in the middle of November 1947. On that day there was an attack on the bus that Amichai and his friend and colleague Ora Haklay were taking to a party on the Carmel. Seeking revenge for the blood of their friends shed by the Lehi, the radical Jewish underground, British soldiers fired on the Jewish bus as it turned near the top of the mountain.[34] Hayim Goldman, a young man sitting with his girlfriend in the seat right in front of Amichai, was killed. Miraculously spared, Amichai wrote to Ruth that the sight of the Carmel from the school window elicited in him the memory of "the place" (ha-makom) where the binding of Isaac happened, as if the innocent Goldman had been a sacrifice, a kind of offering that had been accepted on the Carmel.[35]

Amichai's bus was attacked two weeks before the November 29, 1947, vote for the Partition Plan, after which the war erupted that would cost the lives of 1 percent of the Jewish population in Palestine. In the nascent Israeli literature of the time, the binding of Isaac became a symbol for a generation of young men and women whose lives had been sacrificed for the State of Israel, with no ram to save them. Thus, standing by the window of the Ge'ula School, Amichai foretold the trope that would dominate the poetry of that generation.[36]

At that same time, in the middle of November 1947, the young Yitzhak Kronzon was a third grader at Ge'ula. Amid the growing tension, no one knew how events would turn out, but two weeks later, after the partition vote, the world of Hadar HaCarmel's residents turned upside down, as did that of everyone in the land. Even the littlest children at the school realized that their life routine would be unrecognizably changed. The Ge'ula School was in turmoil. On one floor the draft office of the Hagana resided. Another housed Jewish refugees from the mixed neighborhoods in the lower city.[37] Mrs. Mintzberg, Kronzon's teacher in "class 3-B in the Ge'ula School," bragged to her students that "her Gedalya, who is fifteen years old, lies with a Sten all night and shoots Arabs" and the boy Kronzon was disappointed that his father, a vital worker at the Electric Company, had not been drafted.[38] On December 21 Amichai recorded his students' Hanukkah vacation compositions in his letters. They all complained about the curfew. Moshe wrote that "the Arabs started attacking"; Ziva: "they killed Jews"; Edna: "my father had to be on guard duty"; and Giyora: "a bullet entered the bathroom."[39] It was hard for the teacher to do his job, but he was determined to distract the nerve-wracked children and would rather that they "feel that a mistake in arithmetic is terrible, not the shots outside."[40] Like the other teachers, Amichai tried his best to maintain a sense of normalcy for his pupils.

The Magen David Adom building, which had stood calmly across the street from Ge'ula since they were both built, was seized by a frenzy during that period. Starting in December 1947, Arab forces frequently attacked Jewish vehicles, and the many wounded arrived at the trauma center — the only one in Haifa — bleeding, to be treated. For the first time, Ge'ula students looked out at their familiar neighbor with fear. Amichai wrote to Ruth that at the Magen David Adom near the school, "two buses arrived. . . . The windows were punctured by bullets. . . . The children in the classroom begin to cry. . . . Fifty-one wounded . . . the other passengers stained with blood."[41] The anxiety of the children distressed Amichai and dampened his spirits. He did not yet know that within two months he would share far worse traumas with pupils at a different school.[42]

Likely due to censorship, Amichai did not mention — not even in one word — that Ge'ula was one of the main weapons storage facilities of the Hagana Central Command, even though, as an active member, he surely knew this.[43] Nevertheless, he did hint to Ruth about "matters" that kept him busy during the nights.

On January 23, 1948, Amichai bid farewell to his Ge'ula pupils because he had been transferred to the HaMerkaz School in the heart of the Arab-dominated lower city, which had become a battlefield. In March, after two months away from Ge'ula, he speaks of a visit there and how he was surrounded by the love of the children, his former pupils. In comparison to the school where he now taught, life at Ge'ula seemed almost normal.

On the eve of Passover, on April 22, 1948, the Hagana forces in Haifa took over the city. Eleven days prior to that, Amichai received the Dear John letter from Ruth, ended his correspondence with her, and went south to the Negev, where fierce battles were raging. Amichai's account of Haifa, then, stopped midway. Sixty-eight years later Kronzon fills in the subsequent chain of events at the Ge'ula School. It is as if an unseen hand motivated the seventy-seven-year-old author to reveal what, exactly, happened from Passover 1948 through the end of that fateful school year, at the school that, like the city, was now under full Jewish control. In a story published on Independence Day 2016 in *Ha'aretz*, he writes,

> When we returned to the Ge'ula School after the long Passover vacation, it became clear to us that we would not be able to study in it any longer because it was occupied by refugee children who were forced to leave the kibbutzim of the Jordan Valley. Instead, all the pupils of our school were transferred to the second shift at the technical school at Masada Street, on the corner of Balfour, next to the stone tower that stood there then.[44]

Indeed, before Passover, studies had been conducted in the Ge'ula building despite its role in sheltering crowds of Jewish refugees from Haifa's Arab neighborhoods. But after Passover, when those Jewish refugees could return to their homes, everything changed. The school building was taken over by the Jewish National Authorities to house the evacuees of the Jordan Valley kibbutzim that had been attacked by the Arab armies. Every day between two and six in the afternoon, Ge'ula's regular pupils had to make their way to a farther school building. Kronzon's teacher continued teaching the third grade in its temporary home. She promised her pupils that "on one of the last days of the school year . . . she would teach them the new popular elegiac song that was playing on all the radios, 'In the Vast Plains of the Negev, a Defending Soldier Fell.'"[45] In Haifa war no longer raged. But in Ge'ula once again there were refugees. The former fourth-grade homeroom teacher, Yehuda Amichai, became a "defending soldier" in the terrible battles in the Negev Plains and survived. He never returned to live in Haifa.

After the summer of 1948 Ge'ula returned to being a full-time elementary school, and Kronzon studied there until he graduated at the end of eighth grade. His bar mitzvah in Ge'ula's basement synagogue would later feature in the story "Mother, Sunshine, Homeland." Its climax is the author's belated recognition of the truth behind the bar mitzvah sermon that had been composed for him: "There are three things without which the spirit of man cannot subsist: mother, sunshine and homeland." Of course, when he was thirteen years old, the wisdom of the sermon's words paled in comparison to both the gifts he received and one particular compliment from the school caretaker, Velgreen, who served as the sexton of the synagogue on Saturdays. He "said that he'd never heard anything quite this good."[46]

Unfortunately, the narrator's bar mitzvah success does not reflect his standing in other areas. In "organization and cleanliness," for example, he was known as the "absolute worst" pupil. "Once a month, the nurse Chodorovski came to examine us," he writes. To demonstrate the difference between a clean boy and a dirty one, she chose two children to display in front of the class: "Yoram," who was the "cleanest" child, and the narrator, as a counterpoint, a "dirty child." She listed the details that separated the clean from the dirty: "The clean boy wears polished shoes and his socks are clean and folded down. The dirty boy doesn't wear any socks, and has no lace in his right shoe." Kronzon, the child who was humiliated by the nurse but has since become a successful physician, concludes, with a mixture of humor and bitterness, that this is how he "entered the history books of the Ge'ula School."[47]

In addition to describing his school, Kronzon's narrator repeatedly relates the names of the streets that surrounded it. Their eternal ascents and descents dominate the stories, the fantasies of their author, and the lives of their heroes. The main character of "Musical Education," for example, stops learning the piano because he fears "a large dog that liked to loiter by the *Betar Steps*" at the exact same time that he would "gather the music notes into the dark blue cardboard binder with a gold harp imprinted on it, walk down the *Betar Steps* and then over to *Shiloah Street*, to perform the exercises." The musical career he had begun was cut short because the only alternative to the Betar Steps was a "lengthy route that traversed *Tavor, Bar Kokhba*, and *Arlozorov Streets*, which took hours." This sabotage of his musical education was ironic because his mother was a piano teacher: "Anyone walking on late Saturday mornings along *Ge'ula Street*, from the synagogue to the quarry on the far end of the street, would hear Mother's pupils conscientiously practicing."[48] Everyone played the piano except the son of the piano teacher.

In the overwrought drama of yet another story, the Betar Steps star in an imaginary scene dreamt up by the child narrator. These were the days of the war, and Kronzon, whose father was not drafted, wished that Shaya, his mother's former suitor, would visit. He had never met Shaya, but had seen him in an old photograph, decorated with medals, as a war hero: "I used to look lovingly at . . . the photograph and pray for him to return to our family with his uniform and his pistol. I would fantasize walking down the *Betar Steps* with him, hand in hand and into class 3-B in the Geula School."[49] The Betar Steps become a vital component in the boy's fantasy of parading his hero through the neighborhood.

The sexual development of the narrator of these stories is also bound with the city's topography. On Friday, "the best of days," he and his friends spy on the most intimate moments of the residents of Ge'ula Street. But before he reaches the climax of his story, the narrator must explain the terrain. He lists the bus drop-off points in Hadar HaCarmel for the workers in the Bay Area factories. Indeed, the map of bus stations, apartment buildings, streets, ascents, and steps and the specific relationships of time and distance between them are crucial elements in his story:

> First . . . the Shemen Factory workers arrive because their bus stops next to the yeshiva [on Ge'ula Street]. . . . The ones from Fenitzia . . . disembark from their bus on Herzl Street, and they have to walk much farther through the Betar Steps. . . . Eli, the son of Vackerman, from Fenitzia, got married and started working at the Shemen Factory. *I told you that those from Shemen arrive home earlier.* . . . Every Friday at one, we stand on the terrace . . . and see how Eli Vackerman . . . runs up the hill . . . into their apartment on 28 [Ge'ula] . . . and quickly screws his wife . . . because he has only about a quarter of an hour until his father, who lives with them, gets there via the Betar Steps.[50]

To the great joy of the peeping boys, the young husband hurries home from the bus stop, knowing that he has fifteen minutes of grace thanks to Haifa's hilly topography and the ascent the father must climb from the Herzl Street stop to their home on Ge'ula.

Arlozorov Street and Baerwald's
Residential Designs

The Ge'ula neighborhood and the clusters of houses around it were finally established at the beginning of the 1930s, east of Aliyah (Ascent) Street after a protracted real estate saga. Until then, the street had marked the easternmost border of Hadar HaCarmel, the "garden city" that sprouted up around the Technion in the 1920s on the shoulder of the mountain. Aliyah Street itself, so named mostly due to its steep diagonal route that connected Hadar HaCarmel's main street to the top of the mountain, became, with the establishment of Ge'ula, a central thoroughfare. In fact, only after construction on Ge'ula Street began was Aliyah paved and extended to meet it.[51] Its name was changed to "Arlozorov Street" later, when Chaim Arlosoroff, the young Zionist leader, was assassinated in Tel Aviv in 1933. After an arduous climb up the mountain, this street swerves suddenly, turns westward, and creeps slowly upward, crossing Balfour Street and making its way toward the center of the Carmel.

In 1913, however, when the Jewish artist from Berlin, Hermann Struck, bought a piece of land on the side of the mountain, Hadar HaCarmel did not yet exist, nor did the ascending street that would mark its eastern border. When Struck and his wife, Malka, immigrated to Palestine nine years later, they found temporary housing in the vicinity of the Technion, at the heart of a burgeoning Hadar HaCarmel. The artist asked his friend, the German Jewish architect Alexander Baerwald, who had built the Technion, to design a home for him and his wife on the sloped lot he had acquired a decade earlier. Perhaps due to the ten-year gap between Struck having acquired the lot and the construction of the house and paving of the street, the house's entrance is far below the sidewalk. In fact, because of the steep ground, its roof is almost level with Arlozorov Street.

The many visitors to the Struck home used to walk down the steps and through the well-groomed botanical garden that had been planned along with the beautiful house: "from Aliyah Street [later Arlozorov], one passes through a fragrant garden, iris, cyclamen, pomegranate, all in good taste. On the other side of the fence, the wild, rocky terrain of the mountain still spread," wrote Meir Ben Uri, Struck's loyal student, years later.[52] The artist's dedication to gardening determined not only the nature of the garden but also the plan of the house — in its cellar Baerwald built a private cistern that supplied the water needs of the garden and freed its owner from dependence on the distant well of the Technion.

Thanks to his expertise in horticulture, Struck was Baerwald's partner in designing the Technion and Reali School gardens. But the two Berlin friends shared much more than a love of gardens. Both the architect and the painter were Zionists who believed that construction in the nascent Land of Israel must integrate Jewish and local elements and draw from the eastern lexicon of forms. Struck eternalized his close friend's face in an etching in 1927, and after Baerwald's death in 1930, he painted an image of his tombstone on the Mount of Olives in Jerusalem.

The home that Baerwald built for the Strucks on the steep slope of the Carmel incorporated the geometry of the Arab structures in the region, but the design of its interior was adapted for the needs of its Western tenants.[53] Baerwald used an architectural vernacular that exudes its indigenous nature — a series of interlocking cubical forms lie one on top of the other to become a part of the slope. The arrangement of the cubes in the Struck House creates a dramatic effect and does not blur the geometrical purity of each one of the forms.[54] Yet it is not only the silhouette of the building that is similar to the local houses — both the materials and the pattern declare, so to speak, that they were born here: the deliberately rough chiseling of the stone exterior, the pointed arched openings reminiscent of Islamic structures, and the railing wrought in an Eastern style. The Struck House is a quintessential example of the Baerwaldian residential architecture whose power lies in merging with the topographical environment. His style mimics Arab buildings in mountainous regions, mindful of the climate as well as the building's practical function. Because the house was designed as both the artist's residence and work studio, the large windows were placed in the northern wall, to provide the preferred light. The adjacent external stone steps and the flat roof, typical of Arab construction, perfectly served the artist who wanted to paint from the building's heights.

> When, in the spring at the crack of dawn, the first lights appeared
> over the mountains of the Galilee, illuminating the sky with colors of
> fire and smoke, Struck stood on the roof despite the cold, the brush
> in his hands, his beloved pipe in his mouth, and painted, and looked

Struck House, restored, 2014   *Courtesy of photographer Adi Silberstein*

out . . . and waited . . . for the special clouds that produced an extraordinary atmospheric phenomenon that he loved: . . . the wonderful morning light and the mist gave an otherworldly quality to the color of the bay, the sea and the mountains.[55]

This lyrical scene, recalled by Ben Uri after the death of his teacher, has been interpreted as an expression of the spiritual quest of the religious artist.[56] But it also testifies to Struck's treasured connection to Haifa; the bond with the actual, physical place was a significant component of Struck's fervent Zionism. His desire to settle in Palestine stemmed from his attraction to Haifa and its landscape as much as it did from Theodor Herzl's influence.

Struck was born in an Orthodox Jewish home in Berlin in 1876, and although his family wanted him to be a rabbi, he turned to the Royal Academy of Art in Berlin. When he graduated in 1900, however, the academy prohibited him, as a Jew, from teaching there. Three years later he

embarked on an artistic journey throughout the Mediterranean, including Palestine. Only a year had passed since Herzl, the father of modern
Zionism, had published *Altneuland* and, in it, the prophetic description
of Haifa as "the city of the future."[57] In his literary vision Herzl saw the
slopes of the Carmel covered with charming, white houses and the bay's
port, bustling. When Struck arrived in Cairo during his journey, he met
Herzl in the glamorous Shepherd Hotel, the place where Herzl received
the rulers of Egypt and England.[58] Struck was awed by Herzl, and perhaps
at that point he had already made the decision that if he were to immigrate to Palestine, he would settle in Haifa. On his way back from the east,
Struck visited Herzl in the bosom of his family home in Vienna and made
a sketch of his face. In creating the final etching of Herzl's portrait, Struck
used the *vernis mou* (soft-ground etching) technique, which preserved his
"handwriting," as if the print were a drawing in pencil.[59] Struck captured
the intensity that Herzl's personality radiated and his gaze, like "one of the
prophets of Israel."[60] He managed to show the etching to Herzl, and, when
Herzl died in 1904, Struck's portrait of him circulated all over the world
and was carved into the collective memory of the Jewish people. Sadly,
while this image became iconic, its creator was all but forgotten.

After meeting Herzl, Struck would speak of the leader's beauty and nobility and also strove to look like him—he grew a beard and would be
described as a "tall man, elegant, in a jacket, and a beard, Herzl-style."[61]
Yet Struck's identification with Herzl was deep and essential. In his deeds
Struck achieved what the great Zionist dreamer who died in his prime was
unable to. "Struck . . . fulfilled the goal of his Zionist longing and built himself a home in Haifa," wrote the philologist Victor Klemperer, who met
Struck when they were both in the German army, as he captured the fluc-
tuation of the artist's soul in his own memoirs.[62] Klemperer recognized
that, for Struck, settling in Haifa was the ultimate realization of the Zionist dream, even though one would have expected the religious, Orthodox
Struck to settle in Jerusalem. Struck seemed to his army buddy like a sort
of Don Quixote, a compassionate "knight" with the image of sorrow.

In addition to its connection to Herzl, the natural beauty of Haifa and
the spiritual quality of its vistas attracted the heart of the artist. He decorated his workshop with a painting of the cloudy bay even though he
could see the bay, Acre, and Mount Hermon from his window. When a

Hermann Struck's
portrait of Theodor Herzl
Courtesy of the Open Museum,
Tefen Industrial Park

new student arrived, he would take him up "to the roof of his home, place blank paper and a sharp pencil in his hands, and instruct him to draw Haifa's landscape."[63]

Twenty years after his first trip to Palestine, the artist transported his studio as well as his German furniture from Berlin into the house that looked out from the Carmel over to the sea. His etching press with its heavy rollers and the etching table now lived in Haifa, as did the tremendous book cabinet whose four glass doors guarded a treasure trove of German culture. Outside the entrance, to the left of the door, a marble sign with the artist's name in German welcomed the guests. Inside, above that door, was a pattern of sunrays that echoed the classic cross-vault of the high ceilings. Against the background of the gray floor, the art deco patterns of the hand-painted tiles shone. Those created a "tile carpet" that attracted the eye of all who entered the house. From the stained glass windows in the northeastern wall of the large workroom on the main floor, a soft light floated in.

But it was not just the content of Struck's Berlin house that arrived in Palestine. He brought his artistic talent and the respect that he felt toward all human beings. Struck was the premier Jewish artist in the Land of Israel and its most important authority in the field of etching. His genteel house was a hub for various intellectual circles, especially lovers of art, but it also bustled with many students, for Struck was a superior teacher whose students in Berlin included Marc Chagall, Max Liebermann, and Lovis Korinth.[64] His love for his new homeland was evident in the public and educational work in which he immersed himself. He continuously supported the Tiferet Israel yeshiva that was near his house and served as a member of a number of urban committees, including those that chose the emblems of both Haifa and Hadar HaCarmel.[65] Even during the Italian bombings in World War II, when many left Haifa, Struck not only remained in his home but, "between one bombing and the other," initiated and presented Haifa's first graphic arts exhibition, which attracted an audience of thousands, right in the heart of the city.[66] And beyond Haifa, Struck was among the founders of the Tel Aviv Museum and the initiators of the reopening of the Bezalel Art Academy in Jerusalem. Yet even as he significantly influenced the development of Bezalel in its early years, Struck was not welcome within its artistic establishment.

As improbable as it may seem, the trajectory of Struck's life mirrors that of the fictional heroes of Herzl's utopian novel, *Altneuland*. After leaving Europe in 1902, the protagonists visit Palestine, then disappear for twenty years until they return to Palestine in 1923, whereupon they discover that it has blossomed and Haifa has become a cosmopolitan city. Similarly, Struck embarked on a journey to Palestine in 1903, was absent from that country for two decades, and then returned. The Haifa to which he arrived in 1922 was only at the beginning of its development, but he witnessed Herzl's vision for the city near fulfillment during the British Mandate, when it became an imperial, cosmopolitan crossroads.

Yet while we know nothing about the period during which *Altneuland*'s characters vanish from the plot, the adventures of our flesh-and-blood hero, Struck, could fill an additional novel. Between 1903 and 1922 he achieved international stature and was considered one of the premier etching and print artists of the twentieth century; he created approximately 250 portraits, among them Albert Einstein, Sigmund Freud, Friedrich Nietzsche, Henrik Ibsen, and Oscar Wilde. He also etched a series of anonymous "Jewish faces" that the art critic Arnold Fortlage compared to Rembrandt's portraits.[67] Struck was a member of the Royal Society of Print Artists in London and exhibited his works at the modernist Berlin Secession exhibitions between 1901 and 1912 as a member of that art movement. His book on the theory and art of etching, *Die Kunst des Radierens*, published in 1908 by the Berliner Cassirer Publishing House, became a seminal work. It appeared in five editions through 1922, with the fifth including etchings by Marc Chagall and Pablo Picasso, and it established Struck's fame as a leading print artist, teacher, and theoretician. A German patriot, he volunteered for military service in World War I, serving as a translator, liaison officer, and military artist. In 1917 he became the referent for Jewish issues at the German Eastern Front High Command, and in 1919 he joined the German mission to the Versailles talks as the councilor for Jewish affairs. Soon after he returned to Berlin and witnessed the rise of antisemitism, Walther Rathenau, the Weimar Republic's Jewish foreign minister, was assassinated. Despite his professional success and his connections to German government leaders, this prompted Struck to emigrate to Palestine.

In Haifa his art gradually grew simpler and more essential. The circle of the bay and the straight line of the palm tree became his main artistic motif. The continuous clouds that stretch over the mountains bordering the bay were a means to express his unity with the landscape and, in the 1940s, also his fears of the storm of war and the weakening of his body. Struck continued his extensive artistic, Zionist, and communal activities in Palestine, but during his life — and even after his death in 1944—he did not gain true recognition for his contribution to Israeli art.

In the 1950s and 1960s I often climbed Betar Street, east of the Struck House, and peeked at the hidden structure through the hedgerow. The house was already encircled by apartment buildings, but it was closed. Surrounded by dry plants and desolate, it evoked in us children curiosity mixed with fear. We knew nothing about the original owner of the house, other than the name Struck and that he was an artist.

On the other side of Arlozorov Street, a little lower on the slope than the Struck House, stands its younger brother, the Itzkovitz House, which coincidentally holds a unique, personal connection for me. It is one of the last buildings to bear Baerwald's signature, as it was completed in 1930, the year the preeminent architect died. "The drawings of the architect testify to the talent with which the master approached the study of the entire façade as well as the shape of each opening and its placement inside the entire area of the wall," states an article written about the house in a Palestinian architectural journal seven years later.[68]

The Itzkovitz House is closer to the street than the Struck House, and to this day it looks as though it was born out of the tall, exposed rock on which it was built. Because it rests on the opposite side of the street, those who enter it must go up the stairs rather than down—nevertheless, the genetic features of the common father of the two buildings are obvious. The entirety of the Itzkovitz House is made of local stone; its blocks are unequal in size, one set beside the other asymmetrically; its large, dramatic windows and doors are forged in the shape of pointed arches; and its flat roof testifies to the influence of the vernacular Arab style. Unlike the Struck House, however, here, there are also roofed terraces with arcades of classical columns. But like its older sibling, despite its Eastern appearance, the interior layout attended to the needs of the Western tenant.

The house was commissioned by the physician, Dr. Yitzhak Itzkovitz, the owner of the first radiology clinic in northern Palestine and eventually the head of the Physicians Association in Haifa, and his wife, Aliza. She was the daughter of Jacobus Kann, founder of the Zionist Organization in Holland and an enthusiastic Herzl supporter who financed the Zionist Congress. The Itzkovitz family lived there until 1940, when the Italians started bombing Haifa. Then they sold the house to the city's chief rabbinate, which used it for decades. The wide roof—which Baerwald had planned for the socialite Itzkovitz couple as a space for their popular summer parties—was perfect for weddings. It enabled the rabbinate to raise a *chupah* under the open sky, according to custom, and provided plenty of room for guests. In August 1946 Rabbi Kaniel married my parents on that roof.

My Family's Mythologies and Our Last Home in Haifa

My mother used to tell us often about their wedding at the rabbinate at 16 Arlozorov and how her friend Pnina Benish baked cakes and brought them to that roof. Pnina lived nearby at 26 Arlozorov, the building where my mother resided before she got married. Indeed, it was Pnina's son, Amos, who suggested that my parents name me Nili. They liked the sound of the name, unaware of the fact that "Nili" was the name of an underground Zionist group during World War I. As children, we used to visit my mother's former neighbor quite often, and we knew her well.

In April 1933 my mother arrived in Palestine from Chernovitz, Bukovina, and settled in Tel Aviv, where she had relatives. When her ship neared the Jaffa port, she told me, the "English" — as she called them — boarded, gathered all the passengers in the ship's hall, and interrogated them one by one. In accordance with the British Mandate's policy of limiting Jewish immigration, they decreed that most of the passengers had to return to their country of origin. My mother, who had prepared for this interview ahead of time, pretended to be a tourist: she carried with her only one small suitcase; she had a lot of money to show; and, most important, she had the name of the family of "engineer Gruenfeld," the well-known industrialist, as her supposed hosts. The British were convinced that my mother was indeed only coming for a visit and permitted her to board one of the little boats that awaited the lucky few allowed to come ashore. The ship was ordered to go back to Europe with the rest of the passengers. Upon hearing this, some of them committed suicide by jumping off the deck, while others began a hunger strike. Eventually, the British caved, allowed the ship to anchor in Palestine, and issued official entry certificates to the survivors — it was 1933, and the British were still susceptible to public pressure. On the streets of Tel Aviv my mother would sometimes run into the other passengers. "Some would not say 'hello' to me, thinking I was a traitor. The others would say, 'See? I have a true certificate,'" she recalled. The Gruenfeld house became a second home to her, and the children, Karin and Eli, dear to her heart. Even after we, her own children, were born, she always carried a small photograph of a girl with a bob haircut and a serious, blond two-year-old boy, each wearing a rain cape.

During World War II, when Haifa became the target of air raids starting in 1940, many left the city. My fearless mother, however, decided to move there because she thought, accurately, that the emptying city would offer good job opportunities. When she came from Tel Aviv, she rented a room on the roof at 26 Arlozorov, which stood slightly above the street's sharp curve. It was not far from the Itzkovitz House, whose tenants had by then moved to a different neighborhood, and almost across the street from the Struck House, whose tenants tenaciously remained. At that time the artist's home was crowded not only with visitors but also with refugees from Germany, whom Struck hosted in the various rooms of his big house, including his studio, workshop, and the basement.

A few days after my mother moved to Haifa she became so ill she could not get out of bed. By chance, one of the building's tenants went to the roof to hang her laundry and noticed my mother lying in her room with the door slightly ajar for air. She greeted her, then disappeared. A short while later, however, she returned. The description of the tray that Pnina brought to my mother that day was repeated in my mother's stories in many variations, but it was always set elegantly, with porcelain dishes arranged on a white, ironed cloth napkin; a soft-boiled egg; and dark bread. The striking Pnina looked a bit like the first lady of Hebrew theater, Hannah Rovina—her jet-black hair gathered behind her head in a bun, her features chiseled, and her lips always painted red. Even though Pnina was affiliated with the right-wing, nationalist Herut movement and my mother was a socialist, they remained lifelong friends.

After my mother married my father, she moved from Arlozorov Street into his small apartment on the western end of Hadar HaCarmel. In 1954 all four of us, my parents, my younger brother, and I, moved back east, to the house on 85 Herzl Street, near Arlozorov and Ge'ula. Our new apartment was lovely and airy and seemed as if it had been made just for us.

At the entrance to the apartment is a long, long corridor. You can roll a ball from one end to the other; you can run races or even ride down it on the small bike of a four-year-old. No wonder the poor neighbor who lives underneath us is always angry. "Gadi runs through the rooms and down the long corridor and calls out 'Ima! Where are you?' Nilinka is happy too; she says, 'We have such pure air to breathe!' . . . It is also very close to the store," my father wrote in a letter from October 1954 to a cousin in New York, who would give it to me thirty years later.

To the right of the corridor near the entrance of the apartment, the kitchen opened up. This is where we ate on weekdays, did our homework, and chatted over coffee. This is also where my mother used to quiz me on lists of difficult words when I prepared for spelling tests. Adjacent to the kitchen was a small balcony from whose northern corner we could see the sea.

From a small alcove farther down the corridor, two doors opened to the washroom and the bathroom. *Our bathroom: a kerosene boiler and a small, blue flame that heats water for a shower. I sit on the edge of the tub and follow the ritual of my father's daily shave. With a soft brush, he spreads a mask of thick, white foam over his face. Only his forehead; his soft, red lips; and his kind eyes peek out from the white mask of soapsuds. Afterward, with skilled magician's fingers, he slowly and meticulously uncovers his features from under the mask, shaving his face closely with a straight blade. Sometimes he cuts himself and then wipes the bloody scratch with a purple stick. And on Thursdays we fill the bathtub with water for the two fish we bought from the large pool of carp at the store belonging to our neighbors, the Schechters. Mrs. Schechter hits their heads so they will stay calm until they arrive at our tub. And in the bathroom, for the remainder of the evening, we caress their smooth, slippery backs. The next morning my father kills them. Their entrails and the blood are on the marble counter in the kitchen. I peek in and run away with horror. And at the festive Friday night meal my mother serves the gefilte fish she has cooked, and I refuse to eat it.*

On the left side of the corridor, doors opened into two large rooms, the children's room and my parents' bedroom. Each one had a large casement window with wooden shutters and little metal people as shutter stoppers. Our room was painted a very pale green with a dark blue stencil pattern that I chose, which circled the room just under the molding with blue palm trees, blue balls, and blue children, all of whom kept me company every evening until I fell asleep.

At the first light of dawn, long before we get up for school, we hear Mr. Drimer feeding the pigeons from his balcony as they coo blissfully. Before the pigeons, when it is still dark, we can hear the low growl of the buses on Herzl Street, even though our apartment is in the back of the building. The humming of the buses is our rooster crow. When they begin, that means it is five in the morning, and I usually fall back asleep. My mother comes to wake us up at seven o'clock. "You must get up, wash up, get dressed, and pack your schoolbag," and music from the radio is playing loudly, urging us to hurry. A moment for a sip of coffee with milk and a bite of black bread with margarine, trying to reach school one moment before the bell. On my wrist hangs a hand-sewn, drawstring bag holding a wrapped sandwich and a folded, ironed cloth napkin with wide gold edging.

We entered my parents' bedroom only on rare occasions — on Hanukkah, for example, when we lit candles in the menorah that was placed on the sewing machine near the window, or when the seamstress would come for an entire day of taking measurements and cutting and chatting. As in the other rooms, the windows opened wide and tall, and the treetops peered in at us through them. My mother loved the cool cross-breezes that blew through the house.

At the end of the corridor, facing the entrance, was the capacious living room, which always welcomed me with open arms. There, *there* was the radio, an old, wooden box that sat on the top shelf of a low bookcase. We were all avid radio listeners; there was *The Child's Corner* every day at five in the afternoon: "Hello children, this is me, Esther, talking to you." At seven in the morning, the program *Classical and Light* played throughout the house as we got ready. Sometimes Gadi listened to Arabic music; on Saturdays *Hebrew Songs* and *Folk Songs*, then the festive Shabbat lunch, and at two o'clock my father, a glass of black coffee in his hand and a sugar cube between his teeth, listened to the weekly program of cantorial music —the cantor Yossele Rosenblatt, the Melavsky family, or Moishe Oysher. My mother used to complain that they never played the greatest of them all, Joseph Schmidt, the famous opera singer whom she remembered from Chernovitz and whom she was privileged to meet in the 1930s when he visited Tel Aviv.

On the wall above the radio was a single print by Chagall of a Jew, phylacteries on his arm, and behind his back, a snowy landscape. On the bookcases sat a few of the many children's books that Uncle Chaim had brought us from his bookstore: the pale blue–bound *Greek Myths for Children* and *Norse Myths for Children* with their gold lettering, as well as *Treasure Island* and stories about inventors and their inventions. But most of the books were in German —among them, my father's Bible, with a Hebrew column and a parallel German column in ornate gothic letters. In third grade I began to read it, seated on the rug beneath the large, heavy dining room table in the middle of the room, the table on which we dined only on Friday nights, Shabbat, and holidays. We each sat in our predetermined seat: my mother on the chair closest to the kitchen, my father across from her, Gadi on the east side, and I on the west. Between courses we would run to sit on our father's lap, and he would whisper to us to go to our mother. On the eve of Passover, the table would open and become longer, and, miraculously, a Passover seder would spread over it. On that day the corridor had a special role to fill. Gadi and I had to run the whole length of it to the front door to open it for Elijah the Prophet. For some reason the hallway always seemed very dark, and it was scary to run all the way to the door and open it a crack for Elijah while the grownups were standing and reciting "Pour Thy Wrath." After that they usually put us to bed, but we could still hear a little bit of the singing wafting in from the living room.

But my favorite place in our house was the large terrace, a generous space that spanned almost the entire width of the building. Reading his letter thirty years later, I learned my father shared my love for it: "From our terrace, you see the end of the sea and the bay. What a wonderful view. And it is quiet all around and now we begin living anew." Because our apartment was on the top floor of the northern wing, which faced the bay, the nautical landscape was inextricably linked to it. The railing was high, but even at age six I could look over it to see the curve of the bay and the purple mountains on the other side of it. There was Acre, we knew, and Mount Hermon, and there was Lebanon.

Years later, standing in front of one of Struck's aquarelles, I realized that the artist's roof stood along the same line of sight as our terrace, just a bit higher on the mountain—his view was from the exact same angle as mine. He too had been drawn to this magical vista, and, being an artist, he thought it was the quintessential subject for drawing and tried to replicate its colors in his paintings.[69] When I learned this, my heart went out to this man who so loved the view I cherished.

To the right of our terrace, in the east, lay the green hills of Neve Sha'anan and a little to the north the industrial area, ruled by Haifa's "giant yogurt containers"—the refineries that rise there. But across from us, really close, so very close, was the sea. Sometimes it was blue to the point of pain, endlessly pure and devoid of ships; sometimes gray. In the mornings (I always ran to the terrace when I woke up), the fog used to cover it and were it not for the horns of ships announcing their existence, the bay itself might have disappeared. On Shabbat mornings sailboats glided in red, yellow, and white.

And in New York Kronzon's stories reveal that he, like me, belongs to the fraternity of those who grew up on the large terraces on the northern slope of the Carmel and carry that view wherever they go: flat-roofed white houses, dotted green treetops, the bay, and the ships.

> Uncle Abrasha walked around the terrace, looking at the ships in the port. . . . Suddenly I remembered that Mother always said that Haifa

is the most beautiful city in the world, so that is what I said to my
uncle. He looked at me . . . and asked . . . if I'd seen all the cities of the
world. I said that I hadn't, and he said, "So how can you say that if
you haven't seen them?"[70]

The recurring mentions of the terrace in Kronzon's stories are a melody
that accompanies the history of his family, its joys and disappointments,
its lives and deaths—on a warm Shabbat morning in the middle of the
winter: "mother sits on the terrace, closing her eyes . . . and enjoys herself."[71] And on special days, like the narrator's bar mitzvah, "sixty people
crowded onto the terrace."[72] When Marcus-Ron, "mother's employer" at
the conservatory, came for a Friday night meal, the family took down the
"Czech china service" in honor of the occasion, and they "brought the
table out of the dining room onto the large terrace." But, unfortunately,
when the honored guest began belting out the Kiddush, the Friday night
blessing, the narrator's mother could not hold back and burst into laughter that offended him: "Marcus-Ron stands . . . his face to the sea and the
Carmel at his back . . . his mouth agape . . . and from the depths of his
chest bursts a powerful, ear-deafening, glorious roar that rolls over all of
Hadar HaCarmel all the way to the bay: 'Yom hashishi.'"[73] The large terrace
becomes an active participant in the scene because only against the backdrop of this epic landscape could the catastrophe—his mother's uncontrollable laughter—have reached its mythic proportions.

In another story, when the child narrator suffers a major blow, he turns
to the terrace, as if he can truly unload his sorrow only while facing this
landscape: "I walked into the apartment and went out to the big terrace.
I leaned on the railing, looked out at the ships in the bay of Haifa, and
cried."[74] The terrace, however, plays a part in daily routines as well as cli-
mactic moments. The narrator's father regularly tutors math there. As one
summer day wanes in yet another story, "he sits in a mesh undershirt on
the large terrace and explains. . . . I lie quietly on the sofa and listen. I'm
small and don't understand. . . . Over the port . . . from the sea a cool breeze
starts blowing."[75]

This scene recurs at least twice more, but its subject has become the
father's final tutoring session. Here the words "the large terrace" turn into
the sounds of a requiem. In one story: "My father died on a Friday morn-

ing at 10:45 while tutoring a high school girl in math, on the large terrace of our apartment on Ge'ula Street."[76] And in another: "He died in the middle of a private lesson in math, on the large terrace."[77] The final farewell to the house on 21 Ge'ula Street also takes place against the backdrop of the same landscape, when the visitors who come during the shiva gather on the large terrace for the last time.

Haifa's terraces, then, played many roles. In our house on 85 Herzl Street, we could look out over the roofs of all the houses below us. Across from us lived my friend Ester Peleg, whose apartment was so close that I could call out to her — very loudly — "Ester! Ester!" — and ask about homework (in the 1950s, almost no one had a phone). On one rooftop terrace we could see a man, working day and night, his table loaded with books. Years later I would meet him again. It was Yitzhak Ring, my high school Bible teacher.

On Sukkot Gadi and I built a sukkah on the terrace under the blue table and decorated it with paper chains. Nearby trees sometimes dipped to brush the railing, dewdrops swinging on their leaves on spring mornings, the wind rustling through them. When it rained, we stood near the railing, close enough to feel the light touch of the water sprinkling on our faces but far enough that we didn't get really wet.

On summer evenings our family would eat dinner there, caressed by the moon's rays, surrounded by the lights of the balconies of nearby houses and, over the dark waters of the bay, the sparkles from the sailboats and ships and the breakwater. A gentle breeze would blow through the treetops that circled our house — tall, almost as tall as us as we stood there, but never blocking the view. When autumn came and the school year started, I would prepare arithmetic questions that I supposedly could not solve without my father's help in order to win a few more minutes with him before going to bed. Then I would join my parents' quiet supper and steal a slice of bliss: only the three of us, as "little children" like Gadi had to be in bed already. The table was covered with a tablecloth, and an arc of lights etched the curved line of the bay at night.

Every Friday my father would come home early from the store, and we would listen for his footsteps on the stairs and run to him. For each of us, he would bring a little bag from the sweetshop that opened in the front of our building shortly after we moved in. Beneath the glass that covered the display table that stretched all along the storefront lay the treasures. The chocolate we loved the most we called "tree trunk," because that's what it resembled. Chunks of lop-ended chocolate, three centimeters long — each one looked like an ancient tree trunk, but when it reached our mouths, it would melt and dissolve and its texture was as pleasurable as its taste, the taste of milk chocolate Fridays.

Shortly after the beginning of third grade, we had drills to prepare for a possible war: leave the classroom quickly and run to the shelter in an orderly fashion, without mischief. It was 1956, the days before the Sinai campaign. As in my father's store, the windows in the stores on the ground floor of 85 Herzl Street and all the glass panes of the apartment windows were crisscrossed with a plaid pattern of masking tape to prevent them from shattering in the event of bombings. At night a "blackout" was imposed, and we shrouded these glass panes with blankets so no light could seep through. There was no bomb shelter in our building, so when the sirens sounded, we were to go down to the lowest floor and sit in a windowless space.

My mother sweeps the floor of the corridor. Next to the front door she leans on the mop; her head is lowered. Ima, what happened? You're crying. Eli fell in battle. Eli? Yes, Eli Gruenfeld, the blond kid with the rain cape from the picture. But maybe it's not him. Maybe you're wrong. Let me go down to Kahanovitch to buy the newspaper. And there, among the two lines of the young faces that were printed in black and white in two vertical rows on the sides of the front page, was the face and beneath it, the name: Sergeant Shmuel (Eli) Gruenfeld, nineteen years old. His name is Shmuel, not Eli. Ima, don't cry. Maybe it's somebody else.

I don't recall the sound of the siren, but I vividly remember going down the dark staircase to the Kligers' apartment. I never visited them before or after, but on the night of October 31, 1956, all the house's tenants sat there, in the Kligers' corridor. We crowded on the floor or on low seats and waited for the all clear. My father did not join us. Only Gadi and I were there with my mother. Afterward, I learned that my father had insisted on watching the events that unfolded in the bay. He sat on our terrace and observed the Egyptian warship *Ibrahim El-Awal* shell the city.[78]

Then a French destroyer, anchored in the port, opened fire and the Israeli navy overcame the ship as it tried to retreat out of the territorial waters. In the days after the war, the destroyer was renamed *Haifa*, and, along with many of the children and residents of the city, we went down to the port to see it from the inside. Everybody sang, "It is no legend, my friends, / And not a fleeting dream / Behold, in front of Mount Sinai / the bush is burning again." I will never forget that President Eisenhower stopped food deliveries to Israel to pressure the Israeli government to retreat from the Sinai Peninsula.[79] Suddenly, the salty American butter, which I loved, disappeared from grocery store shelves, and white sugar was nowhere to be found.

But the war was an aberration. Usually, the routine of our lives on 85 Herzl was sweet. Our apartment's proximity to the store meant that my father could now come home every day for a long lunch break, eat with us, then grab a short nap, during which we had to be quiet. As my home was also close to the school, it became a favorite meeting place for friends to do homework together in the children's room or on the large terrace or to play in the generous space provided by the apartment. We were not allowed on the busy Herzl Street, but sometimes we went down to play in the small yard next to the house. At its entrance stood a pomegranate tree, often dotted with red flowers or fruits, and on its other side was a large fig tree that never gave fruit, but in the winter stood bare. The fig tree is one of the only trees that loses its leaves in the Mediterranean winter. So my pride knew no bounds, of course, when *hamora* Sara took us all to see *my* fig tree in third grade when we learned about autumn and how some trees lost their leaves. Friday afternoons and Saturdays continued to be the climax of the week. My father was home. All of us together on Sabbath eve, challah and Kiddush. On Saturday afternoons, after a leisurely *schlafstunde*, my parents' acquaintances would stop by. On the table in the living room the blue-and-white porcelain dishes appeared, a thin gold line around their edges, and a vain porcelain coffeepot—for coffee and cake and chatting and laughing, all in German.

On gray weekdays my father used to sit for hours in the living room at night, alone, making calculations. He had long rectangular ledgers with red margins, which he filled with numbers and dates. Was it these ledgers or the frequent notices from the government that killed him in the end? My parents protected us from the horrors of the overly heavy taxes imposed on them as store owners, but the syllables of *masahakhnasa* (income tax) always made me shudder, even though I did not understand them.[80]

My father had brown-rimmed reading glasses and wavy hair, combed backward, all black and silver threads. After work he would soak his tired feet in the white enameled basin, filled with piping hot water from the kitchen teakettle. I did not understand his exhaustion and fatigue then. I was only happy that he was home.

In the summer between fourth and fifth grade, my father became sick and was hospitalized. He returned home and lay in his bed for weeks, and then, one night, we heard voices from the corridor: "Shh. Don't wake up the children." In the morning it turned out that my father had been readmitted to the hospital. One evening before I fell asleep, my atheist mother told me that she had traveled far for an audience with a great rabbi. He had suggested changing my father's name to Chaim, which means "life," to ensure a long life, but because Chaim was my father's brother's name, that was impossible. My mother told me that she believed this was a bad omen. The rabbi gave her an amulet for my father, on which his name was changed to Raphael—"God heals"—but it was all in vain. Later they took my brother and me to Rambam Hospital. Oxygen tanks stood at my father's side near his head. From the hospital room a small balcony opened over the waves of the sea. I didn't want to stay in that room, so I went out to the balcony.

On that bitter morning of October 22, 1958, as on every morning during those last weeks, my mother came home from the hospital at 7:00 a.m. (she used to visit my father at dawn, return home to wake us up and send us to school, then go to work at the store). This time she told us that she had met *hamora* Sara on the way and learned that there was a teachers' strike. School had been cancelled. And we had to go immediately to our relatives in the suburb of Motzkin. We walked to the 52 bus stop, next to the big synagogue. My mother put us on the bus and told us that Paula and Alfred would meet us at the other end. And, indeed, they did. They took us to their home. I did not understand why there was no teachers' strike in Motzkin, but I was told that there was a strike only in Haifa proper. In the afternoon Alfred's sister, Kathe, came to take care of us. We asked why. Kathe explained that a close friend of Paula and Alfred's had died,

and they had to go to the funeral, so they could not watch us. Perhaps
that's when I knew; perhaps not. Late in the afternoon another relative
arrived, Zvi, who was in no way related to Paula and Alfred. His presence
in their house made no sense. Again we asked. Paula and Alfred took us to
their bedroom. No one was ever allowed into that room, ever, so simply
entering it signaled to us that something very different, something wrong,
had happened. Paula started crying and got out one word, "Abba" (dad),
and I completed her sentence and said, "*met*" (died). Gadi ran to the bathroom and vomited without stopping. And then Zvi took us to the bus station to go home. I remember little of the trip, but when we arrived, I saw
my mother sitting on a low chair in the children's room. As the great poet
H. N. Bialik wrote about the shiva for his father, "Then a dark cloud descended on the house / And crouched there for shelter."[81]

People wanted us to eat dinner, so I told my mother that I would eat
only if she did. And so it was. We ate salami, a food that we never had in
our house. During the shiva, I became sick, and the very kind Dr. Emed
made a house call. Teachers from the school also came to pay a shiva call.
After seven days I went back to school. During homeroom they gave me
a framed plaque from the Jewish National Fund with a tree on it and an
inscription: "For Nili Scharf, your teacher and your classmates planted a
tree in memory of your father, Ya'akov Scharf Z"L."

Belonging to the Scouts

At the end of fourth grade, just a few months before my father's unexpected death, the various youth movements — such as the socialist Zionist HaShomer HaTzair and the labor union–founded HaNo'ar Ha'Oved
— began to woo my classmates and me. These youth movements, and the
kibbutzim that their graduates established, played a major role in the formation of Israeli culture. They were also almost all connected to specific
political parties and often served as instruments of recruitment. My father,
however, instructed, "If you join a youth movement, it must be one that
does not identify with any political party." And this is how I joined the
Scouts, the only nonpartisan youth movement in Israel.

We were small cubs (*ofarim*, literally, "fawns") when we pledged our
loyalty in a scary nighttime ceremony on the mountain. We stood in a *U* in

a large clearing nestled among pine groves. One by one, shuddering with fear, we approached the head counselor, his face illuminated by the burning torch behind him. He pricked our pointer fingers with a sharp pin so that we could swear allegiance to the Scouts not only with our signatures but also with our blood. We then received the metal pin with the symbol of the Hebrew Scouts and learned the three-fingered salute, thumb holding down the pinky finger; and the Scouts' motto, "Be Prepared." They taught us the anthem, "Be prepared to fulfill your duty / Be faithful to your people and homeland / Always help others / Uphold the Scouts' law / Always be prepared." We all took our oath and the commands of the anthem very seriously and, at that moment, were prepared to sacrifice all we had to uphold them. After everyone had pledged their loyalty, we climbed back down the rocky path in the dark.

Now I belonged to the Dror (Freedom) troop, the youngest troop in the large "Ge'ula Tribe." Two to three times per week, in a khaki uniform with a yellow kerchief properly tied around my neck, I would once again climb Bar Kokhba Street toward its intersection with Hermon, then continue up the steeper Betar to the place where it touches HaShiloah. Only today, as I'm writing this, do I recognize the thread that connects the names of the streets of that neighborhood. Gilad and Hermon, Tavor and Shiloah, Betar and Bar Kokhba: mountains and springs, freedom fighters and battlefields in the ancient history and geography of the Land of Israel.

Even before reaching the tip of Betar, I could see my friends gathering on the street corner near the former Magen David Adom building at the intersection of Betar and HaShiloah. The humble, rounded building was no longer a trauma center but a school for girls. The low, stone wall next to it served as a long, comfortable bench where we waited for the counselors to lead us inside the boundaries of the Ge'ula School. In the meantime we would buy sweets from Jimmy at the kiosk on the other side of the street and cluster in groups or pairs, the topics of conversation and the makeup of the groups shifting over the years. At the designated time the counselors arrived, and together we climbed the alley to the gate and entered the large schoolyard. The thick-trunked eucalyptus tree that I remembered from first and second grade welcomed me back, and the large yard appeared friendlier than it had then. On Tuesday afternoons, for us Scouts, it became a drill yard.[82] Our counselors arranged us in threes and taught us to stand at attention and "at ease" and how to march in unison — left, right, left. After the drills we had our meeting.

In the mid-1950s a bomb shelter was constructed at Ge'ula, as in many other places in the land. A portion of the open, roofed area between the two buildings of the Ge'ula School was closed off by a very thick, fortified wall. We called that space "the shelter" (*hamiklat*) even though its main function was to provide a place for our meetings when we stayed within the parameters of the school and did not go up to the mountain. On Tuesdays and rainy Saturdays we would huddle there and sit on long, wooden benches arranged next to the thick walls or on the ground. The counselor would teach us a new song, and afterward we would sing songs we already knew loudly and enthusiastically, such as, "Vanya, oh Vanya, my dear brother / Take me to the war, / You will be a red commissar there / and I will be a nurse." This song was imported from Soviet Russia and, as Kronzon, who sang it as part of a different movement, wrote, "We don't know — and no one explains to us — who Vanya is, what war is discussed, what a commissar is, and how a red commissar is different from one who is not red."[83] Afterward, we would discuss important ideological matters. We conducted a mock trial against Theodore Bikel, the actor-singer who had "traitorously" left Israel. We pondered the morality of euthanasia and the value of white lies. We were so confident that we were right, and we transmitted this certainty to the young cubs who would eventually be our charges when we, ourselves, became counselors.

On Saturday mornings we conquered the mountain with our feet. We would march in formation along Bezalel Street up to the point where it bends southward and suddenly becomes a steep ascent. To overcome the exertion of climbing, we began chanting rhythmically *otto lo otzer ba'aliya*, followed by a stomp — "No auto-mo-bile should stop on the hill [stomp!]. No auto-mo-bile should stop on the hill [stomp!]" — or "dag malu'ah yatza lasu'ah / nichnas lakita vekatav al halu'ah . . . sheh," which means "a herring went for a stroll / entered a classroom, and wrote on the wall / that . . . a herring went for a stroll." And so on until Bezalel meets Ge'ula. With an energetic left-right march in rows of three and Scout songs on our lips, we arrived at the very bottom of the mountain in fifteen minutes, then left the paved road and walked up the wide, dusty path to what was dubbed "The Eucalyptus Grove."

A few years later, when I was almost fourteen, I became a counselor, now wearing a green kerchief. On the side of the shelter, or *miklat,* was a small office that belonged to us — that is, to the Scouts, not the school. And in that little office, as always, without adult supervision, we would sit and plan the meetings and rituals that would enthrall our ten-year-old charges, a new generation of cubs in yellow kerchiefs, children who had just joined the movement. Now I was the one leading the young members of the Arava (Desert Plain) troop up to the mountain. "No auto-mo-bile should stop on the hill [stomp!]. No auto-mo-bile should stop on the hill [stomp!]."

We would leave the school gate, turn left and go up the alley toward Bezalel Street, past the ship-like building of the conservatory, looking down on us from above. I knew it well from the outside, and I loved the way it sat on the mountain as though striving forward toward the sea, where real ships sailed. But it remained stuck on the slope — only the music that burst forth from it soared into the distance.

When I eventually began following the journey of the architect whom I had learned to admire, Benjamin Orell, who planned my beloved Alliance School, I discovered that it was he who built the conservatory in 1947. As in his other creations, here too he ingeniously exploited the steep Haifa slope and turned the constraints of the narrow, triangular lot into an advantage. The rocky landscape facing the sea as well as the port served as inspiration: a ship, pointing northward, and on its sides, portholes. Yet he never forgot the function of the buildings he designed, and as this was to be a conservatory, he forged the window bars of its "portholes" in the shape of lutes.

Our Scout troop did not stop at the conservatory, however, but continued marching toward the mountain to hold our meeting: "We are Scouts / and in our veins / the blood of Judea flows / Hebrew Scout / Be prepared / A Hebrew Scout is always prepared." Onward, on Bezalel and then Ge'ula, after we passed the last houses, there were quarries to our right almost all the way to the Eucalyptus Grove. There, under the trees, we would spread out, choose a comfortable rock or a piece of ground upholstered with leaves, and sit down. I would start the meeting, and all of us, counselors and scouts alike, in khaki uniforms, with carefully folded and ironed kerchiefs around our necks, would sing the old songs together and discuss lofty matters. From far below the Eucalyptus Grove, the sea watched us, a light breeze rustling in the leaves.

In those sun-filled days, when we were Scout counselors and high school students, we no longer needed our supervisors to take us to the mountain. Unlike the beach, to which we had to travel, the mountain, with its green ridges, its valleys, and especially its step paths, was always within arm's — or rather leg's — reach. The Scout meetings continued, but at the same time we would roam over the mountain in small groups, in couples or even alone.

The Green Groves of Mount Carmel

When I was in twelfth grade, studying for my baccalaureate in literature, I stuffed a bag full of books and climbed the mountain to the familiar Eucalyptus Grove to study, far from my house or my friends' houses, far from the noise of cars and the commotion of the city. I spread out a blanket and piled on top of it the Hebrew classics of H. N. Bialik and Shaul Tchernichovsky and the pastoral idylls of David Shimoni. Below, where the wide dust path met the paved road, I suddenly saw a lone man climbing slowly, feigning innocence. I didn't see where he had sprung from — perhaps from one of the caves on the side of the mountain. There was no one else around. And there was no place to hide on the mountain. I decided to retreat slowly, so as not to betray my fear. I got up from my seat, folded the blanket meticulously, put the books in my bag, and tried to cut straight down through the rocks to the road. But the man was almost next to me. He came closer and grabbed me forcefully; the smell of him hit my face. I pleaded, "no more than a kiss," and, indeed, he kissed me on my mouth and let me go. Barely breathing, I jumped from rock to rock until I reached the wide path and, from there, ran to the road and then to a friend's house at the tip of HaShiloah Street, which was closest to the mountain. I did not tell my mother about the incident, but I also never returned to the mountain to study.

Less than two decades later Dahlia Ravikovitch's long poem, "Hovering at a Low Altitude," appeared, with lines that could have been written about me. But her poem tells a much more violent story, and the girl in its verses is much younger than I was:

that man goes up the mountain.
He looks innocent enough.

The girl is right there,
no one else around.
And if she runs for cover, or cries out —
there's no place to hide in the mountain.[84]

Ravikovitch's poem is set on "craggy eastern hills / streaked with ice, / where grass doesn't grow," *not* on the green Carmel. Yet I wondered if, as she wandered on the Carmel, she had run into that sort of man. Either way, the visceral panic the poem evokes, namely that "there's no place to hide," resurrected that memory for me. Most of the time, however, Mount Carmel was a place of magic, and when Ravikovitch, who knew it well, painted it in other poems, it is unmistakably identifiable — green pine groves gliding down its side and the sea, the blue sea, always there, at the bottom.

Throughout high school, on Yom Kippur days, we would gather, five or six girls with blankets and books, and climb up to the Three Pine Trees. We did not take food — for whatever reason, we fasted on this solemn day even though we did not go to synagogue. The Three Pine Trees, with their expansive foliage, stood on a tall, still-bare, hill on the upper border of Hadar HaCarmel. Under the canopy of green needles we used to chat to our hearts' content and read, unbothered by the fast, until the day had almost waned. The three pines that gave the hill its name could be reached in those days only by climbing up the rocks. From its heights we could see green treetops, the magnificent city, and the bay. The port to the west was invisible, so the slice of the sea in front of us was pure and calm and pristine. Only the breakwater drew a line through it.

A few years before we climbed the mountain and gazed down on this landscape, the poem "Painting" by Ravikovitch was published. The poet had spent her youth in Haifa, moving from one foster family to another, living in homes that stood on the side of the mountain.[85] She began writing the unmistakably Haifaian poem-portrait in eighth grade, around the same age we were when we began climbing to the Three Pine Trees:

The woods of green sheep flowed down the slopes
and the sea below splashed and turned blue in the sun.

View from the Three Pines *Courtesy of photographer Nili Gold*

Clouds opened white, like water lilies,
and we were still girls.[86]

Like us, Ravikovitch was hypnotized by those groves, whose green
treetops curl their backs like a flock of sheep on the side of the Carmel.
For a moment, it seems as if they are sliding downward, that their roots are
not planted in the rocky slope. Like us, she was overcome by the sea — the
mirror of the blue sky, glistening in the kind Haifa sun. Ravikovitch saw
this magnificent view, and she painted it in words.

We will never know what her exact lookout point was. Perhaps she
found a rock high on the mountain near her Hugim School, which moved
closer to the top of the Carmel at around that time. But perhaps she sat
on the uncultivated field that spread near the one home that she loved in
Haifa, and where she was loved in return, the home of Rela Harekhavi, at
4 Shamay Street:

And I would go out in the sun to the nearby field
and love the clouds and dream up stories about them,
and I had plenty of time to think about sorrow
from the first day of gray autumn till the end
of yellow summer.[87]

The open field next to Shamay Street, a vertical alley that descends through Hadar HaCarmel, is still bare. In her poem "Painting," Ravikovitch captures not only the landscape but also us, all of whom, like her, were still girls. We savored the views but also suffered growing pains in spite of the wealth of beauty that lay before us. Ravikovitch knew and masterfully depicted the challenges particular to being a girl, especially a girl like her, a girl who dreams up stories, a girl without a father, a girl who imagines "water lilies" everywhere, as they were one of the few details that she remembered from her Shabbat outings with her father before he died, when she still knew "delight beyond delight."[88]

And in Haifa, in the midst of the great sadness that engulfed her "from the first day of gray autumn till the end / of yellow summer," that landscape — comforting and marvelous — became the background of the stories that she told herself, and its pine trees bequeathed her poems. In "Day unto Day Uttereth Speech," a poem whose title is a quote from Psalm 19, she writes,

As in the forests on Mount Carmel
where my soul was filled with yearning —
the pines dropped their needles
when the wind rose
pinecones fell to the ground.
. . . .
King David came to me
. . . .
He'd sit beside me day after day
When he was pleased, he'd play hymns

Ravikovitch was anointed as a poet. The spirit of King David, the handsome poet-king, "rested upon" her, not in Jerusalem, the capital city he built, but in the forests on the Carmel. He bestowed poetry upon her in Haifa.[89]

A. B. Yehoshua and the Steps

And, of course, there were the steps. Climbing them could begin from
anywhere in Hadar, but we often started above the Ge'ula School at the
bottom of the Betar Steps. Then we would continue up flights of stairs
with different names that pass through varied neighborhoods as they ascend elegantly to the top of the mountain. Somehow, they all end up near
the Donkey Steps, whose top reaches, if not heaven, then a similar place
—Panorama Street. The young heroes of A. B. Yehoshua's first novel, *The
Lover*, are unwittingly attracted to those steps. Yehoshua wrote *The Lover*
after he moved to Haifa from Jerusalem and was swept off his feet by his
new city's beauty. The novel takes place in Haifa and uses the city's dis-
tinctive features—deep valleys, seascapes, beaches, and steps—to weave
its plot. It is a story of a Haifa-based upper-middle-class family whose pa-
triarch, Adam, is the prosperous owner of an automobile repair shop and
whose matriarch, Asya, is a high school teacher. Their first child, a deaf
boy named Yigal, was hit and killed by a car at age six because he could
not hear its horn. Their daughter, Dafi, who was born after the accident, is
a rebellious insomniac high schooler. Perhaps due to the little boy's tragic
accident, there is little to no romance between Adam and Asya. Driven
by concern for his wife, Adam finds her a lover, Gabriel, a forlorn young
man who had come to Adam's garage to fix a 1947 blue Morris. Gabriel
had returned to Israel to collect his grandmother's inheritance, only to
find her in a coma. During his visit, however, the brutal Yom Kippur War
erupted; he reluctantly enlisted and then disappeared. The lion's share of
the novel is dedicated to Adam's nocturnal searches for Gabriel, which he
conducts with the help of his daughter and an Arab teenager, Naim, who
works in his repair shop. Dafi and Naim, meanwhile, seem to be destined
for love.

Even though the union between the Jewish girl and the Arab boy does
not take place until the end of the book, it is foreshadowed on the Donkey Steps in the middle of the narrative. The light-haired Dafi is from the
affluent Carmel, while the handsome Naim is a poor car mechanic from a
village in the Galilee. Due to a strange chain of events, Naim spends one
Friday night at his employer's home on the Carmel. The next morning,
Shabbat, Adam and Asya leave the house early, and Dafi is the only one left

at home. The parents ask Dafi to release Naim from his responsibilities for
that day when he wakes up.

Yehoshua wrote the novel using the Rashomon Style, in which each
chapter is recounted in the voice of one of the characters. The experience
of descending the Donkey Steps that Saturday morning is, therefore, recorded in the inner monologues of each of the adolescents, while one consciousness reflects the other. Naim, more aware of his smoldering feelings
for Dafi than she is of her attraction to him, recalls,

> "You want me to come with you?" . . . We started descending the
> mountain. *She showed me steps that go down in the middle of the moun-
> tain.* Inside: flowers, trees, bushes, and greenery. *Like a path in para-
> dise* . . . and all the air around is filled with fragrance.[90]

And Dafi:

> So I said to him, "Just a moment, I'll come with you," because *I
> wanted to show him how to get down* the Carmel *through the steps in the
> middle of the mountain,* where it's nice to walk on a day like this. . . .
> *I showed him the steps going down* and even went a little way with him.
> . . . We carried on walking down among the bushes and flowers.[91]

By showing him the steps going down the mountain, Dafi teaches
Naim a chapter in the book of Haifa's rituals.[92] She initiates him into the
secret society of those who know about the steps. Dafi walks publicly with
Naim, on Shabbat, through the polished, fancy Center Carmel neighborhood while he is wearing filthy worker's clothes. But that walk has a much
deeper significance than merely showing that Dafi pays no heed to status
symbols. The scene on the steps, or the initiation into "Haifaianness," not
only is the first scene in the book that represents a common action between the two characters, but it also foreshadows the consummation of
their love near the novel's closure. Naim describes,

> and it was a long kiss and suddenly I saw that I couldn't stand it any
> longer . . . and I fell on my knees and started kissing her feet . . . but
> she lifted me up and pulled me into the bedroom . . . and then she
> tore off my shirt and said, "Come and be my lover." (421; 340)

And from Dafi's point of view:

> And suddenly we were kissing . . . a deep sort of kiss, like in the movies, . . . and suddenly he let go of me and fell down on his knees and started kissing my feet . . . and I saw he was afraid to stand up . . . so I lifted him up. (421; 340)

Dafi shows Naim the way. First in her city of Haifa, then in her home, and finally in her body. The steps, thinks Naim, are like a fragrant "path in paradise." Yehoshua's image recalls Adam and Eve and the original loss of innocence: "I'm sure I'm the first of all the girls," thinks Dafi (422; 341), and Naim confesses to Adam that "this was the first time in his life" (432; 349). The initiation into the urban space in the heart of *The Lover* — the first descent down the steps in the middle of the mountain — foretells the sexual coming-of-age ritual that culminates it.

The book's title, *The Lover*, is ostensibly for Gabriel, the man Adam introduced to his wife. Yet between the novel's pages, another love is hiding. Adam, who unintentionally caused this love and is also the first witness of its formation, does not understand the relationship growing right in front of him; he does not hear, so to speak, its melody. He is "deaf" to it, as he himself says afterward. "A little lover" (432; 349), thinks Adam, "He fell in love quietly and *I* didn't sense it. . . . It's as if I'm deaf" (434; 351; emphasis mine). Indeed, Naim, the boy that Adam unwittingly ushered into the bosom of his family, is the true, pure lover in the novel. Perhaps a love like this, a love that ignores national identities, could have blossomed only in Haifa, but it is especially surprising against the backdrop of the period. In the mid-1970s, when the events of *The Lover* take place, Israel was still reeling from the Yom Kippur War.

Yehoshua's 1977 novel, like many of his other works, seems to be prophetic and produces meaning on two different levels: personal and national. The great critic and literary scholar Gershon Shaked, who was Yehoshua's teacher at Hebrew University and one of his first readers, said of *The Lover* that it showed the "shadow side of the Israeli existence."[93] Shaked argued that, here, the strong, Ashkenazi Israeli male hero appears in all his weakness, as the author exposes not only his fears and insecurities but also Israel's. Yehoshua's portrayal of Adam as an impotent man may then suggest the author's opinion on the national reality. Israel's founders no longer have the same power and vigor they once did, so to survive they must invite into their homes, so to speak, outsiders from previously marginalized elements in Israeli society.

I would also make the case that in *The Lover* Haifa is an actor rather than a setting. Yehoshua penetrated not only the national Israeli psyche but also the Haifaian one. He foresaw local developments in the city still latent at the time the book was written. The novel's Haifa is beautiful: its sea shimmers from every window, and its Mount Carmel is green, with ranges stretching their arms out in all directions. But within that beauty lurks the eventual deterioration of Hadar HaCarmel, which was bustling in the 1970s but is tellingly absent from the text. The novel foreshadows the decline of Hadar, and the city's future sinking into the periphery: Adam, the Haifaian head of the novel's main household and the owner of an automotive repair shop, is impotent. His wife, Asya, the daughter of a displaced Labor Zionist leader in the city, retreats into the world of dreams, while her daytime occupation — she is a history teacher — revolves around the past. And finally, the only true love that blossoms in the novel — between an Arab and a Jew — is in danger.

Furthermore, throughout *The Lover* Adam desperately tries first to fix and then to find a 1947 model Morris car and, ultimately, succeeds in doing both. If we heed Shaked's interpretation that the 1947 blue Morris is a metaphor for the State of Israel, then perhaps Yehoshua's message is not only one of doom.[94] The dilapidated blue 1947 Morris is being artfully reconstructed in Haifa, of all places, alluding to the potentials presented by the city's mode of life and history. The rejuvenated blue 1947 Morris will one day drive again on the Carmel slopes and can thus be interpreted as Haifa regaining its status as "the city of the future."

And a final note: upon Yehoshua's reluctant departure from the city, the mayor of Haifa expressed the wish to honor the author who had lived there for four decades. Unsurprisingly, they thought to name a square for *The Lover*, Yehoshua's most quintessentially Haifaian novel, a novel that exposes Israel's conflicts but offers a consoling vision — a prophecy of reconciliation.

Forty years after writing this novel, its author still stands by his initial faith in Haifa. As he told me, "Haifa is the model for what I wanted Israel to be." And he added, "It was the city where I lived and where I created and which I loved. . . . I also saw harmony between Jews and Arabs, secular and religious Jews, and a social consciousness. . . . Haifa is Israel at its best."[95]

ACKNOWLEDGMENTS

It takes a town to write a book about one. As I embarked on this book about my hometown of Haifa and walked through its streets, I did not walk alone. With me were writers, architects, friends, and colleagues.

The author Amir Gutfreund was born in Hadar HaCarmel in 1963 and died in the prime of his life in 2015. In October 2010 he traveled from his home in the Galilee to the Carmel to meet with me. "Haifa awakens the muse in me," he said. "In Haifa, the background noises are quiet . . . but if you want to write a convincing Haifa story, you'd better be from Haifa." While his novels fall outside the framework of my book, his spirit hovers over it—as too does the soul of Emil Habibi, the quintessential Haifa man. His landscapes, which are so dear to my heart, also fall outside the parameters of this book. Yet the words he wanted carved on his gravestone, "I stayed in Haifa," accompany me, one who did not stay.

While I wrote, two books of a different nature were always by my side. *Bauhaus on the Carmel and the Crossroads of Empire: Architecture and Planning in Haifa during the British Mandate*, published by Gilbert Herbert and Silvina Sosnovsky in 1993, reconstructs, deed by deed, the almost legendary acts of creation wrought by courageous architects on a stubborn land: planning the city of Haifa and making it a capital of modernism. Hayim Aharonovitch's *Hadar HaCarmel: A Treatise of Labor and a Creation of a Generation of Founders and Builders* appeared thirty-five years earlier. It strings together detail after detail, like beads on a long thread—demographic data, prices of lots, and sewer canals—that sing an ode in prose to Hadar HaCarmel and its builders.

Many people generously gave of their time, ideas, and heart. I'm grateful to each and every one.

There were those who provided invaluable information and documentation: My friend, the architect Waleed Karkabi, head of the Department of Conservation in Haifa, whose love for the city and its buildings was my inspiration from the very first walking tour that I took with him. An overflowing fount of knowledge about architecture and architects in the city, Waleed also opened doors to locked-up archives for me. Eli Roman, a brother in his love of Haifa, sat with me countless hours in his law office, hours that spanned many years and thousands of postcards and documents. Throughout my research and writing, he worked to answer my every question, remove every stumbling block from my path, and introduce me to experts to answer lingering questions. My architectural guide, research assistant, and photographer, architect Adi Silberstein, whose family's roots are in Haifa, gathered for me countless books, articles, and archival documents on the city's structures. Together we walked the route of the book, as she taught me expertly and sensitively how to read a building's design and to appreciate how an architect's creation affects those who use it. Amira Kehat, the ultimate documentarian, has mapped the chronicles of Haifa's houses. She and the Haifa History Society opened the gates of their treasure troves for me.

Particularly meaningful were the walks on which fellow Haifaians took me as they revealed *their* Haifa. Itamar Shoshan, my high school deskmate with whom I explored every nook and cranny of our old school building and yards, related personal memories and gave me his photographs. The former head of city planning, Havah Law-Yone, who coincidentally grew up on my block, guided me through Memorial Park and Herzl Street and taught me the architectural cadences of Hadar HaCarmel. Yovi Sabo nostalgically recounted our childhood as we climbed Haneviim Steps Street together, and he even photographed the neighborhood for this book. Nitza Sabo, his wife, recollected her family's legacy in Hadar HaCarmel as well as her relationship with the poet Dahlia Ravikovitch, who babysat for her. Yovi and Nitza Sabo, like my beloved friends Yosi and Nitza Ben-Dov, hosted me in Haifa and reminded me that even after the intervening decades, Haifa is still home. My cherished colleague and dear friend Nitza Ben-Dov lovingly supported this project from its inception. Yosi, as the executive director of the Hebrew Reali School, gave me a tour of the historical school building and arranged access to its records and rich archives.

My esteemed colleague Yossi Ben-Artzi offered sage advice and kindly made available his huge vaults of books and materials; he and his wife, Orit, cheered me on throughout. The architect Ziva Kolodney, head of Long-Term Municipal Planning in Haifa, expounded on her fascinating work on landscape architecture. Edina Meyer-Maril shared her writings on and intimate knowledge of Alexander Baerwald. Giddon Ticotsky let me in on his discoveries about Dahlia Ravikovitch without reservation. Alon Tam contributed his expertise in Arabic and the region; Regev Nathansohn shared his meticulous documentation and research.

This is the second book on which Julia Holleman has worked with me. Her unwavering integrity, her rare gifts of writing and editing, and her elegant style are interlaced throughout these pages. Julia's identification with my life story and dedication to this intellectual journey motivated me to complete this endeavor. Yuval Moses worked with me on the earliest iteration of the book, in Hebrew. His wisdom and ability to see the essence of things were a driving force at that crucial stage.

The midwife of the book was, without a doubt, Sylvia Fuks Fried, director of Brandeis University Press and my much admired editor and friend, who listened intently and held my hand. With endless tact, she made wise comments to improve the text and enabled me to continue, chapter after chapter. Phyllis Deutsch, editor in chief at University Press of New England, believed in this book from the start and guided it with her keen eye. I also want to thank professors Jehuda Reinharz, Dan Ben-Amos, Yigal Schwartz, and Roger Allen, all of whom read various drafts of the manuscript and made valuable comments. Jessica Kasmer-Jacobs, Jonah Wilkof, and Hannah Spivak helped polish and improve the final product.

One of the pillars on which this book stands are literary works on Haifa. Some of their authors graciously granted me interviews. I am eternally grateful for the time, openness, and inspiration of Esty G. Hayim, Yehudit Katzir, Sami Michael, A. B. Yehoshua, and the late Yehudit Hendel; and for the kindness of Natan Zach and his translator, Vivian Eden.

I want to thank my academic home, the University of Pennsylvania; my colleagues in the department of Near Eastern Languages and Civilizations and especially its chair, Paul Cobb, for his enthusiastic support; Arthur Kiron, curator of Judaica Collections, who encouraged me and who left no stone unturned until he obtained the bibliographic materials I needed; and Sheila Ketchum and Jasmine Shinohara at the Van Pelt Library. I am grateful to the Jewish Studies Program for its support through the Littauer Faculty Research Fund, which made possible the contribution of the talented artist Katherine Messenger. Thanks to her exquisite hand-drawn maps, the path of this book can be followed visually. Thanks also to the Schusterman Center for Israel Studies at Brandeis University for its publication grant.

I am grateful to the architect Amir Tomashov, who advised me and introduced me to the architectural community; Nisim Levi (Nassuma), whose memories and memoir capture the Talpiot Market; Michal Henkin and Adam Prager from Haifa City Archive; Natan Kundinsky, historian of Magen David Adom; Amikam Yas'ur, the star bibliographer who paved the way for my initial research; Moshe Gerstel, cinematographer and the grandson of the great architect; Michael Levin, the art and architectural historian. The Dresner family; Gabriel Laufer, my classmate and amateur photographer; Sara Klai, my classmate; Zvi Roger, the municipal photographer and fellow Scout; Dahlia Levi Eliahu, heiress to Eliahu Bros. Postcards; and Yeri Rimon, the ultimate collector of everything Haifa, all shared their precious photographs and memories with me. My treasured and oldest friend, Rivka Hadar, filled in many blanks about our years in the Scouts.

Lastly, I would like to thank my family. My brother, Gadi Scharf, accompanied this writing journey with photographs, provided precious documents, and chased down connections to sources for me. My son, Avitai, read and edited each chapter with the attention and precision that only a lawyer could bring, along with the love of words that we share. His cheer got me through many difficult crossroads and made it possible for me to finish the book. And Jocelyn, who has become my daughter, always stands by me. My daughter Doria has always believed in me, and her love and caring accompany me. My beloved husband, Billy—my rock and my greatest fan—started seeing and loving Haifa through my eyes and became its champion.

NOTES

Introduction

1. Gilbert Herbert and Silvina Sosnovsky, *Bauhaus on the Carmel and the Cross-roads of the Empire: Architecture and Planning in Haifa during the British Mandate* (Jerusalem: Yad Izhak Ben-Zvi, 1993), 9.

2. Isaiah 35:2 (International Standard Version): "It will burst into bloom, and rejoice with gladness and shouts of joy. The glory of Lebanon will be given to it, the splendor of the Carmel and Sharon."

3. Arnon Sofer, "Haifa and Its Hinterland in the British Mandate Period," in *Idan*, ed. Mordechai Naor and Yossi Ben-Artzi (Jerusalem: Yad Ben-Zvi, 1989), 164–70.

4. Alex Carmel, "Haifa at the End of the Ottoman Period," in *Idan*, ed. Mordechai Na'or and Yossi Ben Artzi, vol. 12 (Jerusalem: Yad Ben-Zvi, 1989), 13; Sofer, "Haifa and Its Hinterland," 164–65.

5. Mahmoud Yazbak, *Haifa in the Late Ottoman Period, 1864–1914: A Muslim Town in Transition* (Leiden: Brill, 1998), 1–13.

6. Alex Carmel, *Ottoman Haifa: A History of Four Centuries under Turkish Rule* (London: Tauris, 2011), 49–56.

7. Yazbak, *Late Ottoman Period*, 15–24.

8. Ze'ev Vilnay, *Heifa: be'avar ubahove* [Haifa: In the past and present] (Tel Aviv: Eretz, 1936), 64–65. There was also a minority of Sephardi Jews of Turkish origin. There are testimonies about this Jewish settlement and its synagogue from 1817, 1833, and 1839. Vilnay cites travelogues by Rabbi Chaim Horvitz (1817), Menachem Mendel from Kamenitz (1833), and Lord Montefiore's diary entry from 1839.

9. Carmel, *Ottoman Haifa*, 77, 80.

10. Ibid., 99, 100.

11. Herbert and Sosnovsky, *Bauhaus on the Carmel*, 17.

12. See, for example, Myra Warhaftig, *They Laid the Foundation: Lives and Works of German-Speaking Jewish Architects in Palestine, 1918–1948*, trans. Andrea Lerner (New York: Wasmuth, 2007), 20, 21, 41, 48, 65.

13. Theodor Herzl, *Old New Land*, trans. Lotta Levensohn (United States: Bloch, 1960), 41, 48, 65.

14. Hayim Aharonovitch, *Hadar HaCarmel: masekhet amal vitzira shel dor meyasdim u'vonim* [Hadar HaCarmel: A treatise of labor and creation of a generation of founders and builders] (Haifa: Publication for the Committee for Hadar HaCarmel, 1958), 22–23, 146–47.

15. Article signed by Abdallah Mukhli in *Al-Muqtabas*, March 15, 1910, qtd. in Yazbak, *Late Ottoman Period*, 221.

16. Yazbak, *Late Ottoman Period*, 89–112.

17. "Balfour Declaration: Text of the Declaration," Jewish Virtual Library, November 2, 1917, www.jewishvirtuallibrary.org.

18. Ziva Kolodney, "Contested Urban Memoryscape Strategies and Tactics in Post-1928 Haifa," *Israel Studies* 21 (Spring 2016): 84–85.

19. Herbert and Sosnovsky, *Bauhaus on the Carmel*, 72, 77–80.

20. Aharonovitch, *Hadar HaCarmel*, 29, 44.

21. Aharonovitch, *Hadar HaCarmel*, 70; Herbert and Sosnovsky, *Bauhaus on the Carmel*, 226–28.

22. Herbert and Sosnovsky, *Bauhaus on the Carmel*, 230.

23. Gilbert Herbert and Silvina Sosnovksy, "The Development of Haifa, 1918–1948: Planning and Architecture," in Naor and Ben-Artzi, *Idan*, 47–58.

24. Silvina Sosnovsky, "Haifa," in *Sur les traces du modernisme: ville et architecture guide* [Guide to the traces of modernism: City and architecture], by Catherine Weill-Rochant (Brussels: Centre International pour la Ville, l'Architechture et le Paysage, 2005), 30.

25. Herbert and Sosnovsky, *Bauhaus on the Carmel*, 251, 238.

26. May Seikaly, *Haifa: Transformation of a Palestinian Arab Society, 1918–1939* (London: Tauris, 1995), 155–58; Mahmoud Yazbak, "The Arabs in Haifa: From Majority to Minority, Processes of Change (1870–1948)," *Israel Affairs* 9 (Autumn–Winter 2003): 123–48, 142–44. David de Vries, "Proletarianization and National Segregation: Haifa in the 1920s," *Middle Eastern Studies*, October 1994, 860–82.

27. Aharonovitch, *Hadar HaCarmel*, 177.

28. Walid Khalidi, "The Fall of Haifa Revisited," *Journal of Palestine Studies* 37, no. 3 (2008): 30–58.

29. Tzadok Eshel, *Hativat "Carmeli"* [The Carmeli Brigade] (Israel: Ministry of Defense, 1973), 132; Ya'akov Markovitzki, "The Battle of Haifa and Its Environs in the War of Independence," and Mordechai Naor, "Haifa and the Struggle," both in Naor and Ben-Artzi, *Idan*, 195–207, 195; 184–94, 189–90.

30. M. Zur, "Zim: The National Shipping Company in Its Development," qtd. in Shlomo Sh'hori, Ariela Re'uveni, and Amos Carmeli, eds., *Heifa: eru'ey 20 shana 1948–1968* [Haifa, 1948–1968: Twenty years of events] (Tel Aviv: Davar, 1968), 31.

31. In February 1962 Sha'ar Ha'Aliya (the gate to immigration) was a camp in Haifa through which more than 360,000 immigrants went; it was opened in 1949 and closed in 1962. "'Gate to Immigration' Camp Closed," *Davar*, February 1962, cited in Sh'hori, Re'uveni, and Carmeli, *Heifa*, 136.

32. "Skyscrapers Will Be Built in the City," *Davar*, January 1950; "Solel Boneh to Its New Building," *Davar*, September 1953, both cited in Sh'hori, Re'uveni, and Carmeli, *Heifa*, 50, 75.

33. "Employment Improvement," *Davar*, September 1952; "Haifa Labor Party to Stop Unemployment," *Davar*, May 1953; "Unemployment in Haifa Worsening," *Davar*, October 1953; "Unemployed Protesting in the City," *Davar*, December 1956; "Unemployed Rioting Near Unemployment Office," *Davar*, January, 1957, all cited in Sh'hori, Re'uveni, and Carmeli, *Heifa*, 68, 74, 76, 100, 101.

34. For the university, see "Humanities Academic Institution Opened," *Davar*, March 1953, in Sh'hori, Re'uveni, and Carmeli, *Heifa*, 81; and Tzadok Eshel, *Abba Hushi: Man of Haifa* (Israel: Defense Ministry, 2002), 195. For the theater, see Eshel, *Abba Hushi*, 229. Planning the theater began in the early 1950s. It was a burden on the budget. "City Theater Opened," *Davar*, July 1961; "City Theater Inaugurated," *Davar*, September 1961, cited in Sh'hori, Re'uveni, and Carmeli, *Heifa*, 132, 133.

35. "Arab-Jewish Youth Center," *Davar*, March 1963; "Pre-University Studies Opened," *Davar*, October 1963; "First Anniversary of the Arab-Jewish Youth Center," *Davar*, June 1964, all cited in Sh'hori, Re'uveni, and Carmeli, *Heifa*, 144, 148, 153.

36. "Underground Digging Completed," *Davar*, May 1953; "The Carmelite Activated," *Davar*, October 1959, both cited in Sh'hori, Re'uveni, and Carmeli, *Heifa*, 103, 117; Eshel, *Abba Hushi*, 219. The tunnel was less than two kilometers long, and it opened on October 6, 1959.

37. The first new building for the Technion was inaugurated in 1953. By October 1965 eleven out of fifteen faculties had already been moved. "The Technion Completes Transfer to New Campus," *Davar*, October 1965, cited in Sh'hori, Re'uveni, and Carmeli, *Heifa*, 163.

1. The Seamline: Where Memory Is Stored

1. See Lionella Scazzosi, "Reading and Assessing the Landscape as Cultural and Historical Heritage," in *Landscape Research* 29, no. 4 (London: Routledge, 2004), 335–55.

2. Waleed Karkabi, head of Building Conservation Team at the Haifa Municipality, architectural walking tour 7, transcribed by Regev Nathanson, Hadar HaCarmel, January 2011.

3. He was forced to give up his post between 1920 and 1927 due to Arab pressure against him because he welcomed Herbert Samuel, the first British governor, who was Jewish.

4. Tamir Goren, *65 shana le'hakamat habinyan: 1942–2007* [65 years for the erection of the building: 1942–2007] (Ramat Gan: Haifa History Society/Haifa Municipality, 2008), 4.

5. Tamir Goren, "Arabs and Jews in the City Council in the Period of the British Mandate," in Goren, *65 shana le'hakamat habinyan*, 21.

6. David Hacohen, "Jews and Arabs in Haifa Municipality," and Avraham Khalfon, "Memories from 'Little Haifa,'" both in Naor and Ben-Artzi, *Idan*, 229, 244. The Hebrew minutes can be found in the Collection of the City Archives.

7. Hacohen, "Jews and Arabs," 233; Khalfon, "Memories from 'Little Haifa,'" 243.

8. Tamir Goren, "The History of the Erection of the Municipal Building," in Goren, *65 shana le'hakamat habinyan*, 4.

9. Ibid.

10. Eli Roman, lawyer and historian of Haifa, interview with the author, Haifa, November 9, 2014. According to Roman, Zechariah Froehlich had a superb memory.

11. Mekteb-i Mülkiye-yi Sahane (Imperial School of Civil Service) is referenced in Carter Vaughn Findley's book *Turkey, Islam, Nationalism, and Modernity* (New Haven, CT: Yale University Press, 2010). The motto "Önce Mülkiye, Sonra Türkiye" (First civil service, then Turkey), which expressed solidarity in civil service among the alumni of the school, was popular in the early twentieth century.

12. Goren, "Arab and Jews," 24. Levi continued this tradition with the support of his two Arab deputy mayors, Tahir Karaman and Shahada Shalah.

13. See Pinchus Margolin's (lawyer and Haifa city council member) 1942 *Haboker* interview and Hacohen, qtd. in Goren's "Arabs and Jews"; Hacohen, "Jews and Arabs," 236–37; and Khalfon, "Memories from 'Little Haifa,'" 241.

14. For the role of Sephardi Jews as intermediaries between Arabs and Ashkenazi Jews, see: Abigail Jacobson and Moshe Naor, *Oriental Neighbors: Middle Eastern Jews and Arabs in Mandatory Palestine* (Waltham, MA: Brandeis University Press, 2016), 57–58, 69, 79–80.

15. Vilnay, *Heifa*, 134; Carmel, "Haifa at the End," 11–12; Khalfon, "Memories from 'Little Haifa,'" 241.

16. Aharonovitch, *Hadar HaCarmel*, 6; Carmel, "Haifa at the End," 5–12; Khalfon, "Memories from 'Little Haifa,'" 241.

17. Carmel, "Haifa at the End," 12.

18. Anat Kidron, "Separatism, Coexistence and the Landscape: Jews and Palestinian-Arabs in Mandatory Haifa," *Middle Eastern Studies* 52, no. 1 (2016): 95–96.

19. Khalfon, "Memories from 'Little Haifa,'" 234.

20. *Ha'aretz*, January 1924, in Goren, "History of the Erection," 2.

21. Gilbert Herbert and Lilian Richter, "The Architect B. Chaikin and the City Hall in Haifa," in Goren, *65 shana le'hakamat habinyan*, 13.

22. For more on this, see chapter 2.

23. The city council allotted 2,500 Palestinian pounds in 1932 for buying the land; see Herbert and Richter, "Architect B. Chaikin," 13.

24. "Preliminary Local Documentation of City Hall," April 24, 2008, City Hall Conservation File [for Landmark Buildings], Department of Conservation, City of Haifa Archive, Haifa, Israel.

25. The members of the committee were Shabtai Levi and David Hacohen and the two Arab deputy mayors, Tahir Karaman and Shahada Shalah; see Goren, "History of the Erection," 5.

26. Ibid. "All the laborers . . . will be Haifa residents. . . . The term 'Haifa resident' means, a person who, to the mind of the employer is a true resident (purity of heart) of Haifa" (5).

27. Tamir Goren, "The Municipality during the War of Independence and After," in Goren, *65 shana le'hakamat habinyan*, 29–34; Yfaat Weiss, *Vadi Salib: hanokhah vehanifkad* [Wadi Salib: A confiscated memory] (Tel Aviv: Hakibbutz Hameuchad/Van Leer Jerusalem Institute, 2007), 30; Benny Morris, *1948* (Tel Aviv: Am Oved, 2010), 166–68; Tamir Goren, *Heifa ha'ivrit be-tashah* [Arab Haifa in 1948] (Sde Boker: Ben-Gurion University of the Negev Press 2006), 8–47.

28. At that time it was called the Cooperative of Haifa Workers of the General Histadrut of the Hebrew Workers in the Land of Israel.

29. The most important cut was that the side wings were built shorter than in the plan. They were elongated in the 1950s, according to Chaikin's original plan (see blueprints in Herbert and Richter, "Architect B. Chaikin," 12). See also Goren, "History of the Erection," 7–9.

30. Goren, "History of the Erection," 8.

31. Shabtai Levi, "Memories from the War of Independence," and Isaac Klein, "Arab Community in Haifa in the Mandate Period," both in Naor and Ben-Artzi, *Idan*, 249–50; 126.

32. Morris, *1948*, 166–68.

33. Khalidi, "Fall of Haifa Revisited"; Mahmoud Yazbak and Yfaat Weiss, eds., *Haifa Before and After 1948: Narratives of a Mixed City* (Dordrecht: Republic of Letters, 2011); Yazbak, "Arabs in Haifa," 132–45; Seikaly, *Haifa*, 65.

34. Goren, "Municipality during the War," 29–34; Weiss, *Vadi Salib*, 30; Morris, *1948*, 166–68.

35. Blueprints, property of Mr. Salim Azam, Building File 351845, Archive of Engineering Administration, Haifa, Israel. The building was probably constructed in 1936.

36. *Horanim* came from *horan*, a poor area in southern Syria.

37. Nili Gold, *Yehuda Amichai: The Making of Israel's National Poet* (Waltham, MA: Brandeis University Press, 2008).

38. Yehuda Amichai's letters to Ruth Zielenziger from August 31, 1947, to April 11, 1948, are housed at HaYisr'elim HaRishonim (First Israelis Archive), Heksherim: The Research Center for Jewish and Israeli Literature and Culture, Ben-Gurion University of the Negev, Beer Sheba, Israel. Further references cite the letter number (as given by Amichai) and the date.

39. Amichai to Ruth Z., letter 53, December 21, 1947; letter 50, December 14, 1947; letter 55, December 25, 1947.

40. Ibid., letter 64, January 16, 1947.

41. Ibid., letter 97, April 7, 1948 (emphasis mine).

42. Sami Michael, *Hatsotsra ba'vadi* [A Trumpet in the Wadi] (Tel Aviv: Am Oved, 1987); Michael, *A Trumpet in the Wadi*, trans. Yael Lotan (New York: Simon and Schuster, 2003); Michael, *Hasut* [Refuge] (Tel Aviv: Am Oved, 2001); Michael, *Refuge*, trans. Edward Grossman (Philadelphia: Jewish Publication Society, 1998); Michael, *Yonim be'trafalgar* [Pigeons at Trafalgar Square] (Tel Aviv: Am Oved, 2005); Michael, *Me'of habarburim* [Flight of the swans] (Tel Aviv: Kineret, 2011); Michael, *Mayim noshkim le'mayim* [Waters kissing waters] (Tel Aviv: Am Oved, 2001). Henceforth all page numbers refer to the Hebrew edition followed by the English translation. If no secondary page number is given for the translation, this means it is my own.

43. This is especially true of *Hatsotsra ba'vadi*, *Hasut*, and *Yonim be'trafalgar*.

44. Michael, *Hasut*, 266; 274.

45. See also Batya Shimony, "The Woman and Homeland in Sami Michael's Works," *Mikan* 12 (December 2012): 192–209. Since 2001 Michael has been the president of the Association for Civil Rights in Israel.

46. Michael, *Hasut*, 267–68; 276.

47. Ami Atias, who assisted the artist in creating the monument, provided this timeline in a phone interview with the author, January 25, 2016; see also Kolodney, "Contested Urban Memoryscape Strategies," 118.

48. Gideon Ofrat's article "Mural Art in Israel in the 1950s" defines Knispel as a member of the small leftist-communist, social realist artists' circle in mid-1950s Haifa, with Yosef Maoz as their ideologue. *Warehouse of Gideon Ofrat*, December 21, 2010, https://gideonofrat.wordpress.com.

49. This view is reinforced by Knispel's participation in the first national monument commemorating Arabs in the State of Israel in the Galilee who fell on Land Day in 1976. See page 119 of Kolodney's "Contested Urban Memoryscape Strategies" for an alternative interpretation of the monument.

50. Sami Michael, private conversation with the author, Evanston, IL, October 8, 2015.

51. Waleed Karkabi, head of Building Conservation Team at the Haifa Municipality, e-mail message to author, August 2, 2015.

52. Elie Rekhess (lecture at the conference "Between Baghdad and Haifa: A Tribute to Israeli Author Sami Michael," Northwestern University, Evanston, IL, November 2015).

53. A house with an open inner space or courtyard into which all the doors of the various rooms face is a common characteristic of the *liwan* style; Karkabi, architectural walking tour 10, November, 19, 2010; see also Waleed Karkabi, "City Hall: Colorful Crossroad of Architectural Styles," in Goren, *65 shana le'hakamat habinyan*, 15–19.

54. Silvina Sosnovsky, 2006, Police Station (aka "small court") Conservation File [for Landmark Buildings], Department of Conservation, City of Haifa Archive.

55. Michael, *Hasut*, 228; 234–35.

56. Michael, *Hatsotsra ba'vadi*, 128, 132; 132, 136.

57. Michael, *Mayim noshkim le'mayim*, 21.

58. The exact parameters of Memorial Park are described in an invitation from the mayor extended to the chief of the armed forces, Mordechai Maklef, to attend the inauguration of Memorial Park, written on April 29, 1953. Abba Hushi to Maklef, April 29, 1953, Haifa City Archives, Haifa Israel.

59. Michael, *Mayim noshkim le'mayim*, 23.

60. Ziva Kolodney, "The Politics of Landscape Production in Haifa between the Mandatory Period and the Sovereign Period" (DSc diss., Technion Israel Institute of Technology, 2010), 70–75. In an interview with Kolodney in preparation for her doctorate in 2006, Sami Michael said that he uses the features of Haifa to describe the emotional facets of the self.

61. Yoel Hoffmann, *Ephraim* (Jerusalem: Keter, 2003), seg. 112. This edition of *Ephraim* is unpaginated, so all numbers refer to numbered segments rather than pages.

62. Ibid., seg. 113.

63. Ibid., seg. 115.

64. Sosnovsky, Police Station Conservation File.

65. Avishai Ehrlich, "English Architect in the Mandatory Palestine," *Tavi* 22, no. 2 (1984): 48–51. These arches likely influenced the design of city hall but are also inspired by the Technion.

66. Ron Fuchs, "Austen St. Barbe Harrison: A British Architect in the Holy Land," (DSc diss., Technion Israel Institute of Technology, 1992), 167–68.

67. Ehrlich, "English Architect."

68. Silvina Sosnovsky, 2006, Courthouse Conservation File, Department of Conservation, City of Haifa Archives.

69. Fuchs, "Austen St. Barbe Harrison," 171–73; Ehrlich, "English Architect."

70. Fuchs, "Austen St. Barbe Harrison," 167–68.

71. Sosnovsky, Courthouse Conservation File.

72. Fuchs, "Austen St. Barbe Harrison," 167–68.

73. Sosnovsky, Courthouse Conservation File.

74. David Kroyanker, *Adrikhalut yerushalayim: habniya bitkufat hamandat habriti, 1918–1948* [Jerusalem architecture: Construction in the time of the British Mandate, 1918–1948] (Jerusalem: Keter, 1989), 436–37; Fuchs, "Austen St. Barbe Harrison," 174–79; Ehrlich, "English Architect."

75. Yohanan Ratner, qtd. in Fuchs, "Austen St. Barbe Harrison," 174–79.

76. Fuchs, "Austen St. Barbe Harrison," 174–79.

77. Ehrlich, "English Architect."

78. Fuchs, "Austen St. Barbe Harrison," 174–79.

79. Ehrlich, "English Architect." The courthouse is one of Harrison's two most modern buildings.

80. Fuchs, "Austen St. Barbe Harrison," 173.

81. Ehrlich, "English Architect."

82. For more on this, see chapter 2.

83. Kroyanker, Adrikhalut yerushalayim, 446–47.

84. Herbert and Sosnovsky, Bauhaus on the Carmel, 248–50.

85. Ibid.

86. In Hebrew city hall is called hekhal ha'iriya, literally, "temple of the municipality."

87. Maoz Azaryahu, "Between Two Cities: The Commemoration of the War of Independence in Haifa and Tel Aviv; A Study in the Shaping of Israeli Collective Memory," Cathedra 68 (June 1993): 98–126.

88. For an alternative account from Azaryahu's "Between Two Cities," see page 126 of Kolodney's "Contested Urban Memoryscape Strategies." Kolodney quotes Zvi Miller, the original landscape designer, who attributes the opposite sentiment to Abba Hushi, saying that he wanted the garden to prevent the office buildings from being built.

89. Herbert and Richter, "Architect B. Chaikin," 10–14.

90. See Benjamin Chaikin, "Municipal Building, Mount Carmel, Haifa," in Builder, July 21, 1939, qtd. in Herbert and Richter, "Architect B. Chaikin," 12.

91. Herbert and Richter, "Architect B. Chaikin," 10–14.

92. "Preliminary Local Documentation," City of Haifa Archive.

93. Ibid.

94. This incident is described in Kroyanker, Adrikhalut yerushalayim, 288. According to Kroyanker, Chaikin turned to his friend, Chaim Weizmann, during the inauguration of the building Ratner designed and said that it ought not seem like a midget next to the nearby public buildings such as the YMCA or Terra Sancta.

95. Nurith Gertz, "Israeli Cinema in the 1960s," in He'asor hasheni, ed. Zvi Zameret and Hannah Yablonka (Jerusalem: Yad Yitzhak Ben Zvi, 2000), 280–97.

96. Foster Hirsch, Otto Preminger: The Man Who Would Be King (New York: Knopf, 2007), 324, 328.

97. Ibid., 330.

98. Michael Jacobson, "Life Is a Movie: Heinz Fenchel, the Best Forgotten Architect in Israel," last modified December 13, 2012, http://xnet.ynet.co.il.

99. Zvi Efrat, Haproyekt Hayisr'eli: 1948–1973 [The Israel project: Building and architecture, 1948–1973], vol. 2 (Tel Aviv: Tel Aviv Museum of Art, 2004), 712. The chapter on luxury opens with a photograph of a lobby that Fenchel designed.

100. Alice Toubi was Mrs. Magdelani's sister.

101. Karkabi, "City Hall," 16.

102. Yossi Vilian, former congregant and lay historian of Hadrat Kodesh, phone interview with the author, November 2014. Vilian, now active in the restoration of Hadrat Kodesh, worshipped at the synagogue as a child and remembers its details vividly.

103. Vilnay, *Heifa*, 135. "In the latter years [early 1930s], synagogues were erected in all the Jewish neighborhoods. One synagogue 'Hadrat Kodesh' is found on the Street of Stairs that ascends from the [lower] city to Hadar HaCarmel" (135).

104. Mordechai Friedman, *Hakipa ba'ir ha'aduma* [The skullcap in the red city] (Jerusalem: Beth El, 2015), 211. Besht is an acronym for Ba'al Shem Tov, the founder of Hasidism, an Ultra Orthodox Jewish sect.

105. The board of trustees of the school at that time demanded German instruction and closed the building to those who wanted Hebrew instruction exclusively. See Sarah Halperin, *Doctor A. Biram ve'bet hasefer hareali ha'ivri* [Dr. A. Biram and the Reali School] (Jerusalem: Reuven Mass, 1970), 77–79. See also chapter 2.

106. Friedman, *Hakipa ba'ir ha'aduma*, 211.

107. According to Vilian, the designated leader of the Vizhnitz Hasidic sect fought there in 1948 (phone interview with the author, January 2015).

108. According to Vilian, Jerusalem's chief rabbi, Rav Abraham Isaac Kook, sent Rabbi Kaniel on a mission to Haifa after the latter survived a sniper's shot in Jerusalem (phone interview).

109. Vilian, phone interview; Yosef Zvi Sabo, congregant of Hadrat Kodesh, interview with the author, Haifa, November 2014. Sabo lived across the street from the synagogue, and both he and Vilian celebrated their bar mitzvahs there.

110. Observant Jews refrain from using their everyday dishes during the holiday due to the biblical prohibition against eating or owning leavened bread. When the special Passover kitchenware was unpacked, homemakers often found themselves missing an item and would run to a store like my father's.

111. From the German saying, *Die Glocke läuten hören, aber nicht wissen, wo sie hängt*, which translates literally to "She heard bells tolling but didn't know where they hung."

112. "Registration of Jewish Property according to the Situation, April 27, 1938," Austrian State Archive, Archive of the Republic, Vienna. I now know the name of the Austrian head manager. Letter from Olga Scharf to Property Authority, December 14, 1938, Vermogenverkehrsstelle (Property Authority Archive), Austrian State Archive, Archive of the Republic, Vienna.

113. The building with the offices was designed by Alexander Baerwald.

114. Vilian remembered that Rabbi Kaniel prayed in my father's synagogue (phone interview).

115. The date of the celebration is confirmed by the invitation sent by the mayor to the chief of the armed forces for the Memorial Park inauguration. See Hushi to Maklef, April 29, 1953, Haifa City Archives.

116. *Iton Rishmi* (Official newspaper) 31, November 5, 1948, 47.

117. Kolodney, "Contested Urban Memoryscape Strategies," 118.

118. The message conveyed by the placement of each language on a sign is discussed in Kidron, "Separatism," 97.

119. Yehuda Amichai, "Sonnet 15," of the "We Loved Here" sonnet cycle in *Shirim: 1948–1962* [Poems: 1948–1962] (Jerusalem: Schocken, 2002), 67 (translation and emphasis are mine).

120. Tower in Hebrew is *migdal*, and lighthouse is *migdalor*.

121. The equation of the port with pain appears in numerous letters and subsequent poems. For example, in letter 3, September 5, 1947, Amichai writes, "A thick fog covered the sea . . . and I only saw the ships as if in a dream, and from time to time, one of them made an opaque sound that always makes me sad." In letter 20, October 12, 1947: "Separation . . . the port, the horn, the sailing, the sea."

122. Tamir Goren, "The Symbol of the City Haifa, Its Origin and Design," *Journal of the Haifa History Society*, no. 1 (January 2004): 14–17; Elan Alon, "A Second Look at the Haifa City Symbol," *Journal of the Haifa History Society*, no. 4 (November 2006): 14–15. According to the latter, the structures in Haifa's emblem are a representation of the towers that used to stand at the entrance to Haifa's ancient port to scare off pirates.

2. The Technion: The Genesis of Hadar HaCarmel

1. Aharonovitch, *Hadar HaCarmel*, 8.

2. The building is now home to the Israeli National Museum of Science, Technology and Space.

3. Shim'on Stern, "Hadar HaCarmel, the Center of Jewish Life in Haifa," in Naor and Ben-Artzi, *Idan*, 39.

4. Aharonovitch, *Hadar HaCarmel*, 151–53.

5. Mendel Zinger, *Shlomo Kaplanski: hayav ufoa'lo* [Shlomo Kaplanski: His life and work], vol. 2 (Jerusalem: Zionist Library, 1971), ch. 23; see also Yuval Dror, "The Beginning of the Hebrew Technion in Haifa: 1902–1950; From a Plan for a Jewish Institution for Higher Education until the End of the Period of the Directorship of Shlomo Kaplanski," in *Iyunim bitKumat Yisrael*, vol. 6 (Sdeh Boker: Ben Gurion University of the Negev/Ben Gurion Institute of Research in Israel and Zionism, 1996), 346.

6. Edina Meyer-Maril, "From a 'New Hebrew' to Moderate Modernism: Alexander Baerwald (1877–1930)," in *The Beauty of Japheth in the Tents of Shem: Studies in Honour of Mordechai Omer*, ed. Hana Taragan and Nissim Gal, vols. 13–14 of *Assaph: Studies in Art History* (Tel Aviv: Tel Aviv University: 2010), 537–46.

7. Eli Liran, Baerwald scholar (lecture at the Haifa History Society, November 2014).

8. Qtd. in Warhaftig, *They Laid the Foundation*, 30.

9. Yossi Ben-Artzi, "The Educational Journey of Alexander Baerwald," *Zmanim*, no. 96 (Fall 2006): 14–21.

10. Meyer-Maril, "New Hebrew."

11. Ada Karmi-Melamede and Dani Price, *Adrikhalut bepalestina-eretz Yisrael bime hamandat habriti: 1917–1948* [Architecture in Palestine during the British Mandate: 1917–1948] (Tel Aviv: Tel Aviv Museum of Art, 2011), 51–52.

12. Abba El-Hanani, *Hama'vak le'atzma'ut shel ha'adrikhalut hayisr'elit bame'a ha'esrim* [The struggle for independence of Israeli architecture in the twentieth century] (Israel: Ministry of Defense, 1998), 16–18.

13. See Carl Alpert, *Technion: The Story of the Israel Institute of Technology* (New York: American Technion Society, 1982), 27, qtd. in Meyer-Maril, "New Hebrew."

14. Karmi-Melamede and Price, *Adrikhalut bepalestina-eretz Israel*, 51.

15. From the memoirs of Saul Sal'i about Abraham Ginzburg. See Amira Kehat, comp., May 20, 2010, 31 Shmaryahu Levin Street (Technion), Building History File 0256, Haifa History Society, Haifa, Israel.

16. Letter 53, December 21, 1947, qtd. in Gold, *Yehuda Amichai*, 278n63.

17. Levin Kipnis, *Shloshet ha'parparim* [The three butterflies] (Petach Tikva: Oranit, 2010).

18. Aharonovitch, *Hadar HaCarmel*, 9–10. The area spreads on the northern slope of the Carmel, seventy-two to a hundred meters above sea level. The funders were Jacob Schiff, the American; and Kalonimu Wissotzky, the Russian. Nathan believed in Herzl's prophecy and was convinced of its industrial and transportational potential. He also thought that Haifa was neutral in terms of religion and nationality, unlike Jerusalem or Tel Aviv.

19. The Russian engineer Gedalya Wilboshevitz was instrumental in finding viable solutions that helped Baerwald with these difficulties.

20. "Zionist Outbreaks Due to Language," *New York Times*, January 19, 1914, qtd. in Meyer-Maril, "New Hebrew." See the discussion of the synagogue in chapter 1.

21. Yitzhak Dimiel (Schweiger), "Hanna'le and Her Shabbat Dress," *Davar Liladim* 20, February 1937.

22. Eli Roman, interview with the author, Haifa, October 15, 2014.

23. Nili Friedlander, friend of Yehoshua Kenaz, phone interview with the author, March 2016.

24. Yehoshua Kenaz, *A Musical Moment* (Tel Aviv: Hakibbutz Hameuchad, 1980), 69, 81; Kenaz, "Musical Moment," in *Musical Moment and Other Stories*, trans. Betsy Rosenberg (Vermont: Steerforth, 1995), 55, 64.

25. Kenaz, *Musical Moment*, 81; Kenaz, "Musical Moment," 64.

26. Yehuda Amichai, *Shalva gedola: she'elot uteshuvot* [The great tranquility: Questions and answers] (Tel Aviv: Shocken, 1980), 18; Amichai, *The Great Tranquility: Questions and Answers*, trans. Glenda Abramson and Tudor Parfitt (New York: Sheep Meadow, 1997), 7. Henceforth all page numbers from *Shalva gedola* refer to the 1980 Hebrew edition and then the 1983 English translation.

27. Nili Gold, *Lo kabrosh: gilgule imagim vetavniyot beshirat Yehuda Amichai* [Not like a cypress: Transformations of images and structures in the poetry of Yehuda Amichai] (Tel Aviv: Schocken, 1994), 82–84.

28. Amichai, *Shalva gedola*, 8; 7. I have slightly altered the English translation for clarity.

29. Gold, *Lo kabrosh*, 82–84.

30. Amichai, *Shalva gedola*, 18; 76.

31. Amichai to Ruth Z., letter 21, October 15, 1947; presumably "yesterday" refers to the fourteenth.

32. Ibid., letters 2, 4, and 10, September 3, 6, and 21, 1947.

33. Ibid., letter 4, September 6, 1947.

34. Ibid., letter 53, December 21, 1947.

35. Shim'on Stern, "Haifa and the Struggle," in Naor and Ben-Artzi, *Idan*, 186; Aharonovitch, *Hadar HaCarmel*, 233–35.

36. Aharonovitch, *Hadar HaCarmel*, 9, 11, 13, 15. Both sat on the Technion's board of directors even before its inception. They supported building it in Haifa and fought for the dominance of Hebrew in its curriculum. Shmaryahu Levin was a Zionist leader who was the first to support Paul Nathan's idea of establishing the Technion, and he became its first executive director in 1912. Ahad Haam, the Zionist thinker, was instrumental in securing the first funds for the Technion's construction.

37. Waleed Karkabi, head of Building Conservation Team at the Haifa Municipality, interview with the author, Haifa, October 2014.

38. Esty G. Hayim, *Anshe pinot* [Corner people] (Israel: Kinneret, Zmora-Bitan, Dvir, 2013).

39. Yehudit Katzir, *Zillah* (Tel Aviv: Hakibbutz Hameuchad, 2013), 322.

40. Stern, "Hadar HaCarmel," 43; Herbert and Sosnovsky, *Bauhaus on the Carmel*, 232; Aharonovitch, *Hadar HaCarmel*, 105–8.

41. Herbert and Sosnovsky, *Bauhaus on the Carmel*, 237.

42. Weill-Rochant, *Sur les traces*, 154; Meyer-Maril, "New Hebrew."

43. Tsafrir Feinholtz, "Vienna in Hadar HaCarmel," accessed March 3, 2016, www.blogsrelease.com.

44. Aharonovitch, *Hadar HaCarmel*, 180, 212, 248.

45. Weill-Rochant, *Sur les traces*, 153.

46. Karkabi, interview.

47. Herbert and Sosnovsky, *Bauhaus on the Carmel*, 229, 241; Aharonovitch, *Hadar HaCarmel*, 157.

48. Karkabi, interview.

49. Herbert and Sosnovsky, *Bauhaus on the Carmel*, 242.

50. Gideon Ofrat, "Mural Art in Israel in the 1950s," *Warehouse of Gideon Ofrat*, December 21, 2010, https://gideonofrat.wordpress.com.

51. Ibid.

52. Hayim, *Anshe pinot*, 217.

53. Michael, *Hatsotsra ba'vadi*, 128; 132.

54. Hayim, *Anshe pinot*, 26.

55. Ibid., 217, 282; Esty G. Hayim, *Corner People*, trans. Sarah Friedman (unpublished manuscript), with author alterations.

56. Hayim, *Anshe pinot*, 110.

57. Ibid., 112–113, 239.

58. Yehudit Katzir, "Disneyel," in *Sogrim et hayam* [*Closing the Sea*] (Tel Aviv: Hakibbutz Hameuchad, 1990), 94; Yehudit Katzir, *Closing the Sea*, trans. Barbara Harshav (New York: Harcourt Brace Jovanovich, 1992), 87–88.

59. On the organic imprint of remembered habits and spaces, see Oded Manda Levy, "Observing and Observing Again: Spaces in Georges Perec," *Resling: Multi Disciplinary Journal* 7 (Summer 2000): 51–53.

60. Yehudit Katzir, private conversation with the author, Tel Aviv, November 2014.

61. Katzir, *Zillah*, 27–28.

62. See the map for chapter 2.

3. Down the Steps: Fragments of Sea and Sky

1. The word *talpiot*, interpreted as "built magnificently," is a biblical hapax legomenon that appears only in 4:4 of Song of Songs.

2. Shabtai Levi, "New Hadar HaCarmel Market Opened," *Palestine Post*, April 10, 1940, 2.

3. See chapter 2.

4. Herbert and Sosnovsky, *Bauhaus on the Carmel*, 245, 246.

5. Aharonovitch, *Hadar HaCarmel*, 171.

6. Ibid.

7. Herbert and Sosnovsky, *Bauhaus on the Carmel*, 246.

8. Nissim Levi, *Nassuma merehov hapijamot* [Nassuma from pajamas street] (Haifa: printed by author, 2009), 47–48 (emphasis mine).

9. Ibid., 49–50. These pages feature an advertisement for Levi's tours.

10. Ya'akov Weiss, *Yaldut nish'kahat: havay venostalgia bsimta'ot Heifa* [Forgotten childhood: Life and nostalgia in Haifa's alleys] (Haifa: printed by author, 2001), 181.

11. Hayim, *Anshe pinot*, 11.

12. Solel Boneh, literally "Paving/Building," was established as a cooperative organization in 1921 and has built many national public projects.

13. Ada Karmi-Melamede and Dan Price, *Architecture in Palestine during the British Mandate: 1917–1948* (Jerusalem: Israel Museum, 2014) 421–22. See also Karmi-Melamede and Price, *Adrikhalut bepalestina-eretz Yisrael*, 417.

14. "The New Central Market in Hadar HaCarmel," *Davar*, April 10, 1940, 4; Feinholtz, "Vienna in Hadar HaCarmel," n26; "New Haifa Market under Way," *Palestine Post*, November 27, 1938, 6; "Palestine-Eretz Israel Exhibition in New York," *Davar*, July 18, 1947, 6.

15. Herbert and Sosnovsky, *Bauhaus on the Carmel*, 247.

16. Karmi-Melamede and Price, *Adrikhalut bepalestina-eretz Yisrael*, 426.

17. Herbert and Sosnovsky, *Bauhaus on the Carmel*, 247.

18. Amir Kolik, "The Growth of Urban Elite: 1918–1948," accessed March 3, 2016, http://humanities1.tau.ac.il.

19. One deputy mayor represented the Christian community; the other, in this case, Karaman, represented the Muslims.

20. Waleed Karkabi and Adi Rosenberg, "Arab-Jewish Architectural Partnership in Haifa during the Mandate Period: Karaman and Gerstel Meet on the 'Seam Line,'" in Yazbak and Weiss, *Haifa Before and After*, 43–68, 59–60.

21. Moshe (Chiko) Gerstel, interview with the author, Tel Aviv, November 2014.

22. *Haifa Encounters: Arab-Jewish Architectural Partnership in the Period of the British Mandate in Haifa*, shown at the Munio Gitai Weinraub Architecture Museum, Haifa, May 10, 2013–September 10, 2013.

23. Weill-Rochant, *Sur les traces*, 156.

24. Weiss, *Yaldut nish'kahat*, 17.

25. Michael Levin, professor of art history and contemporary architecture at Shenkar College, interview with the author, Tel Aviv, November 20, 2014.

26. See Waleed Karkabi, qtd. in Keshet Rosenblum's exhibition review, "When Jews and Palestinians Built Haifa Together," *Ha'aretz*, June 11, 2013.

27. Warhaftig, *They Laid the Foundation*, 204; Rosenblum, "Jews and Palestinians Built."

28. Adi Silberstein, architect (author's assistant and a fourth-year architecture student at the Technion at the time), private architectural tour with the author, Haifa, October 23, 2014.

29. Gerstel, interview.

30. Karkabi gave me a copy of Building Permit 2115/46, dated May 4, 1947, from the Municipal Building and Town Planning Commission. It was the permit for Bet Talpiot, 61 Herzl/62 HeHalutz.

31. Natan Zach, "Casino in Bat Galim, April 1983," in *Anti mehikon* [Anti erasure] (Tel Aviv: Hakibbutz Hameuchad, 1984), 289–90.

32. Ziva Kolodney, Conservation File [for Landmark Buildings], Zone 4, housed in the Department of Conservation of the City of Haifa, January 1994; L. Guterman and A. Silberstein, "The Promenade at Bat Galim," (term paper) (Haifa: Israel Institue of Technology, Faculty of Architecture), 2014.

33. Yitzhak Kronzon, "Givat Brenner," in *Ki mineged tir'e* [See the land at a distance] (Tel Aviv: Am Oved, 2010), 51. Givat Brenner is the name of a kibbutz.

34. Weiss, *Yaldut nish'kahat*, 110.

35. Chava Lo-yon, former head of the Long Range Planning Department in the Municipality of Haifa, architectural tour and interview with the author, Haifa, November 18, 2014.

36. See the 1959 memorandum submitted by Zvi Barzilai, deputy mayor of Haifa, in Weiss, *Vadi Salib*, 66. Document 7252/3, discussing the riots on July, 29 1959, can be found in the State Archives.

37. Eli Nachmias and Ron Spiegel, *Vadi Salib: hamitos veshivro; me'ora'ot Vadi Salib be'mabat mehkari hadash* [Wadi Salib: The broken myth; Wadi Salib events, research from a new point of view] (Haifa, printed by author, 2009), 8; Weiss, *Vadi Salib*, 13. See also footnote 19 on page 66 in Weiss, *Vadi Salib*, for more on the committee report.

38. Yehudit Hendel, interview with the author, Tel Aviv, 2010.

39. See Avraham Blat discussing "The Rationale of the Judges in Giving the Barasch Prize, June 1954," in *HaTzofe*, October, 23, 1955.

40. Barzilai, qtd. in Weiss, *Vadi Salib*, 67.

41. Nachmias and Spiegel, *Vadi Salib*, 118.

42. Yehudit Hendel, *Rehov hamadregot* [*Street of Steps*] (Tel Aviv: Am Oved, 1955), 35; Yehudit Hendel, *Street of Steps*, trans. Rachel Katz and David Segal (New York: Herzel Press and Yoseloff, 1963), 38. Henceforth all page numbers from *Rehov hamadregot* are cited in the text and refer to the Hebrew edition and then the English translation.

43. Report from July 6, 1959, qtd. in Weiss, *Vadi Salib*, 58, 67.

44. In a 1954 interview Hendel said, "You surely know Haifa, it is all built on streets of stairs." *Street of Steps* was adapted into a play, and "Hendel went during the rehearsals for a tour with the director to the very alleys in Haifa." See M. Ahi Yosef and Moshe Ben Alul, "A Story about a Poor Neighborhood," *Davar*, July 2, 1954; and Rivka Katzenelson, "Meetings with Writers," *Ma'ariv*, October 31, 1958, 13.

45. Hendel, interview.

46. Karkabi, architectural tour, Haifa, November 14, 2014.

47. Ziva Kolodney, PhD, landscape architect and head of Long Range Planning Department in the Municipality of Haifa, interview with the author, Haifa, November, 2014.

4. The School and the Synagogue:
At the End of Herzl Street

1. Aluf Orell and Dror Orell, *Binyamin Orell: adrikhal lelo diploma* [Benjamin Orell: An architect without a diploma] (Israel, 2008), 8–9. The authors are the son and grandson of Benjamin Orell. Although Orell's practice built many structures, both in and out of Haifa, it never succeeded financially.

2. Vilnay, *Heifa*, 132–33. "As early as 1881, the Alliance School was established in Haifa by the association Alliance Israelite Française, and in 1936 a large building was erected for that school in Hadar HaCarmel" (ibid.; my translation). See also Moshe Barak, "French, How Pretty You Are: Memories of the French Alliance School," July 30, 2009, www.gshavit.net.

3. Orell and Orell, *Binyamin Orell*, 57.

4. Ibid., 57, 56.

5. Karkabi, architectural walking tour, November, 19, 2010.

6. Silberstein, private architectural tour.

7. Ibid.

8. Barak, "How Pretty You Are."

9. Itamar Shoshan, son of the then vice principal and science teacher, private excursion with the author, Haifa, October 20, 2014.

10. Barak, "How Pretty You Are."

11. Amira Kehat, comp., April 10, 2010, 31 Balfour (Bet Yungerman), Building History File, City Engineering File 372954, Haifa History Society.

12. Barak, "How Pretty You Are."

13. Itamar Shoshan, e-mail message to the author, January–February 2015.

14. David Sasson to the Committee for the Community of Hadar HaCarmel, January 21, 1948, Central Zionist Archives, Jerusalem, Israel.

15. Gold, *Yehuda Amichai*, letter 52, 278n63.

16. Supervisor Mordechai Cohen to the Alliance School, October 23, 1968, file 34019, Israel State Archives, Jerusalem.

17. Asher Yungerman to the Ministry of Education Supervisor, February 22, 1965, file 254/5, Israel State Archives, Jerusalem.

18. Charlotte Wardi, *Le Juif dans le roman français: 1933–1948* [The image of the Jew in the French novel] (Paris: Nizet, 1973).

19. Mordechai Cohen, Ministry of Education Supervisor, "Report of the Supervisor about the School Visit," February 1966, file 34019, Israel State Archives, Jerusalem.

20. Karkabi, architectural walking tour, October 2010.

21. Weiss, *Yaldut nish'kahat*, 70–73; Gabriel Laufer, phone interview with the author, January 2016.

22. Natan Zach, "In the Fields of Then Perhaps," in *Kevan she'ani basviva* [Because I'm around] (Tel Aviv: Hakibbutz Hameuchad, 1966), 20–23.

23. Hoffmann, *Ephraim*; Katzir, "Disneyel," in *Sogrim et hayam*, 81–110, 67–93.

24. Silberstein suggested that the division by the openings "confronts" the feeling of its massiveness (discussion with the author, Haifa, October 9, 2014).

25. Weiss, *Yaldut nish'kahat*, 70–72.

26. Building sign, Central Synagogue, Haifa.

27. Aharonovitch, *Hadar HaCarmel*, 79–80.

28. The contractor Wilboshevitz, whose buildings were always built according to Baerwald's plans, was the one who did the work. Therefore, it seems that the first floor of the synagogue was likely Baerwald's design. This is according to both Eli Liran, who used the Lavon Archive for Wilboshevitz's record, and Edina Meyer-Maril. Eli Liran, Haifa History Society member, phone interview with the author, April 2015; Meyer-Maril, "New Hebrew."

29. Amira Kehat, comp., March 2, 2009, 60 Herzl Street (Central Synagogue), Building History File, Haifa History Society. In Kehat's file of the Central Synagogue, the competition is recorded as being referenced in the journal *Building in the Near East* from March 1936, "Competition to Rework the Plans for the Construction of the Central Synagogue in Hadar HaCarmel, Haifa," and in an architecture survey by the Technion student Avital Kenan, 1980.

30. According to Mordechai Friedman, the Haifa Association for Architects and Engineers protested not using Loeb. See *Hakipa ba'ir ha'aduma*, 208.

31. Aharonovitch, *Hadar HaCarmel*, 255.

32. Edina Meyer-Maril, private research notes from *HaTzofe*, generously shared with the author, September 13, 1938.

33. The work stopped due to lack of funds and quarrels between the Association of Architects and Engineers and the synagogue leadership. See *HaTzofe*, qtd. in Friedman, *Hakipa ba'ir ha'aduma*, 208.

34. Friedman, *Hakipa ba'ir ha'aduma*, 209.

35. Ze'ev Shoham to Va'ad Hadar HaCarmel, November 15, 1942, file 6084; "Report of the Committee for the Clarification of the Matter of the Central Synagogue," committee report, signed by Dr. Gideon Kaminka, chair of the committee, January, 15, 1943, file 4370, both in Haifa City Archives, Haifa. They also decided to (1) pay Loeb compensation of 400 Palestinian pounds (120 in cash and the rest in promissory notes), (2) cover the front in stone, (3) put in windows according to Baerwald's plan and to improve the appearance of the inside, (4) fix the main entrance on Gilad and close the one on Herzl, and (5) wait to complete the top part and leave the temporary roof.

36. Ibid. Ratner also emphasized that they should adjust the plan to meet modern demands, which would require a skilled architect.

37. Edina Meyer-Maril, "The 'Great Synagogue' in Tel Aviv," *Cathedra* 57 (September 1990): 105–19; Liran, phone interview.

38. The Mansfeld/Weinraub plan from 1945 can be found in file 4730 in the Haifa City Archives, but most of their plans and other materials are not accessible because of the ongoing legal dispute and trial.

39. Friedman, *Hakipa ba'ir ha'aduma*, 210.

40. The correspondences between the leaders of the synagogue and the municipality and neighborhood authorities can be found in the Haifa City Archives. They are cited as follows in chronological order: February 26, 1948, file 8740; April 26, 1955, file 3076; July 17, 1955, file 3076; March 6, 1956, file 4730; November 22, 1958, file 4730; letter from 1964, file 4730.

41. January 10, 1964, file 4730, Haifa City Archives.

42. Katzir, "Disneyel," in *Sogrim et hayam*, 95, 89.

43. Ibid.

44. According to Orthodox Jewish law, even a child of five is required to repeat the adult's recitation of the Kaddish.

45. Hoffmann, *Ephraim*, seg. 111.

46. Ibid., seg. 112.

47. *Yitgadal veyitkadash shme raba* are the beginning words of the Kaddish prayer (in Aramaic).

48. Zvi Roger, *Public Art in Haifa*, ed. Inbar Dror Lax (Haifa: Haifa Municipality, 2012), 44–45.

49. See the discussion of the mosaics at the entrances of the underpass in chapter 2.

50. Ofrat, "Mural Art in Israel."

51. "Municipal Announcement Number 6/55," signed by Mayor Abba Hushi, file 3076, Haifa City Archives.

52. "The Result of the Competition of the Engraving on the Front of the Central Synagogue in Haifa," municipal announcement signed by Mayor Abba Hushi, June 13, 1955, file 3076, Haifa City Archives.

53. "Minutes of Meeting Discussion Re: Changes in Engraving of Central Synagogue of Haifa," December 14, 1955, file 3076, Haifa City Archives.

54. Zach, "Fields of Then," in *Kevan she'ani basviva*, 20.

55. Zach uses *yekke*, the derogatory term for German Jews. The source of the expression is the German word *Jake*, which means "jacket," referring to the coats the German Jews used to wear in the 1930s while no one else in Israel did.

56. Zach, "Fields of Then," in *Kevan she'ani basviva*, 20.

57. Ibid., 20, 21

58. Hayim Nahman Bialik, "If the Angel Asks," in *Songs from Bialik: Selected Poems of Hayim Nahman Bialik*, trans. Atar Hadari (New York: Syracuse University Press, 2000), 24.

59. Zach, "Fields of Then," in *Kevan she'ani basviva*, 20, 21.

60. Natan Zach, "The Literature Teacher: For Professor Baruch Kurzweil for His Jubilee," *Ha'aretz*, August 18, 1967, 10.

61. Ibid.

62. Zach, "Fields of Then," in *Kevan she'ani basviva*, 23.

5. Conquering the Slope: Building and Writing the Mountain

1. Amichai lived on Gilad Street 12, care of Schmidt, the owners of a pharmacy on Herzl Street. Amichai to Ruth Z., letter 38, November 21, 1947.

2. Magen David Adom means Red Star of David. It is Israel's emergency medical service.

3. The sense of open space so close to the residence is expressed in the introduction to *The Individual in History: Essays in Honor of Jehuda Reinharz*, ed. ChaeRan Y. Freeze, Sylvia Fuks Fried, and Eugene R. Sheppard (Waltham, MA: Brandeis University Press, 2015), 3: "the children romped freely in the beauty of nature. At the end of the street lay an expansive field."

4. The source of this word is most likely the Sanskrit word *barud*, which means "explosion."

5. Dahlia Ravikovitch, "Tmuna," in *Ahavat tapuah hazahav* [Love of an orange] (1959; repr., Tel Aviv: Sifriyat Poalim, 1974), 36; Ravikovitch, "Portrait," in *The Window*, trans. Chana Bloch and Ariel Bloch (New York: Sheep Meadow, 1989), 8.

6. Yitzhak Kronzon, "The First Day at the Ge'ula School," in *Ki mineged*, 127; my translation. Unless otherwise noted, other translations of Kronzon's work are by Martin Friedlander.

7. Ibid.; Kronzon, "Once in a Hundred Years," in *Ki mineged*, 146.

8. Aharonovitch, *Hadar HaCarmel*, 137, 149, 201–2, 224.

9. Ya'akov Sobuvitch, "The Beginning of Phys Ed and Sports in Haifa," accessed April 25, 2016, www.haifa.org.il. As a teacher in Ge'ula, Amichai also "worked in the Scout movement near the school." Amichai to Ruth Z., letter 26, October 1947.

10. The plaque reads "Alexander Sasha Wilboshevitz." For Gedalya Wilboshevitz's role in building the Technion, see chapter 2.

11. These details are according to the building form, listing number 0287, City File 356840, Haifa History Society.

12. Julius Posner, "About the Schools of Max Loeb," *Habinyan baMizrah haKarov* [Building in the Near East], March 1938, 14–17.

13. Warhaftig, *They Laid the Foundation*, 110.

14. Herbert and Sosnovsky, *Bauhaus on the Carmel*, 127, 131–33.

15. Warhaftig, *They Laid the Foundation*, 110.

16. Friedman, *Hakipa ba'ir ha'aduma*, 208; Amira Kehat, comp., 60 Herzl Street (Central Synagogue), March 2, 2009, Building History File, Haifa History Society.

17. Warhaftig, *They Laid the Foundation*, 111.

18. Posner, "About the Schools," 14–17.

19. Ibid., 17.

20. Aharonovitch, *Hadar HaCarmel*, 253. He reports that an additional wing was built for Ge'ula in 1953.

21. David Sela, ed., "The Ge'ula Neighborhood," *Nostalgia Online*, accessed July 23, 2015, www.nostal.co.il.

22. Thanks to Kiki Hadar for references to the specific marches that were played.

23. Gold, *Yehuda Amichai*, 272–73; Amichai to Ruth Z., letter 35, November 16, 1947.

24. Amichai to Ruth Z., letter 25, October 22, 1947: "routes . . . punishments . . . all those are the main thing"; letter 27, October 27, 1947: "Syntheses between personal care and a strict regimen"; letter 29, November 1, 1947: "The social/educational role of school"; letter 30, November 4, 1947: "Things and rules in the world of the school."

25. Ibid., letter 2, September 3, 1947.

26. Ibid., letter 10, [n.d.; a few days before letter 11, written on September 24], 1947; letter 23, October 18, 1947; letter 40, November 24, 1947.

27. Ibid., letter 42, November 28, 1947.

28. Because Amichai taught English in the higher grades in addition to being a fourth-grade homeroom teacher, he had to be present for both shifts. Ibid., letter 5, September 7, 1947.

29. Ibid., letter 30, November 4, 1947.

30. Ibid., letter 26, 1947; letter 27, October 27, 1947.

31. Ibid., letter 25, October 22, 1947.

32. Yehuda Amichai, *Shirim: 1948–1962* (Tel Aviv: Schocken, 1977), 78; Yehuda Amichai, *The Selected Poetry of Yehuda Amichai*, trans. Chana Bloch and Stephen Mitchell (Oakland: University of California Press, 1986), 12; Amichai to Ruth Z., letter 38, November 21, 1947.

33. Ibid., letter 19, October 10, 1947.

34. *Lehi* is an acronym for "Fighters for the Freedom of Israel," the most militant Jewish underground active during the British Mandate.

35. Genesis, 22:3 (King James Version).

36. This may have been the moment that the association between the national struggle and the binding of Isaac formed in Amichai's mind. It resurfaced in 1980 in Amichai's only explicit Haifa poem. See discussion of "A Meeting with My Father" in chapter 2. Gold, *Yehuda Amichai*, 274. See also Yael Feldman, *Glory and Agony: Isaac's Sacrifice and the National Narrative* (Palo Alto, CA: Stanford University Press, 2016).

37. Amichai to Ruth Z., letter 55, December 25, 1947.

38. Kronzon, "Loot," in *Ki mineged*, 155–59, 156.

39. Amichai to Ruth Z., letter 53, December 21, 1947.

40. Ibid., letter 55, December 25, 1947.

41. Ibid.

42. "Our wounded little school is dying" — ibid., letter 93, late March, 1948; Gold, *Yehuda Amichai*, 285–86.

43. Aharonovitch, *Hadar HaCarmel*, 234–35.

44. Yitzhak Kronzon, "Like a Wall of Steel," *Ha'aretz*, May 11, 2016, 1 of the *Literary Supplement*; my translation.

45. Ibid.

46. Kronzon, "Mother, Sunshine, Homeland," in *Ki mineged*, 133.

47. Ibid., 136–37.

48. Kronzon, "A Musical Education," in *Ki mineged*, 61, 64 (all emphases in Kronzon's quotes are mine).

49. Kronzon, "Loot," in *Ki mineged*, 155–56.

50. Kronzon, "One Says," in *Ki mineged*, 150, 153–54.

51. For the full saga of how the Ge'ula neighborhood became a part of the district of Hadar HaCarmel, see Aharonovitch, *Hadar HaCarmel*, 72–73, 95–96, 112, 136–37, 131–32.

52. Meir Ben Uri, qtd. in Nili Bar Onn, Idit Shlomi, and Rafi Carmi, "Struck House Haifa: Documentation File," April 2011, Struck House Conservation File [for Landmark Buildings], Department of Conservation, City of Haifa Archives.

53. Ibid.

54. Michael Levin, "Five Approaches to the East in Israeli Architecture," *Zmanim*, no. 22 (Fall 2006): 38–47.

55. Meir Ben Uri, "Hermann Struck on His 70th Birthday," *Mekomon Heifa'i*, Adar 11, 1946; newspaper clipping from the Struck archive owned by Mickey Bernstein, Tel Aviv, qtd. in Gidon Ofrat, "Hermann Struck in the Land of Israel: 1922–1944," in *Hermann Struck: 1876–1944 oman hahedpes* [Hermann Struck: 1876–1944; The artist of etching], ed. Ruthi Ofek and Chana Schuetz (Berlin: Stiftung Neue Synagoge Berlin, Centrum Judaicum, 2007), 237.

56. Ofrat, "Hermann Struck," 237.

57. Theodor Herzl, *Altneuland* [Old new land] (Leipzig, Germany: Seemann Nachfolger, 1902).

58. Mickey Bernstein, "Struck and His Work in 1903," in Ofek and Schuetz, *Hermann Struck*, 65–120, 83.

59. *Vernis mou* is a printmaking technique in which the printing plate is coated with a soft, sticky lacquer as the etching ground. Rough, grainy drawing paper is laid on this soft ground (hence the name). The artist draws on the paper, using powerful strokes of chalk or pencil; in the acid bath that follows, the exposed parts of the

printing plate are etched, with the texture of the paper and the stroke of the writing instrument very subtly preserved.

60. Carl Schwartz, qtd. in Bernstein, "Struck and His Work," in Ofek and Schuetz, *Hermann Struck*, 83.

61. Alexander Granach, *Da geht ein Mensch* [Here goes a man] (Augsburg: Olbaum, 2003), 196–97, in Chana Schuetz, "Hermann Struck in Berlin," in Ofek and Schuetz, *Hermann Struck*, 25–63, 60.

62. Victor Klemperer, *Curriculum Vitae: Memories of a Philologist, 1881–1918*, vol. 2 (Berlin, Noack, 1989), 479, 482, qtd. in Schuetz, "Hermann Struck in Berlin," in Ofek and Schuetz, *Hermann Struck*, 25–63n65.

63. Ben Uri, qtd. in Ofrat, "Hermann Struck," 268.

64. Ben Uri, qtd. in "Struck House Haifa."

65. Aharonovitch, *Hadar HaCarmel*, 183.

66. Ofrat, "Hermann Struck," 268.

67. Arnold Fortlage, *Das graphische werk von Hermann Struck* [The graphic work of Hermann Struck] (Berlin: Cassirer, 1911), 5, qtd. in Bernstein, "Struck and His Work," in Ofek and Schuetz, *Hermann Struck*, 68; comparison to Rembrandt's portraits on 91.

68. "A Private House in Hadar HaCarmel," *Habinyan* [The Building] 2 (November 1937).

69. Ben Uri, qtd. in Ofrat, "Hermann Struck," 268.

70. Kronzon, "After the War," in *Ki mineged*, 25.

71. Kronzon, "Two Weeks in Naharia at Czechen Cohen's," in *Ki mineged*, 54; my translation.

72. Kronzon, "Mother, Sunshine, Homeland," in *Ki mineged*, 133; my translation.

73. Kronzon, "Kiddush," in *Ki mineged*, 138; my translation.

74. Kronzon, "The Cake," in *Ki mineged*, 126.

75. Kronzon, "Instead of a Memorial," in *Ki mineged*, 88.

76. Kronzon, "Who Will Get Belgium," in *Ki mineged*, 78.

77. Kronzon, "Instead of a Memorial," in *Ki mineged*, 92.

78. "Special Operations: 1950–1960," Israeli Navy, accessed May 2, 2016, www.navy .idf.il.

79. "Eisenhower Reveals His 1957 Aims to Penalize Israel on Sinai Issue," *Jewish Telegraphic Agency*, September 22, 1965, www.jta.org.

80. In socialist "Red Haifa" even small-business owners were perceived as wealthy capitalists. The municipal authorities overestimated their profits and imposed unrealistic income taxes.

81. Hayim Nahman Bialik, "Shiva," in *Kol kitvei H. N. Bialik* [All the writings of H. N. Bialik] (1938; repr., Tel Aviv: Dvir, 1964), 65, line 1; my translation.

82. Sami Schoenfeld, "The Ge'ula School," Nostalgia Online, April 21, 2016, www .nostal.co.il/search.asp.

83. Kronzon, "The Derby," in *Ki mineged*, 108; my translation.

84. Ravikovitch, "Hovering at a Low Altitude," in Bloch and Bloch, *Window*, 103.

85. Giddon Ticotsky, "Dahlia Ravikovitch: in 'Life' and in 'Literature'" (PhD diss., Tel Aviv University, 2013), 40. In his dissertation on the poet and her life and work, Ticotsky describes her stay in Haifa with the following sentences: "When Ravikovitch moved to Haifa, she was about thirteen years old, and she lived at the expense of the kibbutz with foster families. She changed families on the average of once a year until she went into the army when she was eighteen, [and, Ravikovitch said,] 'each family was worse than the last. Except for the last one.'"

86. Ravikovitch, "Painting," in *Ahavat tapuah hazahav*, 36; Bloch and Bloch, *Window*, 8.

87. Nitza Sabo, interview with the author, Haifa, October 2014, and correspondence with the author, January 2016; Ravikovitch, "Painting," in *Ahavat tapuah hazahav*, 36; Bloch and Bloch, *Window*, 8. During her last two years in high school, 1952–54, Dahlia Ravikovitch lived with the Harekhavi family on Shamay Street. Sabo remembers her babysitting her while she lived with the Harekhavis. Ticotsky, *Dahlia Ravikovitch*, 42. According to Ticotsky, her last two years of high school were a "period of awakening": "the period of the poem 'Painting,' the impressive landscape of the sea facing the woody mountain, the Carmel and the groves, the beginning of the poems of *Love of an Orange*. She then understood that she would be a poet and not a painter, even though the poem 'Painting' is indeed a painting." Additionally, a portion of this poem was composed when she was in eighth grade, but only when this awakening period happened did she complete it.

88. Ravikovitch, "Hemda," in *Ahavat tapuah hazahav*, 48. Ravikovitch, "Delight," in Bloch and Bloch, *Window*, 10.

89. Dahlia Ravikovitch, "Yom le-yom mabi'a omer," in *Kol hashirim ad ko* [The complete poems so far] (Tel Aviv: Hakibbutz Hameuchad, 1995), 167. Ravikovitch, "Day unto Day Uttereth Speech," in Bloch and Bloch, *Window*, 71.

90. A. B. Yehoshua, *Hame'a'hev* [The Lover] (Tel Aviv: Schocken, 1977), 233–34 (emphasis mine). My translation here; the English translation omits this segment.

91. Ibid., 237; A. B. Yehoshua, *The Lover*, trans. Philip Simpson (New York: Harcourt Brace, 1977), 190. Henceforth all page numbers are cited in the text and refer to the Hebrew original, followed by the English translation.

92. A. B. Yehoshua, interview with the author, Givatayim, November 19, 2014. Yehoshua himself discussed how Dani serves as Naim's guide down the Donkey Steps, and thus into Haifa: "When Dafi takes him down the Donkey Steps . . . I walked in those steps. They are fabulous steps!"

93. Gershon Shaked, *Hasiporet ha'ivrit: 1880–1980* [Modern Hebrew fiction: 1880–1980], vol. 5 (Israel: Hakibbutz Hameuchad/Keter, 1998), 60, 93, 168.

94. Ibid., 171.

95. Yehoshua, interview.

INDEX

Note: page numbers in italics refer to images.
Those followed by n refer to notes, with note number.